The ELLE Cookbook

The Art of
French
Cuisine

The ELLE Cookbook

The Art of French Cuisine

Introduction by
Jane Grigson

Translated by R. F. Fullick
Photographs by A. Bouillaud
Ph. Leroy and Y. Jannes

GREENWICH HOUSE
New York

This 1982 edition is published by Greenwich House, a division of Arlington
House, Inc. distributed by Crown Publishers, Inc.

Printed in Singapore

Library of Congress Cataloging in Publication Data

Elle cookbook.
  The Art of French cuisine.

  Previously published as: The Elle cookbook. 1981.
  Includes index.
  1. Cookery, French.   I. Elle.
TX719.E375   1982   641.5944   82-3134
                                        AACR2
ISBN: 0-517-383853

h g f e d c b a

CONTENTS

TRANSLATOR'S NOTES

The Recipes

The recipes in this book have been drawn from a wide variety of sources and are of a very diverse nature. Some are regional recipes in the traditional pattern of la cuisine française, others are creations of the maître-chefs of France's greater hotels and restaurants, while a proportion come from outside France. However, the larger number, one suspects, derive from private or family recipe books and reflect very much the tastes and circumstances of the authors who have been accustomed to preparing these recipes for the enjoyment of their friends and families.

Consequently, with such disparate origins, there will be some inconsistencies and idiosyncracies. No attempt has been made in translation to disguise these or reduce all methods to a bland and common series of procedures; rather, the point of view has been taken that since the original recipe had clearly been successfully made in the way that its originator or contributor had used it, then the reader of it in translation was entitled to know of his or her methods in its original form. No surprise, therefore, should be felt if variations are detected in, say, ways of peeling chestnuts or of preparing the lardons of bacon which figure in so many meat dishes and salads. Let each recipe stand by itself; most people will in any case have kitchen habits which, consciously or unconsciously, will influence the way they use the recipes in this book.

The Ingredients

There are those who by circumstances have the opportunity, and take it, of regularly shopping in one or another of the Channel ports of France but for most of us such a practice is limited to that last frantic dash around the market before catching the ferry back to England. It will be shops in the area where we pass our daily lives that we shall have to turn to when we wish to cook a French dish.

With ingredients therefore it has not been possible to be as purist as with the methods. The growing awareness in this country of the pleasures and possibilities of the French table, initiated in the post-war years so brilliantly by Elizabeth David (who deserves the undying gratitude of all), continued by others and sustained by the ease with which France can be visited and its cuisine experienced, has led to a growing availability of French produce in our shops. Supermarkets seem to become more and more adventurous while much of what is needed for the recipes in this book will be found in delicatessens or on the speciality food counters in large stores.

Nevertheless, in the interests of simple convenience some substitutions have had to be made, although they have been kept to a minimum. The strong regional base of French cooking, founded as it is on an abundance of distinctly local produce, means that in any case it will be impossible to duplicate exactly the intentions of the original cook. For some things, thoroughly acceptable substitutes may be made at home and for these you are referred to the writings of those admirable ladies Jane Grigson, Julia Child or Anne Willan, the practical nature of whose cookery books is not the least of their many virtues. Means of preparing the possible substitutions included in the following list will be found in one or other of their books. Where no substitute can either be made or obtained, an attempt has been made to explain the purpose of the particular ingredient so that the effect of its absence may be understood.

Crème Fraîche
Despite its name, crème fraîche has a hint of sourness which adds a characteristic flavour to dishes in which it is an ingredient. It is increasingly easy to obtain while a substitute is not difficult to make and has good keeping qualities.

The following method is the one recommended by Jane Grigson: Slowly heat to 90°C/194°F soured cream stirred into double its quantity of whipping or double cream. Pour into a pot, cover and put into a warm place overnight. Stir again and then refrigerate. This will keep for ten days.

Herbs
The use of dried herbs where fresh ones are particularly called for must always risk some diminution in the depth and power of the flavour the herb was meant to impart. It may be necessary to tie dried herbs into a muslin bag so that their more spiky nature does not affect the texture of the dish in the mouth: the bag of herbs should, of course, be removed before serving.

Lardons
A number of meat and salad dishes in the book contain small strips of pork belly or bacon, either fried or blanched and then fried. In general, thickly cut streaky bacon has been proposed for use, green where smoked has not been definitely indicated.

Pig's Caul
This web-like membrane serves two purposes: it binds together dishes such as sausages, terrines, stuffed boned joints etc. which might otherwise tend to fall apart during cooking, and it also gives off its fats in cooking, aiding the flavour and texture of the dish. It is unlikely to be found in a shop whose meat is sold plastic-wrapped. The family butcher in the high street should be able to get one for you if you order it in advance; the best source will be a butcher who advertises that he does his own slaughtering.

Calves' Feet and Pigs' Trotters
Meat dishes where these are an ingredient gain in texture from the gelatines which they impart during cooking. Again, a cooperative butcher, or persistence, will find them.

Pork Belly Rind
This is used at the base of the casserole in some of the slowly-cooked meat dishes. It tends to melt during the cooking process, thickening the juices which will make the sauce served with the meat. Green bacon rind can be substituted but its absence would not spoil the dish.

Veal
As this book goes to press, there is some discussion here and abroad about the wisdom of using veal which is the product of factory-farming. Those who do not wish to use this meat will be able to decide for themselves whether pork can be used instead, but certainly for any dish specifying veal escalope or boned veal chops, pork fillet, cut across the grain, will serve very well.

Vegetables
Two vegetable ingredients might be difficult to find at the average greengrocer: the small young turnips the French call navets, and small white onions. Both were probably chosen originally as much for their pleasing decorative appearance as for the flavour they give to a particular recipe. If young turnips cannot be bought, then old turnips – which are coarser and more strongly flavoured – will hardly do, even cut into trimmed pieces. For small white onions, pickling onions are probably a better choice than spring onions, since they are more tightly packed and have a better shape.

Vanilla Sugar
This should not be difficult to find, probably as simple as making your own by immersing two vanilla pods in caster sugar in a screw-top jar. The contents of the sachets in which the French sell it is usually 7½ g, the British packet rather bigger. When using vanilla essence in place of vanilla sugar, the amount of ordinary sugar should be increased by a teaspoon.

Fromage blanc
Again, this is an ingredient found more and more in our shops. Cottage cheese has been suggested as the substitute in case of need but in order to match the texture of fromage blanc, it is preferable to extend it with a little milk and pass it through the blender.

Chantilly cream
This is cream which has been lightly whipped. Preparation is best done by hand, using a wire whisk, so as to get as much air as possible into the cream to ensure its lightness and delicacy. It is sometimes flavoured with vanilla essence.

The Weights and Measures

In all cases, the definitive weight or volume is the one given in metric measurements as in the original French recipe. Most people will by now have a set of kitchen scales marked in both metric and avoir-dupois but for those who do not, the nearest practical equivalent in imperial measurements is given in every case. You should follow either metric or imperial; they are not interchangeable.

Preparation and Cooking Instructions

The information given at the beginning of each recipe is for guidance only. The preparation times will vary according to the expertise of the cook, and the quantities used according to the appetites of the family or guests. Cooking times and temperatures should not give any problems. For dishes cooked in the oven, both oven temperatures and regulo settings are given, while expressions used for cooking on top of the stove, such as 'over a brisk heat' or 'over a very low flame' follow the original French instructions and are intended to be straightforward and self-explanatory.

There may also be room for personal preference in the suggestions, which again follow the original recipes, for serving some dishes at temperatures other than hot or cold.

Conclusion

In carrying out the work of translation, the practical nature of each of the recipes was always evident and the testing of them seemed always to lead to extremely satisfactory and appetising results. The task of selecting from the vast range of recipes available, a chore shared agreeably with the publisher, was far from easy. Throughout, the intention has been to simulate the French domestic table which must remain still the most refined, painstaking and enjoyable on earth.

Roy Fullick

INTRODUCTION
by
Jane Grigson

If you spend time in France, a weekly ritual unmarked in tourist literature or books on folklore will soon catch your eye. You may even find yourself trapped in its excesses. This is the Sunday night return to the city, the weekly rentrée. First you will note, from about 5 o'clock onwards when everyone begins to recover from Sunday lunch, the number of cars in driveways and gardens, by caravans or châteaux, standing with their boots wide open. For the next hour people go to and from the house, feeding the boots with offerings. Eggs, chicken, duck, guineafowl, game in the autumn, fruit, vegetables, wild mushrooms, chestnuts, salads, terrines, rillettes, sausages of all kinds, bottles of wine dusty from the cave, cakes from the pastrycook, dripping fresh cheeses in plastic bags. Delicate items are fitted on to the back window ledge: green radish leaves and dry garlic stalks tickle the passengers' necks agreeably, and in traffic jams solace wafts in from the boot, smelling of melon and strawberries.

Without such supplies, a family could not survive the coming week, or so it feels. An opinion which may surprise a traveller, especially a traveller from Britain, who sees how lavishly and freshly French towns are supplied, and who notes with envy that you can shop at 8 in the morning or 7 at night and on Sunday morning, too.

These well-provided people of France's new prosperity, who cling to the taste of their country origins, are the ones for whom these recipes were first intended, for most of them will take or have a chance to read *Elle* magazine. We have nothing quite like it. *Elle* is the only women's magazine that comes out weekly in France. Tone and make-up are brighter, more sophisticated than in our weeklies. It lacks the brittle trendiness of some of our monthly magazines, and their chintzy shire aspects, too. The appeal is first to youngish women with careers, probably with children, perhaps setting up house for the first time, women who feel that life has more to offer them these days their their mother's kitchen. The inheritors, you might say, of liberation and new wealth. Yet *Elle* is also read by older women, whose lives are centred on their homes, women of formidable expertise in cookery who want to keep in touch with new ideas. A tricky readership to please.

To these women in 1969, *Elle* began to offer the bonus of cookery cards, or rather recipes printed on thick shiny paper that could be torn easily from the magazine and ranged in card index boxes. Those days were boom time for cookery cards. They came with stock cubes and chocolate, with shoe polish and cars. As the boom declined, *Elle* kept – and still keeps – going, to the pleasure of its readers. Form and audience demand that explanations be brief yet comprehensive, thorough but unpatronising. Choice of recipes must be compatible with the new image women have of themselves, without shattering its fragility. Kitchen novices want to give dinner parties without making fools of themselves: the menu must reflect their professional status without reflecting on their lack of skill. People with knowledge and no time for new ideas or old classics brought up to date discreetly with 'convenience' ingredients that do not show too much. The better-off or those with expense accounts who eat in *nouvelle cuisine* and other smart restaurants, want to reproduce something of the new style at home.

Elle has taken notice of all this, summarising the changes and developments over the last twelve years in nearly two thousand recipes. From them, for this first translation into English, Jenny Dereham from the publishers has chosen and put together the sort of compendium and reference that many people have been wanting for years. And Roy Fullick, printer by trade, gourmet by choice, has turned the culinary French into neat English. From his knowledge of France and its food, he has known exactly where to add helpful notes. But these have been kept to a discreet minimum. Nothing intrudes on the real thing – a collection of dishes chosen for the French by the French and, in the main, from the French tradition.

You will find fashionable dishes of the recent past (*boeuf Stroganoff, en croûte, au poivre,* sorbets, eggs benedict, a number of recipes using green peppercorns). The *nouvelle cuisine* restaurants have provided the new dishes, *magrets de canard* (duck's breast steaks), salmon rillettes and fish terrine, *salade composée,* the 'cooking' of herrings in lemon juice, and original associations of fruit with meat, fish and salads. Every so often a classic dish comes in like a sight of home – *rognons bonne femme* after the new *rognons aux trois moûtardes, poulet au vinaigre* followed by the favourite *poulet à l'estragon.* The romantic names of French cookery are there, too, Reine de Saba chocolate cake and Marie Leszczinska's *bouchées à la reine.* We go after Curnonsky and his disciples, all goggles and dust coats in their first cars, as they braved regional France and came up with a store of dishes that have become classics in their turn. Among the recipes is a number from outside France: veal with a tunny sauce from Italy might be expected, but not *empanadas* from Mexico or hamburgers with peanuts – or *rødgrød* of red fruits from Denmark. A judicious blend that keeps interest going from page to page.

In this compendium, 362 dishes are described and shown as they should – and well could – appear on our tables. No gloss of the over-garnished kind to spoil our confidence, but food displayed in or with brown stoneware jugs and rillettes pots, petalled white Chinese bowls, heads of garlic, sturdy pepper mills, Sabatier knives and scrubbed chopping boards, all the items we have adopted from France in the last twenty years to set beside our own pudding basins and pot-bellied casseroles. Many will adopt *The Elle Cookbook* with as much warmth. It slips neatly into the gap between *nouvelle cuisine* manuals and the informative exhilaration of Elizabeth David's *French Provincial Cooking* and its better progeny.

ARTICHAUT AUX CREVETTES
Artichokes with prawns

PREPARATION TIME: 25 minutes
COOKING TIME: 30 minutes
FOR SIX

250 g (9 oz) frozen, peeled
prawns
6 good-sized artichokes
1 wine glass vinegar
salt
4 lemons
2 egg yolks

1 tablespoon Dijon mustard
1 tablespoon wine vinegar
500 ml (18 fl oz) oil, preferably
peanut
1 tablespoon each chopped
tarragon, chives, parsley,
chervil

Plunge the frozen prawns into 1½ litres (2½ pints) boiling water for 2 minutes. Remove and drain. Cut the stalks from the artichokes and remove the outer leaves. With a sharp knife, cut off the top 1½ cm (about ¾ in) from the leaves. Wash the artichokes under a running tap and leave them to soak for 15 minutes in vinegar and water.

Bring to the boil a large saucepan of water to which salt and the juice of 3 lemons have been added. Once boiling, cook the artichokes for 25–30 minutes. Remove and drain, and allow to cool. Pull off the central leaves and scoop out the choke from the middle of the vegetable, taking care to remove all the fine inedible fibres.

Make a mayonnaise with the egg yolks, mustard, wine vinegar and oil. Mix in the chopped herbs and lemon juice. Take half of this mayonnaise and mix it with the prawns. Fill the artichokes with the mixture and serve the remainder of the mayonnaise separately.

Elle suggests that this is a first course worthy of your best dinner parties.

FONDS D'ARTICHAUT GRATINÉS
Gratin of artichokes hearts

PREPARATION TIME: 30 minutes
COOKING TIME: 40 minutes
FOR SIX

6 good-sized artichokes
juice of 2 lemons
70 g (2½ oz) flour
300 g (10½ oz) button
mushrooms
80 g (scant 3 oz) butter

200 g (7 oz) smoked ham
500 ml (18 fl oz) milk
salt, pepper, nutmeg
50 g (scant 2 oz) grated
Emmenthaler cheese

Break off the stalks from the artichokes and remove the outer leaves. Take a good sharp knife and, turning the artichokes in a circular fashion, cut off the remaining leaves and the choke, so that only the heart remains. Put all the hearts into water to which lemon juice has been added.

In a large saucepan bring to the boil 2½ litres (about 4 pints) of water. As soon as it is bubbling, add and mix in well 30 g (1 oz) of flour which has been made into a smooth paste with a little cold water. Put in the artichoke hearts and cook for 15–20 minutes, keeping the water on the boil.

While the artichoke hearts are cooking, slice the mushrooms and put them in a saucepan with 30 g (1 oz) of butter. Put over a brisk heat until the moisture in the mushrooms has evaporated. Then mix in the chopped ham, remove from the heat and put to one side.

In another saucepan make a white roux with the rest of the butter and flour. Beat in the milk and let the sauce boil for 5 minutes, stirring all the time. Then salt slightly and add pepper and grated nutmeg to taste. Remove from the heat and add the mushroom and ham mixture and three-quarters of the grated cheese. Mix thoroughly.

When the artichoke hearts are cooked, remove them from the boiling water and drain. Arrange them on an ovenproof dish and cover each one with the mushroom, ham and cheese sauce. Sprinkle on the remainder of the grated cheese, and brown in a very hot oven 230°C/450°F/Gas Mark 8 for 15 minutes.

PAPETON D'AUBERGINES
Baked aubergines

PREPARATION TIME: 40 minutes
COOKING TIME: 30–35 minutes
FOR SIX

1½ kg (3¼ lb) aubergines
  (egg-plant)
olive oil
salt, pepper, thyme

5 eggs
50 g (about 2 oz) grated Gruyère
  cheese

Trim the stalks from the aubergines and slice them crossways into thin rounds. Put the slices into a cloth, roll it up and squeeze in order to extract as much liquid as possible.

Heat the oil in a pan, add the drained aubergine slices and brown them. Then make a purée of the browned slices by sieving them through a vegetable sieve. Drain off any unabsorbed oil, add salt, pepper and the leaves of 3 stalks of fresh thyme (or the equivalent in dried thyme). Beat in the eggs, one by one. Pour the aubergine mixture into a flat, round ovenproof dish that has been lightly greased. Put into an oven pre-heated to 220°C/425°F/Gas Mark 7.

As soon as the surface of the mixture becomes firm, sprinkle on the grated Gruyère, reducing the oven temperature to 180°C/350°F/Gas Mark 4. Continue cooking for 25–30 minutes, keeping an eye on the colour. The dish will be perfectly cooked when the blade of a knife can be inserted and withdrawn quite clean.

Elle suggests that this dish can be served either hot or cold. If hot, it is a delicious accompaniment to grilled or roasted meat. If allowed to get cold, it can be cut into slices as an hors d'oeuvre.

AUBERGINES FOURRÉES
Stuffed aubergines

PREPARATION TIME: 30 minutes
COOKING TIME: 45 minutes
FOR SIX

2 red peppers (green peppers
  may be used instead but they
  don't have the mellow, ripe
  taste of the red peppers)
olive oil
4 large onions
3 good-sized aubergines
  (egg-plant)

cooking oil
3 tomatoes
200 g (7 oz) of Tome or other
  white cheese which can be
  sliced, such as Cheshire or
  Lancashire
sprig of parsley
3 cloves garlic

Cut the peppers in half, remove the seeds and slice into strips. Gently heat 2 tablespoons of olive oil in a pan and slowly soften the strips of pepper. Remove from the pan and keep on one side.

Peel and chop the onions and, in the same pan, slowly cook them until they are transparent. Also put them aside.

Cut off the stalks from the aubergines and partially cut them lengthways into slices so that they remain attached at one end. Sprinkle them with a little salt and leave them to sweat for 30 minutes.

Heat some cooking oil in a deep pan, drain the aubergines and put them into the hot oil, one by one, being careful not to break them. While they are cooking, turn them and also keep the slices separate by inserting a metal spatula from time to time. When the aubergines are browned on all sides, remove, drain and wipe with kitchen paper to remove any surplus liquid. Stuff the aubergines alternately between the slices with the tomatoes cut into rounds, slices of cheese and the cooked strips of red pepper.

Cover the bottom of a round baking dish with the cooked, chopped onions and place the stuffed aubergines on top. Sprinkle with a tablespoon of olive oil, followed by the parsley and garlic, both chopped fine.

Cook in a very hot oven, 230°C/450°F/Gas Mark 8 for about 35 minutes.

GRATIN D'AUBERGINES
Crusted aubergines

PREPARATION TIME: 40 minutes
COOKING TIME: 20 minutes
FOR SIX

2 kg (about 4½ lb) aubergines
  (egg-plant)
2 tablespoons sea-salt
cooking oil
750 g (about 1¾ lb) tomatoes
2 cloves garlic

5 good leaves of fresh basil
thyme and parsley
1 tablespoon olive oil
salt, pepper
100 g (3½ oz) grated
  Emmenthaler cheese

Cut the stalks from the aubergines. Cut them lengthways in 1 cm (½ in) slices. Put the slices in a colander or strainer and sprinkle with the sea-salt. Leave to sweat for 30 minutes.

Wash the slices under running water to remove all the salt, drain them and dry them off well in a cloth or with kitchen paper. Heat plenty of cooking oil in a deep pan and fry the aubergine slices until they are brown. Remove, drain and keep warm.

Separately, prepare a tomato sauce. Cut the tomatoes in half, remove the pips and put them into a casserole with the garlic, basil, thyme, parsley and olive oil. Cook over a brisk heat until any liquid in the tomatoes has evaporated. Put the mixture through a sieve or Moulinette, and lightly salt and pepper it.

In a flat ovenproof dish, put in first a layer of tomato sauce, a layer of aubergine slices and then a sprinkling of the grated cheese. Continue with further layers, finishing with cheese. Put into a hot oven until the surface is golden-brown, about 20 minutes.

This dish is equally good hot or cold.

FLAN AUX ASPERGES
Asparagus tart

PREPARATION TIME: 15 minutes
COOKING TIME: 45 minutes
FOR SIX

1¼ kg (2¾ lb) asparagus
50 g (scant 2 oz) flour
4 eggs
500 ml (18 fl oz) milk

50 g (scant 2 oz) butter
salt, pepper, nutmeg
250 g (9 oz) ham

This recipe comes from the Touraine.

Cut off any hard root parts of the asparagus, wash them and cut into 2–3 cm (1 in) lengths. Put them in a strainer and plunge for 5 minutes into boiling salted water. Drain, run cold water over them and drain again.

In a bowl, work the flour and eggs together, dilute with the milk and the butter (just melted), add salt, pepper and grated nutmeg. Butter the inside of an ovenproof dish, set out the cut pieces of asparagus and the ham, cut into dice, pour on the batter mixture and cook in a very hot oven, 230°C/450°F/Gas Mark 8 for 35–40 minutes.

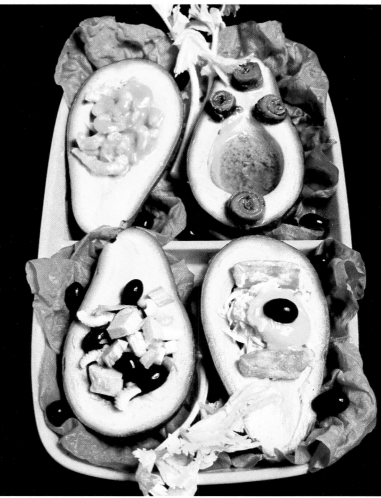

AVOCATS AUX OEUFS DE SAUMON
Avocado with caviar

PREPARATION TIME: 10 minutes
COOKING TIME: nil
FOR SIX

3 ripe avocados
2 lemons
salt

tabasco sauce
50 g (about 2 oz) salmon roe (or
    Danish caviar)

Cut the avocados in half lengthways, take out the stones and remove all the flesh. Put the flesh through a blender, moistening it with the juice of the lemons. The mixture should be lightly salted and several drops of tabasco sauce added to heighten the flavour.

Fill the avocado shells with the mixture, garnish with the salmon roe and serve immediately.

Elle suggests that this quickly-made dish should be prepared at the last minute: once exposed to the air, the flesh of an avocado soon discolours. If the dish has to be prepared in advance, sprinkle lemon juice over the surface of the avocado mixture and add the roe just before serving.

AVOCATS GARNIS
Stuffed avocados

PREPARATION TIME: 30 minutes
COOKING TIME: nil
FOR SIX

3 avocados
1 lemon

1 lettuce
150 g (about 5½ oz) black olives

Cut the avocados in half lengthways and remove the stones. Sprinkle with lemon juice to prevent darkening of the flesh. The avocados should be served chilled, upon a bed of lettuce leaves and surrounded by black olives. A simple vinaigrette sauce may be preferred with this dish, or alternatively, it may be garnished in the following ways:

With vinaigrette and anchovies Make a vinaigrette sauce in the proportions of four-fifths olive oil to one-fifth vinegar or lemon juice, flavouring the sauce with mustard and a teaspoon of anchovy essence. Garnish with rolled anchovy fillets.

With prawns Allow a level tablespoon of peeled prawns for each half avocado, together with some chopped celery and a dessertspoon of mayonnaise which has been thinned with a few drops of tabasco sauce and water.

With crab Proceed as with the prawns, but garnish with black olives.

With tunny fish (tuna) Flake the tunny fish and mix with an equal quantity of chopped celery which has been steeped in either a vinaigrette sauce lightly flavoured with mustard, or in a mayonnaise lightly thinned with water. Allow a good tablespoon of mixture for each avocado half.

[12]

CÉLERI RÉMOULADE
Celeriac salad

PREPARATION TIME: 20 minutes (one hour before serving)
COOKING TIME: nil
FOR SIX

1 celeriac root
1 teaspoon salt
1 lemon
2 tablespoons chopped parsley
(optional)

For the rémoulade sauce
1 egg yolk
2 tablespoons french (Dijon)
mustard
salt, pepper, vinegar
250 ml (9 fl oz) salad oil

Peel the outer skin of the celeriac and cut into thick slices that will fit into a vegetable shredder (using the fine disc). Dip the slices into lemon juice so that the celeriac will not darken after it has been shredded.

Put the finely shredded celeriac into a dish and sprinkle with salt and the juice of half a lemon and leave to sweat for ½ to 1 hour. Drain it, squeezing it between the hands, and then put into the salad bowl from which it will be served.

Make a mayonnaise with the listed ingredients for the rémoulade sauce. If it is too thick, it can be lightened with a teaspoon of water or milk.

Add the sauce little by little to the celeriac, stirring well so that the sauce and shredded celeriac are thoroughly mixed. Since the amount of sauce required will depend on the size of the celeriac root used, do not add all the sauce at once.

The dish should be allowed to stand, after mixing, for half an hour and served (according to taste) with or without a sprinkling of chopped parsley.

CROUTES GRATINÉES
Golden toast

PREPARATION TIME: 15 minutes
COOKING TIME: 10 minutes
FOR SIX

50 g (scant 2 oz) butter
6 slices of good white bread
(cottage loaf or french bread
sliced diagonally)

6 slices of ham
150 g (5 oz) grated Emmenthaler
cheese

Melt half the butter in a frying pan. Fry the slices of bread on each side until they are golden. Drain on kitchen paper. Put a slice of ham on each slice of bread and trim the ham to suit the shape of the bread.

Lightly butter a flat fireproof dish, arrange the bread and ham slices and liberally sprinkle them with the grated cheese and with small knobs of butter. Put them under a grill which has been allowed to heat for 10 minutes in advance and cook until golden brown. Serve immediately.

Elle suggests that, accompanied by a green salad, this simple dish is sufficient for a light meal.

CHOUX AUX FROMAGE
Cheese puffs

PREPARATION TIME: 20 minutes
COOKING TIME: 4 minutes per batch if fried
10–12 minutes, according to size, if in oven

FOR SIX

100 g (3½ oz) butter	75 g (about 2½ oz) grated
150 g (5 oz) flour	Gruyère cheese
5 eggs	pepper, nutmeg, salt
	frying oil

In a large casserole, bring 250 ml (9 fl oz) of water and butter to the boil together. Add the sifted flour all at once and beat vigorously until the dough comes away clean from both the dish and the spoon. Remove from the stove and continue to beat the dough for a further minute. Add one whole egg and stir vigorously until it is thoroughly mixed with the dough. Stir in the remaining eggs one by one, in the same way, and then the grated cheese. Keep working the dough, having added pepper, a little grated nutmeg, and salt in moderation (because of the cheese) until it is all completely smooth.

Heat a deep-fat frying pan of oil but do not allow it to smoke. Take 2 rounded soupspoons and filling one with dough, use the other to shape a ball which is then rolled into the hot oil. When the puffs are golden-brown, they are ready. Take them from the hot oil and drain them on kitchen paper. Serve hot.

If small puffs are to be served as an hors d'oeuvre, they may be cooked in a hot oven, 220°C/425°F/Gas Mark 7. Butter a baking sheet and, using a forcing bag, form pastry puffs to about the size of a walnut.

FEUILLETÉS AU ROQUEFORT
Cheese in puff pastry slices

PREPARATION TIME: 25 minutes
COOKING TIME: 15 minutes
FOR SIX

1 packet of frozen puff pastry (370 g, 13 oz, size)	200 g (7 oz) of Roquefort cheese 1 egg

Buy the puff pastry the day before and let it thaw overnight in the refrigerator. Bring it out into the kitchen 1 hour before you are ready to begin.

Lightly flour a pastry board and roll out the puff pastry, keeping its oblong shape, until it is about 3 or 4 mm (say ⅛ in) thick. Cut the pastry into rectangles each about 7½ cm × 11 cm (3 in × 4½ in) making 16 in all. Take 8 rectangles and on each place a piece of Roquefort cheese about the size of an index finger.

Score the remaining 8 rectangles diagonally with the point of a knife. Beat the whole egg and with a pastry brush moisten all 4 edges of the rectangles on which the cheese is placed, to a width of about 1 cm (½ in). Lay the scored rectangles on to the cheese and press the edges together with the fingers. Brush the scored surface with the beaten egg, taking care not to let it run over the edges.

Lightly butter a baking sheet, dust it with a little flour and place the cheese slices on it. Cook in a very hot oven, 240°C/475°F/Gas Mark 9 for 10 minutes, without opening the oven door. Then leave the oven door ajar and cook for a further 5 minutes. Serve either warm or hot.

Elle suggests that made half size, this dish is delicious served with aperitifs.

CROQUETTES AU FROMAGE
Cheese croquettes

PREPARATION TIME: 20 minutes (the day before) 1 hour resting time
COOKING TIME: 30 minutes
FOR SIX

75 g (about 2½ oz) butter
75 g (about 2½ oz) flour
500 ml (18 fl oz) milk
3 egg yolks
250 g (9 oz) grated Emmenthaler
   cheese
salt, freshly-ground pepper,
   nutmeg
frying oil

For the coating
flour
2 eggs
100 ml (3½ fl oz) milk
150 g (5 oz) fine white
   breadcrumbs (fresh)

In a casserole, make a white roux by melting the butter over a low heat, adding and whisking in the flour and cooking for about a minute; stir continuously. Remove from heat and add the milk, stirring it in quickly, and return to the stove to cook for 10 minutes, stirring all the time. Remove the sauce from the heat, add first the egg yolks one by one, beating vigorously, then the grated cheese. Season with a little salt and pepper to taste, and sprinkle on a little grated nutmeg.

Take a greased rectangular baking dish and spread out the mixture to a depth of 1½ cm (about ⅝ in). Smooth the surface with a spatula, and leave in a cool place for 6 or 7 hours, or overnight.

Cut the mixture into strips each 6 cm × 1½ cm (about 2½ in × ⅝ in). Form them into sausage shapes and roll them first in flour, then into the eggs and milk beaten well together, and lastly into the breadcrumbs. Let the croquettes stand for an hour in the refrigerator.

Heat the oil and fry the croquettes, turning them frequently so that they are lightly browned all over. As soon as they are done, remove and drain on kitchen paper. Keep each batch warm until the remainder is done.

Elle suggests that these croquettes can be served as a first course, but they also make an attractive hors d'oeuvre with aperitifs.

CORNIOTTES
Cheese hors d'oeuvre

PREPARATION TIME: 30 minutes
COOKING TIME: 20 minutes
FOR SIX

300 g (10½ oz) cottage cheese
4 eggs
4 tablespoons crème fraîche

250 g (9 oz) Emmenthaler
   cheese
salt, pepper
500 g (1 lb 2 oz) short pastry

In a bowl, whip together the cottage cheese, 3 whole eggs and the cream. It is preferable to drain the cottage cheese through a fine sieve before mixing. Add the Emmenthaler cheese, cut into dice, lightly salt and pepper to taste. Roll out the pastry until it is paper thin. With a round pastry cutter, make discs of 8–10 cm (3½–4 in) in diameter. Put 2 or 3 spoonfuls of cheese mixture into the centre of each disc. Beat the remaining egg and brush the edges of the pastry discs. Pull up the edges in 3 or 4 places and press them together firmly, so as to form the shape of a cocked hat. With the rest of the beaten egg, brush the surface of each corniotte.

Cook on a greased baking dish in a moderate oven, 180°C/350°F/Gas Mark 4 for 20 minutes.

This recipe from Vosges will make a first course or an excellent hors d'oeuvre with aperitifs.

ROULÉS AU FROMAGE
Cheese snaps

PREPARATION TIME: 40 minutes
COOKING TIME: 20 minutes
FOR SIX

50 g (scant 2 oz) butter
60 g (2 oz) flour
500 ml (18 fl oz) milk
100 g (3½ oz) grated cheese,
   Gruyère for preference

salt, pepper, nutmeg
1 packet frozen puff pastry
   (370 g, 13 oz size)
1 egg

Make a béchamel sauce with the butter, flour and milk. Let it cool and then mix in all but 3 spoonfuls of the grated cheese. Lightly salt, add pepper to taste and sprinkle with grated nutmeg.

Roll out the defrosted puff pastry to a thickness of 4 mm (about ⅙ in) cut into rectangles of 10 cm × 12 cm (4 in × 4¾ in) and fold into 3 along the long edge. Brush each piece with beaten egg and score the top surface with a fork.

Leave in a cool place for 20–30 minutes and then place in a very hot oven, 240°C/475°F/Gas Mark 9 and cook for 15 minutes without opening the oven. Check the colour is not over-brown and leave for 5 further minutes. Remove from the oven and put in a cool place.

When the pastries are cold, push the handle of a wooden spoon lengthways through them to form tubes. Using a forcing bag, fill each roll from both ends with the sauce, then dip each end in the rest of the grated cheese which was kept aside.

Before serving, re-heat the cheese rolls in the lowest part of a cool oven, 140°C/275°F/Gas Mark 1. Serve very warm.

BOUCHÉES À LA REINE
Chicken vol-au-vents

PREPARATION TIME: 30 minutes
COOKING TIME: 1 hour
FOR SIX

salt, pepper
bouquet garni (parsley, thyme
   and bay leaf)
1 carrot
1 onion
2 wing portions of chicken
150 g (5 oz) mushrooms
1 lemon
1 small sweetbread

100 g (3½ oz) butter
4 tablespoons flour
nutmeg
1 small tin of chicken quenelles
   (optional)
3 egg yolks
125 ml (4½ oz) double cream
6 medium-sized vol-au-vent
   cases (frozen are excellent)

Boil 1½ litres (a good 2½ pints) of water which has been salted and peppered, add the bouquet garni, the carrot and onion and simmer until the carrot is tender. Take out the herbs, put in the pieces of chicken and simmer for 20 minutes. Take out the chicken, remove the skin and bones and dice the meat. Strain off the liquid and set aside.

Slice the mushrooms and sprinkle with lemon juice. Plunge the sweetbread into boiling, salted water for 10 minutes. Take it out, remove all pieces of skin and dice the meat.

Make a roux with the butter and flour, add ¾ litre (about 1¼ pints) of the strained liquid, mix thoroughly together and bring to the boil. Add the diced chicken and sweetbread and the sliced mushrooms and grate in a little nutmeg.

Let it all simmer over a low heat with the saucepan uncovered. Add more strained liquid if any remains. From time to time, skim the surface of the sauce as it reduces and thickens. When the scum stops coming to the surface, remove the saucepan from the heat and add the quenelles which have been cut into rounds, and the yolks of the 3 eggs beaten into the cream. Stir everything gently into the sauce and put the pan back on a low heat, taking care that the sauce does not stick.

In the meantime, the vol-au-vent cases should have been heated in the oven to the point where they are lightly browned. Remove the caps, fill with the hot mixture from the pan and serve.

CRÈME D'OEUFS AUX CREVETTES
Scrambled eggs and prawns

PREPARATION TIME: 10 minutes
COOKING TIME: 15 minutes
FOR SIX

300 g (about 10 oz) peeled
  prawns
2 tablespoons of cooking oil
50 g (scant 2 oz) butter
50 ml (1¾ fl oz) white rum or
  whisky

salt, pepper
12 eggs
100 ml (3½ fl oz) crème fraîche
pinch of cayenne pepper

If using frozen prawns, plunge them into a pan of well-salted boiling water, bring back to the boil, remove the prawns and dry on kitchen paper. Put the oil and half the butter into a pan and when hot, gently heat the prawns for 5 minutes. The rum or whisky should now be poured over the prawns and flamed. Then remove the pan from the fire and cover with a lid.

Melt the remainder of the butter in a double-boiler, salt and pepper the beaten eggs and pour them into the melted butter. With a wooden spoon, stir vigorously until the mixture has the consistency of smooth cream. Add the cream and a pinch of cayenne to the prawns, return to the heat until the sauce thickens.

Put the eggs into a warmed serving dish, pile the prawns into the centre and serve while still hot.

Elle advises that the cooking time will be reduced if the eggs are cooked directly over a low heat rather than in a double-boiler.

PIPÉRADE
A Basque egg dish

PREPARATION TIME: 40 minutes
COOKING TIME: 40 minutes
FOR SIX

4 red or green peppers
1 kg (2¼ lb) tomatoes
olive oil
1 onion

1 clove of garlic
salt, pepper
6 thin slices of smoked ham
6 eggs

Cut the peppers in half and remove all the seeds, then grill them open side downwards until the thin outer skin blisters and curls, when it can be peeled off. Cut the peppers into small pieces. Peel the tomatoes and remove their pips and mash the flesh into a pulp.

Heat 2 tablespoons of olive oil in a heavy pan, slowly cook the chopped onion and add the chopped peppers. When the mixture is almost cooked, add the tomato pulp and the crushed clove of garlic. Season with salt and pepper and let it cook slowly until it has the texture of a smooth, thick sauce.

While the sauce is cooking, grill the slices of ham over a drip-pan. Remove and keep warm. Deglaze the pan with 1–2 tablespoons of the sauce and then add the mixture to the sauce.

Remove the saucepan from the heat and stir in the beaten eggs. Return to the heat and cook over a gradually increased heat, stirring continuously so that the mixture remains smooth and no lumps are formed. When everything is thoroughly mixed together and of a thick, even consistency, pour into a warmed serving dish and garnish with the grilled slices of ham.

OEUFS POCHÉS BÉNÉDICTINE
Eggs Benedict

PREPARATION TIME: 10 minutes
COOKING TIME: 20 minutes
FOR SIX

6 slices of white bread
3–6 slices of York ham,
  depending on size
6 egg yolks
6 tablespoons crème fraîche
400 g (14 oz) butter
salt, pepper
1 lemon
6 eggs (very fresh)

Cut the crusts from the bread and lightly toast each slice. Cut the ham into pieces of the same size as the bread.

In a double-boiler, whisk together the 6 egg yolks and the cream into a smooth sauce. Slowly melt the butter and having removed any froth which may have formed, stir it little by little into the sauce. Season with salt and pepper and add the juice of half a lemon. Keep the sauce warm in the double-boiler over a low heat.

Poach the eggs in the traditional way (in vinegar and water brought to the simmer and held there) for 3 minutes. Remove, dry them off on kitchen paper and trim off any threads of egg white.

Set out the pieces of toast on a warm serving dish, put a slice of ham on each and then a poached egg. Cover with the sauce and serve immediately.

The chef of the Paris restaurant, 'Paul Chêne', from where this recipe comes, advises that a good Muscadet be drunk with this dish.

OEUFS COCOTTE A L'OSEILLE
Coddled eggs with sorrel

PREPARATION TIME: 15 minutes
COOKING TIME: 6–8 minutes
FOR SIX

200 g (7 oz) sorrel
80 g (scant 3 oz) butter
salt, pepper
250 ml (9 fl oz) crème fraîche
1 loaf (stick) French bread
butter
chives, parsley
12 eggs

If sorrel is not available, substitute the same quantity of spinach with a squeeze of lemon juice.

Strip the sorrel leaves from their stalks, wash them and dry them and put into a casserole with 30 g (1 oz) of butter. Season with salt and pepper. Cover the pan and cook for 1 minute, then remove the lid to let any liquid evaporate. Bring the cream to the boil in a small saucepan, season with salt and pepper. Gently stir in the cooked sorrel and bring to the boil 2 or 3 times. Put to one side.

To make the bread sticks, cut the loaf into pieces of about 12 cm (4½ in) long and slice each piece in half lengthways. Butter each slice thinly. Finely chop the chives and parsley together and sprinkle on the buttered sides, then cut each piece in half again lengthways so that each length of loaf gives 4 sticks.

Take 6 ramekin dishes, butter the insides and season. Crack 2 eggs into each dish, taking care not to break the yolks. Put the ramekins into a flat ovenproof dish half-filled with hot water and cook in an oven heated to 200°C/400°F/Gas Mark 6. Watch the progress of the cooking carefully; the eggs will be cooked when the whites have become opaque and the yolks are still liquid (although this is very much a matter of taste, some people preferring both whites and yolks to be well-cooked).

Remove the ramekins from the oven and pour the sorrel sauce over them. Serve very hot, with the bread sticks.

The chef of the restaurant 'Julius' at Gennevilliers in the Hauts-de-Seine from where this recipe comes, recommends a chilled white Burgundy with this dish.

OEUFS FRITS AU RISOTTO
Fried eggs with rice

PREPARATION TIME: 20 minutes
COOKING TIME: 25 minutes
FOR SIX

2 medium-sized onions
50 g (scant 2 oz) butter
100 g (3½ oz) risotto rice
2½ times the rice's volume of
　water
pepper and salt

a pinch of saffron
3 tomatoes
12 thin slices of smoked bacon
　cooking oil
6 eggs

Finely chop the onions and cook slowly in butter until transparent. Add the rice and cook together for 3–4 minutes, stirring constantly. Bring the well-salted water to the boil, add pepper, colour it with the saffron and pour on to the rice. Reduce the heat, cover the pan and cook wihout stirring for 20–25 minutes. The rice will be done when the water has been absorbed. Keep to one side in a warm place.

Cut the tomatoes in half and grill them cut-side upwards, having moistened each one with a drop of oil and lightly sprinkled them with salt. Grill the bacon without any added fat or oil.

Take a small saucepan and put in cooking oil to a depth of 4 cm (about 1¾ in). Heat the oil and just as it begins to smoke, carefully pour in from very close to the surface an egg which has been broken into a cup. The white should completely surround the yolk, although it may be necessary to help it, using a wooden spoon. The egg will be ready when it floats on the surface of the oil. Remove and drain on kitchen paper.

When all the eggs are done, arrange them around the rice on a warmed serving dish, together with the grilled tomatoes and bacon.

OEUFS AU VERT
Eggs in a green sauce

PREPARATION TIME: 30 minutes
COOKING TIME: 6–7 minutes
FOR SIX

12 eggs
1 bunch watercress
1 bunch chervil
4 stalks parsley

mayonnaise
6 tablespoons double cream
several small tomatoes (optional)

With a needle, prick the rounded end of each of the eggs so that they will not crack while being cooked. Put them in boiling water for 6–7 minutes, then plunge them into cold water. Peel them under a running cold tap, dry them off and arrange them in a serving dish having taken a thin slice from one side so that they will stay in place.

Chop the watercress and herbs extremely fine: the better this is done, the more delicate the sauce will be. Make a stiff mayonnaise and extend it by stirring in the cream. (Note: the cream will not be needed if prepared proprietary mayonnaise is used.) Add the chopped herbs, mix well in, and cover the eggs with part of the sauce, serving the remainder in a sauceboat.

Garnish each egg with a leaf of cress: if desired, the dish may be eaten with tomatoes.

Elle suggests that the cream can be substituted by a low-fat soft white cheese, the kind which can be bought in a tub from delicatessens.

[19]

OEUFS AUX HERBES
Eggs with herbs

PREPARATION TIME: 5 minutes
COOKING TIME: 15 minutes
FOR SIX

75 g (about 2½ oz) butter
6 eggs
300 ml (10½ fl oz) crème fraîche
cornstarch

2 tablespoons chopped parsley
2 tablespoons chopped chives
salt, pepper

Melt a little butter in 6 individual fireproof serving dishes, break an egg into each and cook over a very low heat.

During this time, reduce the cream in a saucepan to about half its volume; thicken it with a level teaspoon of cornstarch mixed to a paste with a few drops of water. The sauce should be sufficiently thick just to coat the back of a spoon. Chop the herbs and mix thoroughly into the sauce, season with salt and pepper and pour it over the eggs. Serve immediately.

Elle advises that if using porcelain fireproof dishes, be sure to cook the eggs over an asbestos mat.

OEUFS BROUILLÉS PRINTANIERS
Scrambled eggs and asparagus

PREPARATION TIME: 15 minutes
COOKING TIME: 30 minutes
FOR SIX

500 g (generous 1 lb) asparagus
12 eggs

salt, pepper
100 g (3½ oz) butter

Cut off the tips of the asparagus to a length of about 5 cm (2 in) and slice the tender part of each remaining stalk into short lengths. Blanch the asparagus in salted, boiling water for 10–15 minutes; at the end of this time they should still be almost crunchy. Remove, and drain them and complete the cooking, slowly, in 40 g (about 1½ oz) butter. They will remain quite firm and keep all their flavour.

Break the eggs into a round-bottomed saucepan, season with salt and pepper, add 60 g (2 oz) of butter and put over a fairly brisk heat. Beat the eggs with a whisk until they begin to thicken and continue with a wooden spoon, making sure that the mixture does not stick to the bottom of the pan. Reduce the heat and let the mixture continue to thicken; while it is still just runny, remove pan from the heat and continue to stir the mixture for a further minute.

Mix in half of the asparagus and transfer to a serving dish. Hollow out the centre and put the remainder of the asparagus into it, keeping aside sufficient of the asparagus tips to decorate the surface of the dish.

Elle suggests that this elegant dish is worthy of being the first course at a dinner party or formal occasion.

EMPANADAS
Mexican pasties

PREPARATION TIME: 30 minutes
COOKING TIME: 15–18 minutes
FOR SIX

100 g (3½ oz) fat bacon
2 onions
1 green pepper
500 g (1 lb 2 oz) minced beef
1 tablespoon tomato purée
50 g (about 2 oz) seedless
 raisins
2 tablespoons stoned green
 olives

1 hard-boiled egg
salt, pepper
sugar
thyme
tabasco sauce or cayenne
 pepper
1 packet frozen puff pastry, 400 g
 (14 oz) size
1 fresh egg

Chop the bacon and onions together and cook in a heavy pan over a moderate heat until the onion is transparent. Cut the pepper in half and remove all the seeds and the stalk, dice the flesh and add to the cooking pan. When the pepper is soft, add the minced beef and continue cooking quickly over a raised heat until the meat is done.

Remove from the heat and stir in the tomato purée, the raisins which have been allowed to swell by immersing them in warm water, and the olives and hard-boiled eggs, both chopped. Season and sprinkle on a pinch of sugar and a level teaspoon of chopped thyme. Flavour with about 10 drops of tabasco sauce (or a good pinch of cayenne pepper), stir all together and taste. The mixture should have a distinctly piquant flavour. Return the pan to the heat and simmer without the lid on for a further 10 minutes. Remove, and allow to cool.

Roll out the pastry to a thickness of 4 mm (⅙ in) and, using a small plate, cut out 6 rounds about 13 cm (5½ in) in diameter. Shape them into an oval and put a sixth of the mixture on to each piece of pastry. Beat the egg and moisten the edges of the pastry rounds; fold over into a turnover shape and press the edges firmly together. If the back of a fork is used, it will give a firm bond and decorate the turnover at the same time. Brush the top surface of each turnover with the remaining beaten egg and cook in a very hot oven, 220°C/425°F/Gas Mark 7, for 10–15 minutes.

CROUSTADE AU JAMBON
Ham and cheese flan

PREPARATION TIME: 30 minutes
COOKING TIME: 45–50 minutes
FOR SIX

For a 24-cm (9½-in) flan dish
1 packet frozen puff pastry (or
 short pastry if preferred), 400 g
 (14 oz) size
2 slices cooked ham

250 g (9 oz) Gruyère or
 Emmenthaler cheese
60 g (2 oz) butter
3 eggs
225 ml (8 fl oz) single cream
salt, pepper, nutmeg

When the pastry has quite unfrozen, it should be rolled out and folded over twice (to give three thicknesses). This should be repeated a second time before finally rolling it out to the shape of the flan dish. Grease the inside of the tin lightly with butter, powder it with flour and line with the pastry, trimming off any surplus from the edges.

Cut the ham into strips and half of the cheese into thin slices. Melt 20 g (¾ oz) of butter in a pan and quickly heat the ham through: line the flan with slices of cheese and the cooked ham. Then pour over a mixture of the eggs beaten into the cream, seasoned with the salt, pepper and a little grated nutmeg. Grate the rest of the cheese and sprinkle it over the surface of the mixture, finally adding a few knobs of butter.

Put in a fairly hot oven, 200°C/400°F/Gas Mark 6 and when the surface is golden-brown, reduce the temperature to 180°C/350°F/Gas Mark 4 until the cooking is completed. The flan is done when the pastry base becomes firm: this can be checked by carefully lifting the flan from the tin with the end of a spatula.

The flan should be served hot.

MOUSSE DE POIREAUX
Leek mousse

PREPARATION TIME: 15 minutes
COOKING TIME: 30 minutes
FOR SIX

2 kg (4½ lb) small young leeks   *200 ml (7 fl oz) crème fraîche*
125 g (4½ oz) butter   *1 tablespoon salad oil*
salt, pepper

Strip off any tired outer leaves of the leeks, trim the root-ends and cut off the top third of the green leaves. Wash the leeks well in several changes of water. Poach 5 or 6 of the leeks for 5 minutes in well-salted boiling water, remove, drain, and put to one side.

Chop up the remaining leeks, heat 50 g (about 2 oz) of butter in a sauté pan and slowly cook the chopped leeks for about 30 minutes, stirring frequently. Pass the cooked leeks through the fine disc of a Moulinette (or, better still, through a blender) and season with salt and ground pepper. Put the purée into a double-boiler.

In a small saucepan, melt the remainder of the butter and heat it to a nut-brown colour. Using a wooden spoon, gradually incorporate the melted butter into the leek purée, followed by the cream.

Remove from the heat and transfer the purée to its serving dish. The whole leeks which were put aside should be lightly brushed with oil and used as decoration.

Elle suggests that this delicious mousse goes perfectly with any roast of meat or poultry.

FLAMICHE AUX POIREAUX
Leek flan

PREPARATION TIME: 30 minutes
COOKING TIME: 1½ hours
FOR SIX

For an 26/28.-cm (10/11.-in) flan dish

For the pastry
250 g (9 oz) flour
1 egg yolk
125 g (4½ oz) butter

For the filling
2½ kg (5½ lb) leeks

125 g (4½ oz) butter
1 thick slice of ham, about 250 g (9 oz)
4 eggs
250 ml (9 fl oz) crème fraîche
salt, pepper
250 ml (9 fl oz) milk
30 g (1 oz) grated cheese (optional)

To prepare the short pastry: sift the flour into a mixing bowl, make a well in the centre and put in a pinch of salt, the yolk of an egg, the butter cut into small pieces and 100 ml (3½ fl oz) of cold water. Using the finger tips, work the ingredients together as quickly as possible to achieve a dough which is pliable and not soft and sticky to the touch. Roll the dough into a ball and leave it to rest in a cool place for 1½ hours.

Then roll out the dough, fold it into three and roll it out again, repeating the process three times altogether. Lightly butter the flan dish and line it with the rolled-out pastry, trimming the edges and pricking the pastry all over. Return to a cool place.

While the pastry is resting, trim the leeks, retaining only the white parts. Cut these into pieces about 2 cm (¾ in) long. Heat 75 g (about 2½ oz) of butter in a sauté pan and cook the sliced leeks over a low heat for 1 hour, stirring constantly. The leeks should not darken at all.

Cut the ham into dice and fry them lightly in the rest of the butter. Fill the pastry-case with the cooked leeks and ham. Beat together in a bowl the 4 eggs and the cream, season with salt and pepper. Add the milk and pour the mixture over the leeks and ham, then sprinkle with grated cheese if wished, and dot with knobs of butter.

Cook in a cool to moderate oven, 160°C/315°F/Gas Mark 2–3 for 30 minutes.

MATAFAN
Batter with bacon

PREPARATION TIME: 10 minutes
COOKING TIME: 20–25 minutes
FOR SIX

For 24-cm (10-in) frying pan	salt, pepper
300 g (10½ oz) flour	250 ml (9 fl oz) milk
4 eggs	50 g (scant 2 oz) butter

Start by heating the oven to 240°C/475°F/Gas Mark 9.

Sieve the flour into a mixing bowl, make a well and break in the 4 eggs. Season. Beat the eggs and flour together, moisten with the cold milk and sufficient cold water to give a smooth batter, somewhat thicker than a pancake batter.

Heat the butter in the pan over a brisk heat. As soon as it begins to turn brown, pour all the batter in at once, shaking the pan to prevent it sticking. Do not stir the mixture in the pan although a fork may be used to keep the edges of the batter from sticking to the sides of the pan.

When the batter is hot, reduce the heat, continue cooking until the base of the batter is golden-brown and quite detached from the pan while the centre is still very moist, possibly still a little liquid. At this point, put pan and batter into the hot oven: it will rise and become golden-brown, when it is ready to serve.

If the Matafan is to be served as a dish by itself, it can be garnished with small strips of bacon which have been blanched in boiling water for 10 minutes and then fried lightly in a pan without added fat. The garnish should be added to the batter while it is still liquid enough to cover it. Small chipolata sausages also make a good garnish. A green salad should be served with a garnished Matafan.

CROÛTES AUX CÈPES
Creamed mushrooms

PREPARATION TIME: 15 minutes
COOKING TIME: 15 minutes
FOR SIX

100 g (3½ oz) dried mushrooms (cèpes)	250 ml (9 fl oz) crème fraîche
1 onion	salt, pepper
300 g (10½ oz) butter	lemon
	6 slices of white bread

Soak the dried mushrooms in hot (but not boiling) water for 10–15 minutes and then wash them under a running tap to remove any foreign matter. Thoroughly drain them and dry on kitchen paper. Slice them and put to one side.

Chop the onion finely and, in a large pan, cook slowly in 25 g (about 1 oz) butter until it becomes transparent. Add 75 g (about 2½ oz) butter and as soon as it sizzles, add the sliced mushrooms to the cooked onion, stir them together and continue to cook slowly for a further 5 minutes.

Bring the cream to the boil and pour it over the mushrooms, season and add the juice of the lemon. Stir all the ingredients together and, with the pan uncovered, leave the mixture to thicken.

In the meantime, melt the rest of the butter in a separate frying pan. It should be very hot without being allowed to burn. Fry the slices of bread on both sides until they are crisp and golden.

Pile each fried slice of bread with mushrooms and serve.

QUICHE AU CHAMPIGNONS
Mushroom flan

PREPARATION TIME: 30 minutes
COOKING TIME: 45–50 minutes
FOR SIX

For a 24-cm (9½-in) flan tin
400 g (14 oz) of puff pastry
  (frozen or fresh)
1 egg for glazing
400 g (14 oz) cultivated
  mushrooms

1 lemon
2 shallots
40 g (scant 1½ oz) butter
3 eggs
300 ml (10½ fl oz) single cream
salt, pepper

If using frozen puff pastry, make sure that it is completely defrosted. Roll out the pastry to a thickness of 4 mm (⅙ in) and line the flan tin which has been lightly greased and dusted with flour. Prick the base of the pastry with a fork, brush with beaten egg and put in a low oven for 10–12 minutes.

Cut the stalks from the mushrooms, wipe them with lemon juice which has been mixed with 2 or 3 parts of water, and then slice them, sprinkling the slices with lemon juice to prevent discoloration.

Finely chop the shallots and cook them in the butter in a medium-sized casserole until transparent. Add the mushrooms and when any liquid has evaporated, remove from the heat and allow to cool.

Beat the eggs and the cream together, pour over the mushrooms and mix together. Season, and pour the mixture into the flan. Cook the flan in a fairly hot oven, 200°C/400°F/Gas Mark 6 for 20 minutes, then finish the cooking at a moderate heat, 180°C/350°F/Gas Mark 4. Serve warm.

CHAMPIGNONS AU GRATIN
Gratin of mushrooms

PREPARATION TIME: 30 minutes
COOKING TIME: 30 minutes
FOR SIX

1 kg (2¼ lb) cultivated
  mushrooms
2 lemons
2 shallots
40 g (scant 1½ oz) butter
1 clove garlic

200 ml (7 fl oz) double cream
8 tablespoons milk
1 egg yolk
1 teaspoon cornflour
salt, pepper

Cut the stalks from the mushrooms, then wipe them with lemon juice which has been mixed with 2 or 3 parts of water. Slice them and sprinkle with juice of the second lemon to prevent discoloration.

Chop the shallots finely and slowly cook them in butter, and add the sliced mushrooms. Raise the heat and, over a brisk heat, evaporate most of their liquid. Stir constantly and do not let the mushrooms dry out.

Take an ovenproof gratin dish and rub it all over inside with the peeled clove of garlic. Beat together the cream, milk, yolk of egg and cornflour, and season.

Put the mushrooms in the gratin dish and pour over the cream mixture, making sure it thoroughly blends with the mushrooms. Dot the surface with several knobs of butter.

Cook in a fairly hot oven, 200°C/400°F/Gas Mark 6 for 30 minutes, reducing the heat if the mixture bubbles too furiously.

CHAMPIGNONS MONTAGNARDS
Mushrooms Savoy

PREPARATION TIME: 10 minutes
COOKING TIME: 35 minutes
FOR SIX

500 g (generous 1 lb) button mushrooms	*1 clove garlic*
	100 ml (3½ fl oz) wine vinegar
1 lemon	*300 g (10½ oz) tomatoes*
olive oil	*bouquet garni*
2 onions	*salt, pepper*

Trim the mushroom stalks and wipe them with lemon juice diluted with 2 or 3 parts of water. Then cut each mushroom into quarters.

Heat some oil in a pan until it is almost smoking, put in the mushrooms and fry them over a brisk heat. Continue cooking until any liquid given out by the mushrooms has evaporated.

Meanwhile, in another pan, heat 3 tablespoons of olive oil and gently cook the chopped onion and garlic until they are transparent, then add the vinegar and, over a brisk heat, reduce it to half its volume. Add the tomatoes (which should have been peeled, seeded and chopped), the bouquet garni, and season. Cook slowly, without covering the pan, for about 25 minutes. Remove the bouquet garni, and mix the mushrooms in with the tomato sauce; leave to cool and serve cold.

Elle suggests that this delicious dish is probably better prepared in advance.

CHAMPIGNONS FARCIS
Stuffed mushrooms

PREPARATION TIME: 40 minutes
COOKING TIME: 25 minutes
FOR SIX

12 large mushrooms	*The béchamel sauce*
6 medium-sized mushrooms	*95 g (3¼ oz) butter*
1 lemon	*95 g (3¼ oz) flour*
30 g (1 oz) butter	*250 ml (9 fl oz) crème fraîche*
2 thin slices of ham	*500 ml (18 fl oz) milk*
60 g (2 oz) grated Gruyère cheese	*2 egg yolks*
	salt, pepper, nutmeg

Wipe the mushrooms clean with damp kitchen paper. Remove the stalks from the large mushrooms and chop them up, together with the medium-sized mushrooms. Sprinkle with lemon juice and put to one side.

Melt half the butter in a pan and gently cook the large mushrooms whole. Remove and keep warm. Melt the rest of the butter and cook the chopped mushrooms until all the liquid has evaporated. Chop the ham, mix it with the chopped mushrooms, heat through and put to one side.

Make a béchamel sauce with the butter, flour, crème fraîche and milk. Add the beaten egg yolks and season with salt, pepper and grated nutmeg.

Take half the béchamel sauce and add it to the chopped mushrooms, together with a tablespoon of grated cheese. Check the seasoning. Fill the centre of each large mushroom with a good measure of the mixture and spread what remains over the bottom of an ovenproof serving-dish. Arrange the stuffed mushrooms in the dish and cover with the other half of the béchamel sauce which has had the remainder of the grated cheese stirred in; it will probably need thinning with a little milk.

Put into a hot oven until the surface is browned and the dish heated through.

TARTE À L'OIGNON AU FROMAGE
Onion and cheese flan

PREPARATION TIME: 10 minutes (2 hours beforehand if making the pastry)
COOKING TIME: 15 minutes (if making the pastry)
30 minutes for the filling
FOR SIX TO EIGHT

For a 26-cm (10½-in) flan tin	2 tablespoons oil
The pastry	2 or 3 pinches paprika
250 g (9 oz) flour	500 g (generous 1 lb) grated
pinch salt	Emmenthaler cheese
130 g (about 4½ oz) butter	2 eggs
1 egg yolk	125 ml (4½ fl oz) crème fraîche
The filling	100 ml (3½ fl oz) milk
1 large onion	salt, nutmeg

If making the pastry, pile the flour on to a pastry-board, make a hollow and put in the salt, the butter which has been softened and cut into knobs, and the egg yolk. Work quickly with the fingers into a dough, moistening with only enough water to give a good consistency. Form the dough into a ball and let it rest for 2 hours in a cool place.

At the end of this time, roll out the pastry (or the thoroughly defrosted frozen pastry) to a thickness of 4 mm (⅙ in) and line the buttered flan tin. Blind-bake the pastry case by lining the inside with a sheet of greaseproof paper which is covered by a layer of dried beans, and baking for 15 minutes in centre of a pre-heated oven, 200°C/400°F/ Gas Mark 6. Take out the pastry, remove the dried beans and grease-proof paper, and leave to cool.

While the pastry is resting prior to cooking, chop the onion finely and put it into a thick-bottomed casserole with the oil and cook gently over a low heat until the onion becomes transparent. Stir in the paprika and remove the casserole from the heat.

Sprinkle half the grated cheese into the pastry-case, then put the chopped onion in a layer, followed by the remainder of the cheese. Beat together eggs, cream, milk, 2 or 3 pinches of salt and an equal amount of grated nutmeg, and pour the mixture into the pastry-case. Cook for about 25 minutes in an oven pre-heated to 200°C/400°F/Gas Mark 6. Serve hot or just warm.

PISSALADIÈRE
Olive and anchovy flan

PREPARATION TIME: 30 minutes
COOKING TIME: 75 minutes
FOR SIX TO EIGHT

1 kg (2¼ lb) onions	1 egg
olive oil	about 30 anchovy fillets in oil
pepper, salt	30 black olives
1 packet frozen puff pastry, 400 g	
(14 oz) size	

Chop the onions and cook them in oil over a low heat until they are just transparent; this will take about 35 minutes. Lightly pepper and barely salt them.

Roll out the pastry to a thickness of 4 mm (⅙ in) and put it onto a greased and floured baking sheet: cut strips of pastry and make a rim, or border, of a depth of 1.5 cm (⅝ in), brushing the edges with egg-white in order to ensure firm adhesion of the strips.

Spread the cooked onion evenly over the inside of the pastry-case and arrange the drained anchovies in a lattice pattern over the surface of the onion. Brush all round the pastry border with beaten egg.

Pre-heat the oven to 240°C/475°F/Gas Mark 9 and cook the flan for 20 minutes. Reduce the heat to 200°C/400°F/Gas Mark 6 and continue until the base of the flan is cooked: this can be checked by lifting the edge of the flan with a spatula. Remove from the oven and garnish with black olives.

Elle says that true pissaladière from Nice is made with bread-dough. The use of frozen puff pastry not only reduces cooking time, but makes a more subtle dish.

[26]

OMELETTE BRAYAUDE
Peasant omelette

PREPARATION TIME: 30 minutes
COOKING TIME: 10 minutes
FOR SIX

250 g (9 oz) sliced ham
300 g (about 10 oz) peeled
   potatoes

100 g (3½ oz) butter
6 eggs
salt, pepper

Buy the ham in a slice about 1 cm (⅖ in) thick. Cut it into dice and taste a piece: if it tastes salty, plunge the ham into boiling water for 5 minutes, drain and dry off.

Cut the peeled potatoes into dice and fry them in half the butter. When they are cooked, add the ham and let them sizzle together without becoming brown.

In the meantime, beat the eggs together and season. Add the ham and potato pieces and make the omelette in the usual way, using the rest of the butter. Note that the omelette should not be folded but turned over with the aid of a plate and cooked on both sides. Care should be taken not to overcook the omelette, or a leathery texture will result.

Elle says that, in the Auvergne, 2 or 3 tablespoons of cream are sometimes poured over the omelette after cooking; it is then sprinkled with grated Gruyère and lightly browned under the grill. This refinement, which prolongs the cooking, may not be to everyone's liking.

OMELETTE AUX FOIES DE VOLAILLE
Chicken-liver omelette

PREPARATION TIME: 10 minutes
COOKING TIME: 5 minutes
FOR SIX

500 g (1 lb 2 oz) chicken livers
   (with hearts attached, if
   possible)

100 g (3½ oz) butter
13 eggs
salt, pepper

If using fresh chicken livers, the heart will be attached. Frozen chicken livers do not normally include the heart: they are perfectly adequate used on their own but the dish will not have exactly the same flavour.

Separate livers and hearts: cut the livers into large dice, remove any fat and sinews from the hearts and cut them into quarters. Heat 75 g (about 2½ oz) of butter in a pan, add the liver and heart pieces and cook gently until they are sealed (i.e. have an all-over grey colour). Season and put on one side in a warm place.

Beat the eggs; season. Heat the rest of the butter in an omelette pan until it foams and add the beaten eggs. When the omelette begins to take, add the liver and hearts and continue cooking until the omelette reaches the desired consistency.

Elle advises that since few kitchens will contain an omelette pan big enough for 13 eggs, it is preferable, with this number, to make two separate omelettes.

CHIPOLATAS EN CRÊPES
Sausage pancakes

PREPARATION TIME: 10 minutes (once the batter has been prepared)
COOKING TIME: 20 minutes
FOR SIX

For the pancake batter to make 9 crêpes
500 g (1 lb 2 oz) flour
6 eggs
30 g (1 oz) sugar
1 litre (36 fl oz) milk
80 g (scant 3 oz) butter
3 tablespoons oil

For the filling
9 chipolatas
mustard
50 g (about 2 oz) grated Gruyère cheese

These crêpes are usually made for a pancake party.

Begin by making the pancakes. Mix all the batter ingredients together thoroughly, taking care to avoid any lumps. To be certain, pass the batter through a sieve. The amount of butter and oil in the batter means that it should not be necessary to grease the griddle each time: it will also avoid smoke and fumes. A knob of butter to cook the first pancake should suffice. Make the pancakes as thin as possible. This means that the pancakes should not be tossed but turned over with a spatula.

If, having made the required number of pancakes, some batter is left over, it can be kept under refrigeration in a sealed jar for 5 or 6 days.

The French chipolatas which can be found in continental food shops, are longer and of a different texture from the sausage sold under that name in English shops. Prick the chipolatas and poach them in water which is simmering but not boiling for 10 minutes. Remove and allow to cool.

Roll each chipolata in a pancake which has been lightly smeared with mustard. Put the sausage-pancake in an ovenproof dish, sprinkle with the grated cheese and heat in a warm oven until the surface is golden-brown.

CRÊPES FARCIES
Stuffed pancakes

PREPARATION TIME: 25 minutes
COOKING TIME: 20–25 minutes
FOR SIX

12 pancakes 13–15 cm (5–6 in) in diameter
500 g (generous 1 lb) cooked green vegetable (spinach, beetroot leaves)
100 g (3½ oz) butter
salt, pepper, nutmeg

3 hard-boiled eggs or 100 g (3½ oz) chopped ham (optional)
150 g (5½ oz) grated Gruyère cheese
100 ml (3½ fl oz) cream

Make the pancakes in advance, following the method given in the previous recipe. They can be kept wrapped in foil in the refrigerator.

Blanch the vegetables in boiling salted water just long enough to soften them. Remove and drain off all the water and either chop the vegetables or leave whole, according to your taste. Heat the butter in a pan and toss the vegetables until all the moisture has evaporated. Season with pepper, grated nutmeg and very little salt. Add one-third of the grated cheese and mix together. (Either chopped hard-boiled egg or chopped ham can be added at this stage.)

Arrange a heaped tablespoon of the mixture on to each pancake, roll them and arrange them in an ovenproof dish. Pour the cream over, sprinkle on the rest of the grated cheese and dot with 1 or 2 knobs of butter.

Put the dish in a fairly hot oven at 200°C/400°F/Gas Mark 6. The grated cheese will brown while the pancakes heat right through.

FOIE GRAS DE VOLAILLE
Chicken-liver pâté

PREPARATION TIME: 15 minutes
COOKING TIME: 3 minutes
FOR SIX TO EIGHT

500 ml (18 fl oz) dry white wine
1 kg (2¼ lb) chicken livers
400 g (14 oz) butter
4 tablespoons port wine

salt, pepper
pinch of quatre-épices
1 truffle (optional)

Bring the white wine to the boil in a saucepan. Put in the chicken livers and bring the wine back to the boil; with a very careful eye on the clock, cook the livers for exactly 3 minutes. Remove them quickly with a perforated spoon, allow them to drain and cool.

Put the livers through a blender, adding the softened butter knob by knob. Then mix in the port wine and season with salt, pepper and the quatre-épices. Finally, the pâté should be passed through a sieve so a homogeneous mixture is obtained.

Put the pâté into a terrine, pressing it down very well. Cover the surface with foil and refrigerate. Decorate with slivers of truffle before serving if you are lucky enough to have one. Serve with toast.

Elle advises that it is essential to observe the correct cooking time for the livers. They should, when cooked, still be pink inside but without any trace of blood.

Quatre-épices can be bought in some continental shops in this country, but it is worth bringing back from France. It contains pepper or allspice, nutmeg, cloves and cinnamon and can be finely ground in the proportions of 7 : 1 : 1 : 1.

PÂTÉ DE FOIE DE PORC
Pork-liver pâté

PREPARATION TIME: 40 minutes
COOKING TIME: 1½–1¾ hours
FOR TEN

1 kg (2¼ lb) pig's liver
300 g (10½ oz) lean pork
700 g (1½ lb) salt fat bacon (or belly of pork)
4 shallots
1 clove garlic
1 teaspoon fresh thyme

1 teaspoon quatre-épices (see previous recipe)
60 g (2 oz) cornflour
salt, pepper
1 pig's caul (if obtainable)
2 or 3 bay leaves
100 g (3½ oz) lard
gelatine (optional)

Every ingredient in the above list as far as the cornflour should be finely minced together; the pâté's smooth consistency will depend upon it. If necessary, pass everything twice through the mincer.

Line the inside of the terrine in which the pâté is to be made with the pig's caul which should have been thoroughly rinsed in warm water. Put the minced ingredients into the dish, pressing down well. Bring the pig's caul over the top surface of the pâté, trim off any overlap and press down all around the edges. Arrange the bay leaves on top.

Put the terrine into a dish containing water (a bain-marie) and cook in a fairly hot oven at 200°C/400°F/Gas Mark 6. When the surface of the pâté is golden-brown, cover the dish with its lid.

From time to time, lift the lid; when the surface of the pâté has fallen by 1 cm (about ⅖ in), it is properly cooked. Let the pâté cool with its lid on, then remove the lid and put a wooden board, thoroughly weighted down, on to the surface while the pâté becomes quite cold.

Smooth off the surface of the pâté and then pour the melted lard over it. When this is quite cooled (it will have a dead white appearance), the pâté can have a layer of gelatine poured over it. The pâté should be covered with foil and refrigerated for 24 hours before being eaten.

Elle says that this delicious pâté will keep for a week after the first slice has been cut. The cut surface should always be covered with foil before the pâté is put back into the refrigerator.

SOUFFLÉ AU FROMAGE
Cheese soufflé

PREPARATION TIME: 25 minutes
COOKING TIME: 25–30 minutes
FOR SIX

For 2 soufflé dishes sized about 16 cm (6½ in)
500 ml (18 fl oz) milk
1 level teaspoon salt
pepper

100 g (3½ oz) butter
100 g (3½ oz) flour
25 g (scant oz) cornflour
6 eggs
100 g (3½ oz) Gruyère cheese

Bring the milk to the boil together with the salt and a pinch of freshly-ground pepper. Melt the butter in a large saucepan and throw in the flour and cornflour thoroughly mixed together. Remove from the heat and whisk the mixture, making sure that there are no lumps. Pour on the hot milk and, continuing to whisk vigorously, bring the mixture back to the boil. As soon as it reaches boiling point, remove from the heat.

Leave the mixture to settle for 1 minute and then thoroughly beat in the egg yolks, 2 at a time. Cut the cheese into thin strips, and add to the mixture.

Beat the egg whites until they are really stiff and then gently fold together the mixture and the egg whites. The soufflé dishes should have been well buttered and they should be exactly filled to the brim with the soufflé mixture.

The oven should have been pre-heated for 25 minutes at a temperature of 200°C/400°F/Gas Mark 6. Cooking time should also be about 25 minutes but after 15 minutes the progress of cooking should be noted (opening the oven door as little as possible) so that the top of the soufflé does not become overbrowned.

Elle advises that if a larger soufflé dish is used, it is doubtful whether the soufflé will rise to the extent shown in the illustration.

SOUFFLÉ AU JAMBON
Ham soufflé

PREPARATION TIME: 30–35 minutes
COOKING TIME: 30 minutes
FOR SIX

For a 16-cm (6½-in) soufflé dish
100 g (3½ oz) boiled ham
100 g (3½ oz) button mushrooms
salt, pepper, nutmeg
250 ml (9 fl oz) milk

50 g (scant 2 oz) butter
50 g (scant 2 oz) flour
20 g (¾ oz) cornflour
3 eggs

Cut the fat from the ham and mince the lean. Slice the mushrooms, heat a knob of butter in a pan and quickly sauté them so any moisture evaporates. Mix ham and mushrooms together and put to one side.

Add salt, pepper and (optional) a pinch of grated nutmeg to the milk and bring it to the boil. Heat the rest of the butter in a fairly large pan: as soon as it begins to froth, add all at once the flour and cornflour which have been mixed and sieved together. Remove from the heat and whip the mixture until there are no lumps.

Pour in the boiling milk and, continuing to whisk, bring everything back to the boil. Remove at once from the heat and carefully incorporate first the 3 egg yolks, one by one, and then the ham and mushroom mixture.

Whisk the egg whites until stiff and then combine them with the ham mixture, taking care to fold them together gently.

Fill the well-buttered soufflé dish to the brim with the soufflé mixture. Put into an oven pre-heated to 200°C/400°F/Gas Mark 6. The soufflé should take between 30 and 35 minutes to cook properly but progress may be carefully observed, opening the oven door as little and as infrequently as possible, from 15 minutes onwards.

TARTE AUX ÉPINARDS
Spinach flan

PREPARATION TIME: 20 minutes
COOKING TIME: 50 minutes
FOR SIX

For a 25-cm (10-in) flan dish
500 g (generous 1 lb) cooked
  and chopped spinach
salt, pepper, grated nutmeg
60 g (2 oz) butter

2 tablespoons flour
250 ml (9 fl oz) single cream
4 eggs
1 packet of frozen puff pastry,
  370 g (13 oz) size

Either fresh, frozen or tinned spinach may be used. Once cooked and chopped, it should be squeezed in a cloth to remove all surplus liquid. Then season with salt, pepper and grated nutmeg.

Melt the butter in a pan and stir the flour well in. Cook for 2 minutes, continuing to stir, then add the cream and allow the mixture to thicken. Add a little more seasoning.

Remove from the heat and add the well-beaten eggs. Take two-thirds of this mixture and stir into the chopped spinach; check seasoning.

Roll out the pastry to a thickness of ½ cm (⅕ in) and line the flan dish which should have been lightly buttered and floured. Prick the surface with a fork. Pour in the spinach mixture and cover it with the remainder of the egg mixture.

Pre-heat a warm oven (190°C/375°F/Gas Mark 5) for 15 minutes and cook the flan for about 40 minutes. The colour should be observed from time to time and the progress of cooking checked by shaking the dish: the flan will be cooked when the filling and the base are both firm.

After 40 minutes, turn out the oven and leave the flan in it for a further 5 or 10 minutes. Remove and leave to cool; this dish is better served warm rather than hot.

BEIGNETS AUX ÉPINARDS
Spinach fritters

PREPARATION TIME: 45 minutes
COOKING TIME: 3–4 minutes each batch
FOR SIX

500 g (1 lb 2 oz) bread dough
500 g (generous 1 lb) spinach
2 tablespoons olive oil
50 g (scant 2 oz) pine kernels

1 continental chipolata sausage
salt, pepper, nutmeg
cooking oil

Buy bread dough from your baker. It should be bought in advance and left to rise in a warm place.

While this is happening, strip the spines from the spinach leaves, wash thoroughly, drain and dry and cut them into strips.

Heat the oil over a fairly brisk heat and, stirring constantly, soften the spinach but do not let it brown and crispen. When it is tender, remove with a perforated spoon and then put the pine kernels and the chipolata into the pan, the nuts coarse-chopped and the sausage skinned and crumbled. Warm these through for a minute or two, remove from the heat and mix in the spinach. Season the mixture and allow to cool.

Roll out the dough on to a floured pastry-board to a thickness of 3–4 mm (about ⅛ in). Make rings with a 10 cm (4 in) diameter pastry-cutter and roll them out into ovals. Put a tablespoon of the spinach mixture into the centre of each oval, brush the edges of the dough with water, bring the edges together and form each piece into a rough ball.

Heat plenty of oil in a deep fat fryer to a point where it is not yet smoking. Cook the fritters in the oil until they are golden-brown. The fritters can be eaten either hot or cold.

TOMATES FOURRÉES AU POISSON
Tomatoes stuffed with fish

PREPARATION TIME: 25 minutes
COOKING TIME: nil
FOR SIX

6 large tomatoes
200 g (7 oz) flaked poached cod
100 ml (3½ fl oz) crème fraîche
2 shallots
juice of half a lemon

several leaves of tarragon
salt, pepper
1 lettuce heart
black olives
parsley

Cut the tops off the tomatoes, scoop out the flesh and the seeds lightly salt the insides and turn them upside-down. Put on one side.

Blend together the fish, shallots, cream, lemon juice, tarragon and seasoning into a smooth cream. Shake any excess liquid out of the tomatoes and fill each one with the fish mixture.

Arrange the stuffed tomatoes on a serving dish and garnish with small pieces of lettuce heart, black olives and chopped parsley. Chill before serving.

TAPENADE
Anchovy paste

PREPARATION TIME: 20–25 minutes
COOKING TIME: nil
FOR 250 G (9 OZ) OF PASTE

200 g (7 oz) large black olives
100 g (3½ oz) anchovy fillets
2 heaped tablespoons capers

pepper
olive oil
lemon juice

Pass each of the three main ingredients (having stoned the olives) separately through a blender, and then through a fine sieve which will ensure that a smooth cream of each ingredient is produced. Mix them together, season with pepper, and extend the mixture (as if making a mayonnaise) by dripping in the olive oil. From time to time, flavour to taste with 1 or 2 drops of lemon juice. The result should be a thick paste of even consistency.

Tapenade should be kept in the refrigerator in a sealed glass jar.

Elle suggests that this typically Mediterranean preparation, the basis for a number of sauces, makes a delicious appetiser when spread on buttered toast or bread.

POTAGE AUX HARICOTS
Bean soup

PREPARATION TIME: 15 minutes
COOKING TIME: 45 minutes–1hour
FOR SIX

250 g (9 oz) dried haricot beans	4 or 5 sticks celery
or 500 g (generous 1 lb) fresh	2 leeks (the white part only)
shelled haricot beans	60 g (2 oz) butter
bouquet garni	4 large tomatoes
1 medium-sized onion	salt
1 clove garlic	2 egg yolks

Cook the beans together with the bouquet garni, the peeled and halved onion and the garlic in 2½ litres (4½ pints) of boiling water until they are cooked. Do not salt the water.

Slice the celery and leeks into small pieces and gently cook them in half the butter: when tender, add the tomatoes, chopped whole and including the skin and seeds. Let this mixture simmer over a low heat until the cooking of the beans is complete.

Remove the onion and the bouquet garni from the beans (retaining the cooking liquid) and add the celery mixture. Put this mixture through a blender and then through a fine sieve, discarding any skin or pips. The aim is to have a smooth, creamy and digestible soup.

Return the soup to the saucepan, salt to taste and bring it back to the boil. Just before serving, remove from the heat and add the 2 egg yolks which have been beaten together with 2 spoonfuls of the soup and the remainder of the butter. The soup must not be allowed to boil after the eggs have been added.

The soup should be served with croûtons which have been fried in oil.

POTAGE AU CRESSON
Watercress soup

PREPARATION TIME: 10 minutes
COOKING TIME: 30 minutes
FOR SIX

1 bunch watercress	salt
30 g (1 oz) butter	2 egg yolks
2 or 3 potatoes	100 ml (3½ fl oz) single cream

Cut the coarse stalks from the watercress, wash the leaves well, drain thoroughly and put aside several of the best leaves as decoration for the tureen.

Put the butter into a large saucepan and brown the peeled and sliced potatoes for about 5 minutes. Add the watercress and let it simmer until it is softened: add 2 litres (3½ pints) of water and season with salt. Keep the pan just on the boil for 25–30 minutes, then put the soup through a blender. Season to taste and return to the saucepan.

Just before serving, take the pan off the heat and stir in the egg yolks and the cream which have been beaten together. Return to the heat, but do not allow the soup to boil again.

Decorate the tureen with the leaves of watercress kept back for this purpose, and serve with golden croûtons.

POIS CASSÉS EN SOUPE
Split-pea soup

PREPARATION TIME: 20 minutes
COOKING TIME: 1 hour for the peas; 10 minutes for the soup
FOR SIX

250 g (9 oz) split peas
half a pig's trotter
1 head of celery
bouquet garni

1 onion
bowl of croûtons fried in butter
4 tablespoons of single cream

Put the peas, the pig's trotter, the celery, the bouquet garni and the peeled onion into 2 litres (3½ pints) of cold water. Bring to the boil and cook until the peas are tender. Drain the peas, retaining the cooking liquid which should be kept warm. Remove the other ingredients. Pass the peas through a blender; then extend the purée of peas with the cooking liquid until you have a soup of a texture which suits your taste. If necessary, add more water.

Pick the meat from the pig's trotter and prepare the croûtons. Stir the cream into the soup and bring it back to the boil. Serve with the croûtons and the pieces of pig's trotter.

SOUPE AUX CHOUX DU ROUERGUE
Cabbage soup

PREPARATION TIME: 30 minutes
COOKING TIME: 2–2½ hours
FOR SIX

250 g (9 oz) pork belly
1 onion
4 carrots
2 small turnips
1 small green cabbage

3 potatoes
salt, pepper
bread
200 g (7 oz) Roquefort cheese

Wipe and dry the pork belly and cut into thick strips. Put them into 2 litres (3½ pints) of cold water, bring to the boil, skim and continue just on the boil for 30 minutes. Add the peeled and sliced onion, the carrots and turnips cut into strips, and continue cooking.

In the meantime, cut the cabbage into quarters and plunge it into boiling water for 10 minutes. Remove and rinse it through with cold water. Remove the hard core of the cabbage and slice the rest into thin strips.

After the other ingredients have been cooking for 1 hour, add the cabbage and continue cooking at the same temperature (i.e. just on the boil). After a further 30 minutes, add the potatoes cut into large slices.

The soup will be ready after 2 hours but can be allowed to continue cooking.

Check that the soup is seasoned to taste. Serve by putting a slice of bread into each soup plate; place on each slice a piece of Roquefort cheese about the size of a (French) sugar-lump. Pour the boiling soup over the bread and cheese: the cheese will melt and if stirred will give to the soup both a creamy texture and a most agreeable aroma.

Elle reminds that the Rouergue is the district from which Roquefort cheese comes.

VELOUTÉ DE LAITUE
Cream of lettuce

PREPARATION TIME: 15 minutes
COOKING TIME: 10 minutes
FOR SIX

3 lettuce hearts
50 g (scant 2 oz) butter
50 g (scant 2 oz) flour
2 litres (3½ pints) chicken stock

salt, pepper
2 egg yolks
125 ml (4½ fl oz) crème fraîche

Wash and thoroughly drain the lettuces and, using a large knife and a chopping board, cut them into thin strips. Melt the butter in a sauce pan and add the sliced lettuces: soften them while constantly turning them over with a wooden spatula. Sprinkle the flour over the lettuce and blend it in, then add the hot stock bit by bit. Continue cooking for a further 10 minutes, still constantly stirring the mixture. Season.

Beat the egg yolks into the cream. Remove the soup from the heat and quickly add the eggs and cream but it is essential not to let the soup boil after they have been added. Serve immediately.

POTAGE PARMENTIER
Potato and leek soup

PREPARATION TIME: 20 minutes
COOKING TIME: 50 minutes
FOR SIX

2 leeks
4 potatoes
1 teaspoon salt
100 ml (3½ fl oz) crème fraîche

30 g (1 oz) butter
2 egg yolks
bowl of croûtons

Cut the leeks into quarters lengthways and then slice into small pieces. Peel the potatoes; if the soup is not to go through a blender, cut them into small dice. If it is to be blended (which will produce a smooth soup), they can be cut into quarters.

Put the leeks and potatoes into 2 litres (3½ pints) of salted cold water, bring to the boil and cook for 40–45 minutes. Skim if necessary.

According to taste, the soup may now be put through a blender, returned to the saucepan and brought back to the boil. The egg yolks and cream should be beaten together with 1 or 2 spoonfuls of soup mixed in; just before serving, the saucepan should be removed from the heat and the beaten egg mixture stirred in.

The soup should be served with croûtons which have been fried in butter.

GASPACHO ROSE
Pink gaspacho

PREPARATION TIME: 30 minutes
STEEPING TIME: several hours
FOR SIX

500 g (generous 1 lb) tomatoes
200 g (7 oz) stale white bread
clove of garlic
4 tablespoons olive oil

2 tablespoons wine vinegar
salt, ice-cubes
cucumber, green pepper, onions
bowl of croûtons

Skin and seed the tomatoes. Soak the bread in water and then squeeze it dry. Put bread, garlic and tomatoes into a blender to make a smooth mixture: add the oil and vinegar and a pinch of salt (but no pepper).

Thin the mixture with ¾ litre (27 fl oz) water and put the soup into the refrigerator for 2 hours. Before serving, add a tray of ice-cubes to the tureen.

The gaspacho should be accompanied by slices of cucumber, green pepper cut into very small dice, chopped onion and croûtons which have been fried in oil.

Those who do not like raw vegetables may have the soup by itself while others can garnish the soup according to their own taste. Gaspacho is usually served in cups or bowls rather than soup plates.

POTAGE FROID AU CONCOMBRE
Cold cucumber soup

PREPARATION TIME: 15 minutes (2 hours before serving)
COOKING TIME: nil
FOR SIX

1½ cucumbers
75 g (about 2½ oz) peeled
  walnuts
6 individual pots of natural
  yoghurt

2 tablespoons fresh fennel herb
  (or mint, if not available)
4 cloves garlic
3 tablespoons olive oil
salt, pepper

Peel the cucumbers and cut them in half lengthways. Scrape out the seeds and cut the flesh into very small dice; put them into a dish and sprinkle them with salt. Let the cucumber sweat for 30 minutes. Then rinse the cucumber in water and dry off in a cloth or on kitchen paper.

Mix the cucumber, chopped nuts, yoghurt, fennel and crushed garlic together in a bowl, season, and then add the oil drop by drop, stirring together. When the mixture is complete, keep in the refrigerator until the time of serving.

Elle advises that this soup from Bulgaria is usually presented in individual bowls. Add a tablespoon of crushed ice to each bowl before serving and decorate with a slice of cucumber.

BAR FARCI
Stuffed bass

PREPARATION TIME: 40 minutes
COOKING TIME: 40–50 minutes
FOR SIX

1 bass of 1¾–2 kg (4–4½ lb) in weight
For the stuffing
150 g (5 oz) salmon roe (or Danish caviar)
3 medium-sized quenelles de brochet
80 g (scant 3 oz) butter
1 shallot, finely chopped
1 teaspoon dried thyme

1 tablespoon each of chopped parsley, chervil and watercress
salt, pepper
Cooking and the sauce
1 lettuce
1 carrot
1 large onion
3 sticks celery
¼ litre (9 fl oz) dry white wine
120 g (scant 4½ oz) butter

Ask your fishmonger to remove the scales from the bass and to gut it through the back, removing the spine in the process.

Mix together well all the ingredients for the stuffing. The salmon roe may be quite salty so taste the mixture before seasoning, which should in any case be done sparingly. Make a sausage of the stuffing and insert it into the cavity of the fish. Close the mouth of the cavity.

Take the green outer leaves of a lettuce and plunge them one by one into salted boiling water for just a second, and then dry them on kitchen paper. Wrap the fish entirely in these lettuce leaves and loosely tie them to keep them in place. Put the fish into a baking-tin.

Chop all the other vegetables and simmer them together in a tablespoon of butter until they are lightly coloured. Arrange them around the fish. Pour a little of the white wine into the baking-tin and cook the fish in a fairly hot oven (200°C/400°F/Gas Mark 6). Moisten with a little wine from time to time; it won't be necessary to use it all.

The fish should be served whole on a dish. Remove any ties, open the envelope of lettuce and draw it back around the fish. Stir the remainder of the wine into the juices in the baking-tin, season to taste and boil for 5 minutes. Strain the sauce and bring it back to the boil. Remove from the heat and whip the sauce while adding the remainder of the butter, knob by knob. Serve in a warmed sauce-boat.

CABILLAUD EN COCOTTE
Cod and tomato casserole

PREPARATION TIME: 5 minutes
COOKING TIME: 30 minutes
FOR SIX

3 large cod fillets
2 onions
3 cloves garlic
3 tablespoons olive oil

5 tomatoes
bouquet garni
200 ml (7 fl oz) dry white wine
salt, pepper

In a fireproof dish, slowly cook the chopped onion and garlic in olive oil until they are transparent, add the peeled and seeded tomatoes cut in quarters, raise to a brisk heat and add the bouquet garni, the white wine and seasoning. Stir well together and, when bubbling, reduce the heat and cook uncovered for 15 minutes. Add the cod fillets, lightly season with salt and cook slowly, still uncovered, for about 10–15 minutes until the fish is done.

Elle suggests that the fish should be served in the dish in which it was cooked, accompanied by boiled rice.

[37]

CABILLAUD AU GRATIN
Gratin of cod

PREPARATION TIME: 30 minutes
COOKING TIME: 30 minutes
FOR SIX

350–400 g (about 12–14 oz)
  cooked cod fillet
6 medium-sized potatoes
250 g (about 8 oz) button
  mushrooms
lemon juice
50 g (scant 2 oz) butter

1 shallot
40 g (scant 1½ oz) flour
400 ml (14 fl oz) cold boiled milk
salt, pepper, nutmeg
50 g (scant 2 oz) grated Gruyère
  cheese

Prepare the fish in individual fireproof dishes. Left-over white fish may be used but in any case the fish used should have been poached in a court-bouillon.

Cook the potatoes in their skins, peel them while they are still warm, slice them and line the bottom of each serving-dish.

Slice the mushrooms, sprinkle them with lemon juice and fry them in butter together with the finely-chopped shallot. When the liquid has evaporated, sprinkle them with flour and cook for a further minute, stirring all the time. Add the cold milk and continue stirring and cooking while the mixture thickens. Season, add grated nutmeg and the flaked cod fillet and mix together.

Divide the mixture among the serving-dishes and sprinkle each one with grated cheese. Put in a fairly hot oven (200°C/400°F/Gas Mark 6) until each dish is heated through and the cheese has formed a brown crust.

Elle suggests that this dish can be prepared in advance, and kept in a refrigerator before cooking in the oven.

CABILLAUD PORTUGAISE
Cod Portuguese

PREPARATION TIME: 20 minutes
COOKING TIME: 30–40 minutes
FOR SIX

3 good-sized cod steaks
flour
olive oil
12 small onions
4 good-sized tomatoes
2 cloves garlic

1 red pepper
1 green pepper
thyme, rosemary
100 ml (3½ fl oz) dry white wine
salt, pepper

Buy cod steaks about 2–3 cm (1 in) thick. Wipe them, salt both sides and leave for a few minutes. Roll them in flour and cook in oil in a pan until golden-brown on both sides, taking care not to let the oil burn. Remove the fish to a casserole in which the dish will cook and be served.

In the same oil, first brown the small onions and add them to the cod. Then put in the peeled and seeded tomatoes, and the crushed garlic. Cut the peppers in half lengthways, remove the seeds and inner membranes and soften them under a grill until the skin can be peeled off. Cut the peppers into strips, add them to the tomato mixture and then pour it all over the fish.

Sprinkle in a level tablespoon of chopped fresh or dried thyme, and a few leaves of rosemary. Moisten with white wine, season with freshly ground pepper and cook uncovered over a moderate heat, without stirring the dish, for 20 minutes. Then reduce the heat further, cover the dish and let it simmer for about 5 more minutes.

Elle suggests that this dish may be served either with boiled rice or boiled potatoes.

MORUE AUX OIGNONS
Salt-cod with onions

PREPARATION TIME: 24 hours of soaking
COOKING TIME: 45 minutes
FOR SIX

1 whole salt-cod	50 g (scant 2 oz) flour
1 kg (2¼ lb) potatoes	frying oil
4 large onions	20 black olives
200 ml (7 fl oz) olive oil	3 hard-boiled eggs
2 cloves of garlic	pepper

Use a small sharp knife to skin the salt-cod. Cut the flesh into pieces and steep it in plenty of cold water for 24 hours to remove the salt. The water should be changed at least three times during this period.

On the day of cooking, put the pieces of salt-cod in a saucepan with plenty of cold water and bring it slowly to the boil. As soon as it bubbles, remove from the heat.

Cook the potatoes in their skins, then peel them and cut them into slices. Remove the salt-cod from its pan with a perforated spoon and flake it. Peel the onions, cut them into slices and separate into rings. Keep enough rings on one side to decorate the dish. Heat half the olive oil in a pan and slowly cook the onion rings until they are transparent. Add the crushed garlic and stir frequently.

Take an ovenproof dish and put in alternating layers of potato, flaked salt-cod and onion rings. Pour on the remaining olive oil and cook for 20 minutes in a fairly hot oven (200°C/400°F/Gas Mark 6).

While the dish is cooking, roll the remaining onion rings in flour and drop them briefly into a pan of hot oil. Remove and drain them.

Take the dish from the oven and decorate it with black olives, slices of hard-boiled egg and fried onion rings.

Elle suggests that a green salad goes well with this dish which comes from Portugal.

BRANDADE DE MORUE
Salt-cod pâté

SOAKING TIME: 12 or 24 hours
PREPARATION TIME: 10 minutes
COOKING TIME: 1½ hours
FOR SIX

1200 g (2¾ lb) salt-cod or 2 tins	300 ml (10 fl oz) olive oil
of salt-cod fillets	150 ml (5¼ fl oz) boiled milk
2 or 3 cloves of garlic	1 potato (optional)

Soak the fish in plenty of cold water to remove the salt; 24 hours in the case of a whole fish, 12 hours for the tinned fillets. The water should be changed from time to time.

Put the fish in a large saucepan of cold water and bring to a slow boil (where the surface of the water quivers without bubbling). Keep at this temperature for 10 minutes, then remove from the heat and keep the fish in its cooking water for a further 10 minutes.

Pick out the skin and bones and flake the filleted fish. Pound it in a mortar to a paste, adding 2 cloves of garlic; put it in a saucepan and, over a medium heat, stir vigorously while alternately adding little by little the olive oil and the warm milk. Care must be taken to see that the mixture does not boil. When it is stiff enough to peak, stop adding the liquids.

The behaviour of the mixture during this stage of preparation can be capricious! If it persists in remaining too soft and fluid, thoroughly mix in potato which has been boiled in its skin and mashed. Again, add only enough to ensure a mixture of the right consistency.

This dish should be served very hot, garnished with triangles of bread lightly rubbed with garlic and fried in olive oil, and with black olives.

MATELOTE D'ANGUILLES
Eel stew

PREPARATION TIME: 10 minutes
COOKING TIME: 1 hour
FOR SIX

2 kg (4½ lb) eels
2 tablespoons flour
100 g (3½ oz) butter
small glass of Armagnac
1 bottle of white wine (Riesling or Anjou)
salt, pepper

bouquet garni
20 small button mushrooms
lemon juice
20 small white onions
sugar
6 or 8 triangles of white bread
oil

Cut the skinned and prepared eel in 5 cm (2½ in) pieces. Coat them lightly with flour. Heat a tablespoon of butter in a casserole and put in the pieces of eel. Let them cook long enough to seal without taking on colour, remove from the heat and sprinkle them with the Armagnac. Leave for a few minutes.

Pour in enough white wine to cover the eel thoroughly, season and add the bouquet garni. Bring to the boil. After 3 or 4 minutes, remove the eel from the casserole and put it in a warm place. Continue cooking the sauce over a low heat for a further 20 minutes.

The mushrooms which, after peeling, should have been sprinkled with lemon juice to prevent discoloration, should now be added to the sauce. Cook the onions very slowly in butter, so that they neither break up nor are browned. Glaze them with a teaspoon of caster sugar, add salt.

Work butter and the rest of the flour together in equal quantities. Remove the casserole from the heat and extend the flour and butter mixture with small quantities of sauce: return this mixture to the sauce and stir well in. Bring back to the boil, replace the eel and keep to a slow boil (the surface of the water quivering but not bubbling) for 10 minutes. Add the onions.

Serve from the casserole into soup plates. Garnish with triangles of bread which have been fried in oil and butter.

If a red wine matelote is prepared, the method is the same except that the sauce is cooked for 10 minutes longer.

ASSIETTE DES PÊCHEURS
Fisherman's platter

PREPARATION TIME: 20 minutes
COOKING TIME: 45 minutes
FOR SIX

1 small bass of 400 g (14 oz)
1 John Dory of 400 g (14 oz)
1 piece of salmon of 250 g (about 8 oz)
12 scallops
18 langoustines
chopped chervil
250 g (scant 9 oz) butter

For the court-bouillon
200 g (7 oz) carrots
200 g (7 oz) onions
200 g (7 oz) leeks, white part only
1 stick of celery
1 bottle of dry white wine (Muscadet)
bouquet garni
salt, freshly-ground black pepper

Trim and wash the vegetables and cut them all into thin (julienne) strips. Melt 50 g (scant 2 oz) of butter in a saucepan, put in the cut vegetables and simmer them gently. Pour in the white wine and 1 litre (1¾ pints) of water; add the bouquet garni. Salt sparingly and season with pepper. Continue cooking for 30 minutes and then strain the court-bouillon.

Ask your fishmonger to fillet the bass and the John Dory. Cut off the heads and legs of the langoustines (small crayfish), take the scallops from their shells and cut the white parts in two if they are too thick. Wash and dry all the fish and shellfish.

Poach each separately in the court-bouillon for about 2 or 3 minutes, remove and keep warm in a double-boiler. Then reduce the court-bouillon over a brisk heat by about a quarter. Take it off the heat and whisk in the remaining 200 g (7 oz) butter, knob by knob.

Divide the fish and shellfish among individual warmed dishes, cover with the sauce and sprinkle with chopped chervil.

The chef of 'Le Domaine' restaurant in Orvault (Loire-Atlantique), from where this recipe comes, recommends that a chilled Chablis should be drunk with the dish.

HADDOCK AU CURRY
Smoked haddock in a curry sauce

PREPARATION TIME: 20 minutes (2 hours in advance)
COOKING TIME: 40 minutes
FOR SIX

1 kg (2¼ lb) smoked haddock
  fillet
½ litre (18 fl oz) milk
60 g (2 oz) butter
6 onions

clove of garlic
2 tablespoons curry powder
tablespoon of flour
200 ml (7 fl oz) dry white wine
200 ml (7 fl oz) double cream

Cut the fish into squares and leave it to soak for 2 hours in the milk, together with enough water to cover it completely. Then drain and dry the fish.

Melt the butter in a pan and heat through the pieces of haddock until they just begin to swell. Remove from the pan. Gently cook the finely-chopped onion in the same pan until the onion is transparent. Add the curry powder and a level tablespoon of flour and, stirring frequently, cook for a few minutes. Pour in the wine, cover the dish and let the mixture simmer for 15 minutes. Stir in the cream and add the haddock. If the sauce is too thick, it can be extended with a little boiling water.

Cover the dish again and continue cooking over a very low heat for 12–15 minutes, trying not to let the sauce boil.

Serve the dish sprinkled with chopped parsley, together with either boiled potatoes or rice.

HADDOCK CHARENTAISE
Smoked haddock Charente

PREPARATION TIME: 10 minutes
COOKING TIME: (FISH): 10–15 minutes
           (SAUCE): 20–25 minutes
FOR SIX

3 or 4 small smoked haddock
  fillets
500 ml (18 fl oz) boiled milk
250 ml (9 fl oz) crème fraîche

60 g (2 oz) butter
salt, pepper, nutmeg
lemon juice

Try to buy small fillets. Lay them full-length in a fireproof dish and just cover them with the milk and added water. Bring the liquid to the boil, remove from the heat and leave the fish to continue to poach in the cooking liquid for 10–15 minutes (according to the size of the fish).

To make the sauce, put 6 tablespoons of the cooking liquid into a warm (but not boiling) double-boiler and mix in the crème fraîche and the butter knob by knob. Continue whipping until the sauce coats the back of a spoon. Season to taste, add a little grated nutmeg and several drops of lemon juice.

The sauce is served separately from the fish. Boiled potatoes or rice will go well with this dish.

HARENGS À LA DIABLE
Devilled herrings

PREPARATION TIME: 15 minutes
COOKING TIME: 20–25 minutes
FOR SIX

6 herrings
100 g (3½ oz) Dijon mustard
cayenne pepper
dried breadcrumbs
100 g (3½ oz) butter

Gut the herrings and take out the soft or hard roes.

Put the Dijon mustard in a bowl and stir in a pinch of cayenne pepper. Slash the herrings two or three times on each side. Take the roes and brush them with mustard and put them back inside the fish. Brush the fish all over with mustard and roll them in dried breadcrumbs.

Put the fish under a grill, moistening them from time to time with melted butter. Turn them over carefully so as not to break the fish and cook the other side similarly.

Serve with fried or chipped potatoes.

Elle suggests that mackerel may also be cooked in this way. The method has the merit of reducing the cooking smell.

HARENGS MARINÉS AU CITRON
Herrings in lemon juice

PREPARATION TIME: 15 minutes
MARINADING TIME: 3 hours
COOKING TIME: nil
FOR SIX

1 kg (2¼ lb) herrings with soft roes
500 g (generous 1 lb) juicy lemons
½ orange
salt, pepper
olive oil
chopped mixed herbs

Using a thin sharp knife, detach the whole fillets from the herrings. Break up the raw soft roes by putting them through a fine sieve, mix with the juice of all the lemons and the half-orange. Lay the herring fillets out full-length in an earthenware dish, season and cover with the marinade. Leave in a cool place for 3 hours.

Just before serving, draw off half the liquid and pour a tablespoon of olive oil over the fish. Season lightly and sprinkle with chopped herbs.

The dish should be eaten on the day it is prepared.

The chef of the 'd'Olympe' restaurant in Paris from where this recipe comes, recommends a Gewurztraminer with these delicious herrings.

HARENGS SAUCE MOUTARDE
Herrings in a mustard sauce

PREPARATION TIME: 20 minutes
COOKING TIME: 30 minutes
FOR SIX

6 herrings
For the sauce
70 g (scant 2½ oz) butter
40 g (scant 1½ oz) flour

3 egg yolks
salt, pepper
2 teaspoons of strong Dijon
   mustard

The herrings may be cooked as you wish, either fried in a spoonful of oil or, better still, slashed on both sides and grilled. This latter method has the advantage of driving a lot of the fat from the fish, and of reducing the cooking smell.

For the sauce, melt 40 g (1½ oz) butter in a pan, mix in the flour and cook for 1 minute, stirring continuously. Pour in 300 ml (10½ fl oz) cold water all at once, reduce and thicken the mixture. Beat the egg yolks, stir in a little of the mixture and then add the egg to the pan. Season and let the sauce boil for 2 minutes, adding the mustard a little at a time.

Take the sauce from the heat and, just before serving, glaze it by stirring in the 30 g (1 oz) butter, knob by knob.

Boiled potatoes are the usual accompaniment to this dish, but some prefer either fried or chipped potatoes.

BROCHETTES DE LOTTE
Kebabs of monkfish

PREPARATION TIME: 20 minutes (1 hour in advance)
COOKING TIME: 10 minutes
FOR SIX

1 kg (2¼ lb) monkfish
150 g (5 oz) smoked bacon
For the marinade
150 ml (3½ fl oz) olive oil
15 coriander seeds

teaspoon of fennel seeds or dried
   fennel
juice of 1 lemon
salt, pepper

Cut the fish into cubes 3 cm (a good inch) in size. Put all the ingredients for the marinade into a flat dish, stir them together and then add the pieces of fish. Let them marinate for an hour, turning them over from time to time.

Cut the bacon (which should be in thick slices) into squares and thread bacon and fish alternately onto kebab skewers, beginning and ending with a piece of bacon. Brush each kebab with marinade.

If the kebabs are to be cooked on a barbecue, light it at least 30 minutes in advance and make sure the grill can be raised and lowered. If using an oven grill, heat it 10 minutes in advance and cook the kebabs in the intermediate position. Turn the kebabs occasionally while they are cooking.

Serve with saffron rice.

Elle suggests that, to save time, the marinating could be done the day before, leaving it overnight in the refrigerator. If doing this, be sure to remove the fish at least an hour before making up the kebabs.

MAQUEREAUX PROVENÇALE
Provençale mackerel

PREPARATION TIME: 30 minutes
COOKING TIME: 25–30 minutes
FOR SIX

6 medium-sized mackerel
salt, pepper
150 g (5 oz) button mushrooms
2 medium-sized onions
1 shallot
1 small clove of garlic (optional)
40 g (scant 1½ oz) butter
3 tablespoons vinegar

Gut the mackerel without taking off the heads. Wash and wipe the fish and slash them two or three times on each side. Roll them in a mixture of salt and pepper, and put them under a grill. (If you have no grill, buy good mackerel fillets, season them and coat them in flour, then fry them in oil. The dish will not look as attractive, but will taste as good.)

Chop up the mushrooms, the onions, the shallot and the clove of garlic. Cook them all gently together in butter until the liquid from the mushrooms has evaporated. Add the vinegar, season and bring to the boil for 2 minutes.

Arrange the fish in a serving dish, pour the mushroom mixture over them and garnish with stuffed tomatoes.

Although this is a simple and inexpensive dish, with stuffed tomatoes it is good enough for a supper party.

MAQUEREAUX AU VIN BLANC
Mackerel in white wine

PREPARATION TIME: 5 minutes
COOKING TIME: 20 minutes
FOR SIX

6 medium-sized mackerel
1 sachet of powdered
  court-bouillon
½ litre (18 fl oz) dry white wine
1 large onion
2 carrots
1 lemon
6 peppercorns
2 cloves
salt

Gut the fish through the gills, wash and wipe them. Lay them in a flat fireproof dish, sprinkle on half of the court-bouillon powder and pour the wine over them, together with ½ litre (18 fl oz) of water. Add the lemon and the carrot, both cut into thin slices, the onion cut into separated rings, the peppercorns and the cloves. The fish should be completely covered by liquid.

Cover the dish with aluminium foil and put over a medium heat. When the liquid is bubbling, cook for a further 5–12 minutes (according to the size of the fish) and then remove from the heat.

Let the fish cool in their liquid. Then put them into a serving dish, garnished with onion rings and with slices of lemon and carrot from the court-bouillon. If necessary, reduce the court-bouillon over a brisk heat, season with salt and when cool strain it through a sieve on to the fish.

If this dish is eaten hot instead of cold, accompany it with boiled potatoes.

LOTTE À LA BRETONNE
Gratin of monkfish

PREPARATION TIME: 15 minutes
COOKING TIME: 50 minutes – 1 hour
FOR SIX

1 kg (2¼ lb) monkfish
1 sachet of powdered
*   court-bouillon*
50 g (scant 2 oz) butter
flour

250 ml (9 fl oz) single cream
salt, pepper
2 tablespoons grated Gruyère
*   cheese*

Cut the flesh of the tail of the monkfish into even-sized pieces, removing the spine as this becomes possible. Put the pieces of fish in a saucepan, arranged in a single even layer. Sprinkle on the court-bouillon powder, pour in enough water to completely cover the fish and, with the lid on, cook over a brisk heat. As soon as the liquid boils, reduce the heat and let it simmer for 30 minutes.

Remove and drain the fish and arrange the pieces in an ovenproof dish. Keep in a warm place.

Strain the cooking liquid and reduce it over a brisk heat by a good third. Make a white sauce with the butter, two level tablespoons of flour and add a glass (5 fl oz) of reduced liquid and all the cream. The sauce should have the consistency of a light béchamel. Season and, if necessary, add a bit more of the court-bouillon.

Drain off from the serving dish any liquid given off by the fish. Cover it with the sauce, sprinkle with the grated cheese and put into a very hot oven (240°C/475°F/Gas Mark 9) until the surface is golden-brown and the dish heated right through.

LOTTE RÔTIE
Baked monkfish

PREPARATION TIME: 10 minutes
COOKING TIME: 20–25 minutes
FOR SIX

1200 g (2¾ lb) monkfish
2 cloves of garlic
100 ml (3½ fl oz) olive oil
several twigs of dried fennel
salt, pepper

a sprig of thyme
1 bay leaf
1 lemon
Pernod (optional)

Wash the piece of fish and take off the fine skin that covers it, and remove any fins. Dry the fish on kitchen paper. Peel the garlic, slice it and stick the pieces into the fish. Tie up the fish as if it were a roast of meat.

Pour the oil into an ovenproof dish, arrange the twigs of fennel and place the piece of monkfish on them. Season, add the thyme and the bay leaf, sprinkle on the juice of a lemon and cook in a fairly hot oven (200°C/400°F/Gas Mark 6).

Elle suggests that, if wished, the dish can be flamed just before serving with a small glass of Pernod or Ricard.

LOTTE EN BOURGUIGNON
Burgundian monkfish

PREPARATION TIME: 50 minutes (in advance)
COOKING TIME: 35 minutes
FOR SIX

1¼ kg (2¾ lb) monkfish
3 carrots
1 leek
200 g (7 oz) small onions
3 shallots
bouquet garni
8 peppercorns
pinch of cinnamon
pinch of grated nutmeg

pinch of quatre épices (see page 29)
salt
1 bottle of red burgundy
tablespoon of oil
90 g (3 oz) butter
30 g (1 oz) flour
2 tablespoons sugar

Rinse and dry the monkfish and cut it up into pieces. Put them into an earthenware dish and add the sliced carrot, the leek cut into three, the peeled onions, the shallots, bouquet garni, the peppercorns, all the spices and a pinch of salt. Add the bottle of wine and leave overnight.

The next day, take out the pieces of fish, and wipe them. Put the marinade through a sieve and, separately, reserve both the liquid and the vegetables.

Heat the oil and 30 g (1 oz) of butter together in a pan and brown the fish on all sides. Remove with a perforated spoon and arrange the pieces in a casserole. In the same fat, cook the vegetables from the marinade. Add them to the fish and put the casserole on one side.

Heat the marinade (wine) in a saucepan, bringing it to the boil. Thoroughly mix together the flour and 60 g (2 oz) butter with a fork. Add this mixture little by little to the wine, whisking thoroughly all the time. Then make a tablespoon of caramel by heating the sugar mixed with a few drops of water; add it to the sauce which should simmer for 20 minutes. Add to the fish and cook for a further 15 minutes.

For vegetables, both boiled potatoes and salsifis cooked in butter go well with this dish.

The chef of the Paris restaurant 'La Bonne Table', from which this recipe comes, recommends that a good Burgundy be drunk with it.

LOTTE SAUCE ROSE
Monkfish in pink sauce

PREPARATION TIME: 20 minutes
COOKING TIME: 40 minutes
FOR SIX

1 kg (2¼ lb) monkfish
1 kg (2¼ lb) tomatoes
4 shallots
4 tablespoons olive oil
sprig of thyme

2 bay leaves
salt, pepper
150 ml (5 fl oz) single cream
2 eggs
cayenne pepper

Cut the monkfish up into pieces. Peel and seed the tomatoes and chop them into large pieces. Chop the shallots and put them into a pan with the cold oil; gently heat them until they become transparent. Add the chopped tomatoes, the thyme and the bay leaves, season and cook together over a brisk flame for 10 minutes. Add the pieces of fish and as soon as the liquid returns to the boil, lower the heat, cover the pan and let it simmer for 20 minutes.

Take out the fish and arrange the pieces in a warmed serving dish. Reduce the sauce to a creamy consistency and pass it through a sieve into another pan. Mix the cream and beaten egg yolks together and add them to the sauce. Season with a little cayenne and warm through over a low heat, taking care not to let the sauce boil, and stirring constantly. The sauce is ready when it coats the back of a spoon.

Pour over the fish and serve immediately, with a dish of hot buttered rice.

MULET BOHÉMIENNE
Grey mullet Bohéme

PREPARATION TIME: 30 minutes
COOKING TIME: 45 minutes–1 hour
FOR SIX

1 grey mullet about 1200 g
  (2¾ lb)
300 g (10½ oz) chopped onion
100 ml (3½ fl oz) oil
1 large green pepper

3 or 4 tomatoes
salt, pepper, cayenne pepper
1 clove garlic
4 or 5 twigs of dried fennel
150 ml (5¼ fl oz) white wine

Ask your fishmonger to gut the fish through the gills and to clean it out carefully. Wash and wipe the fish and season the interior.

In a casserole, gently cook the chopped onion in the oil, stirring frequently until it becomes transparent. Cut the pepper in half lengthways, remove the seeds, stalk and inner membranes and slice the flesh into thin strips. Add them to the onion and, when they have become soft, add the peeled and seeded tomatoes. Season and stir in a small pinch of cayenne pepper. After 25–30 minutes of gentle cooking, add the crushed garlic.

Arrange the dried fennel twigs in the bottom of an ovenproof dish and pour the sauce over them. Place the fish on top. Put the dish into a fairly hot oven (200°C/400°F/Gas Mark 6). When the sauce starts to bubble, pour the wine over the fish.

Check the progress of cooking by inserting the point of a knife into the back. When cooked, the knife should slip easily along the length of the spine.

Serve the fish in the dish in which it was cooked, with either boiled rice or boiled potatoes. To prevent the tail scorching in the oven, cover it with aluminium foil.

MULETS AU CITRON VERT
Mullet with limes

PREPARATION TIME: 10 minutes
COOKING TIME: 20 minutes
FOR SIX

6 grey mullet
1 small tin of anchovy fillets
sprig of basil
sprig of parsley

bunch of chives
4 limes
salt, pepper

Gut and scale the mullet, and wash them well in running water.

Pound the anchovies into a paste in a mortar together with the herbs and the juice of one lime. Cut the other 3 limes into round slices. Make four cuts through the backbone of each fish and insert a slice of lime into each. Spread the anchovy paste over the fish and then lightly season them.

Cut six rectangles of aluminium foil and wrap each fish separately. Bake them in a very hot oven (230°C/450°F/Gas Mark 8) for 20 minutes. Serve with boiled rice or boiled potatoes.

Elle suggests that the anchovy paste can be quickly and effectively made in a blender.

MOULES AUX AMANDES
Mussels with almonds

PREPARATION TIME: 30 minutes
COOKING TIME: 15–20 minutes
FOR SIX

60 mussels
1 crushed clove of garlic
2 tablespoons ground almonds
3 tablespoons chopped fresh
  parsley
3 tablespoons melted butter
1 tablespoon lemon juice
salt, pepper

Scrub and wash the mussels very carefully and cook them quickly in boiling water over a brisk heat until they open. Discard any which remain closed. Break off the lid of each mussel at the hinge and arrange the bottom halves by tens in individual ovenproof serving dishes.

Mix all the other ingredients together, season and put a teaspoon of the mixture on to each mussel. Heat an oven to its maximum and put in the dishes; when the mixture starts to bubble, the mussels are ready to serve.

Brown toast is usually served with this dish.

Elle suggests that with smaller or larger helpings, this dish can be served as an hors d'oeuvre or a main course.

MOULES POULETTE
Mussels in a cream and wine sauce

PREPARATION TIME: 25 minutes
COOKING TIME: 25 minutes
FOR SIX

3 litres (5 good pints) mussels
1 onion
80 g (scant 3 oz) butter
100 ml (3½ fl oz) dry white wine
10 peppercorns
bouquet garni
1 tablespoon flour
2 egg yolks
200 ml (7 fl oz) single cream
1 lemon
tablespoon chopped parsley
salt, pepper

Scrub and clean the mussels very carefully. Chop the onion finely and cook gently in a tablespoon of butter until transparent. Add the wine, peppercorns, the bouquet garni and bring to the boil for 1 minute. Add the mussels and as they open, take them out, remove the lid at the hinge and arrange them in a warmed serving dish. Discard any mussels which do not open. This dish should be put over a pan of hot water so that it remains warm.

Strain the cooking liquid and put aside. Melt the rest of the butter in a saucepan, stir in the flour, add the cooking liquid and reduce it. Beat the egg yolks and mix them into the cream, together with the juice of half a lemon; add this to the saucepan and stir well together. Check the seasoning, add the chopped parsley and while the sauce is still boiling, pour it over the mussels.

Should there be any delay in serving, cover the dish so that the mussels do not dry out.

[48]

MOULES MICHEL
Mussels cooked in cream

PREPARATION TIME: 20 minutes
COOKING TIME: 5–8 minutes
FOR SIX

3 litres (5 good pints) mussels
3 shallots
50 g (scant 2 oz) butter
300 ml (10½ fl oz) crème fraîche
1 tablespoon of white wine vinegar
pepper

Scrub the mussels and wash them several times in plenty of cold running water without, however, letting them stand in water.

In a large pan, put the chopped shallots, the butter, the cream, the vinegar and the mussels. Season with plenty of freshly-milled pepper and cover the pan. Put it over a brisk heat, shaking the pan vigorously from time to time. As soon as all the mussels have opened, serve at once with country bread and salted butter. Discard any unopened mussels.

The chef from the Atlantic-Hotel, Wimereux, from where this recipe comes, suggests a Loire wine to go with it; either a Muscadet or a Gros-Plant, or a Sancerre or Pouilly-Fumé.

ROUGETS EN PAPILLOTES
Red mullet in a paper bag

PREPARATION TIME: 30 minutes
COOKING TIME: 15–18 minutes
FOR SIX

6 red mullet, about 150–180 g (5–6½ oz) each
3 medium-sized onions
olive oil
fennel seeds
salt, pepper

Cut heart-shaped pieces of greaseproof paper large enough to enclose the separate fish and to allow the edges to be folded together.

Chop the onions and brush each fish on both sides with olive oil. Put a sprinkling of chopped onion, a few fennel seeds and a small pinch of pepper and salt on to one half of each paper shape. Place the fish on this half and season its upper side in exactly the same way. Fold the paper over and close the envelope by rolling or folding the edges together.

Arrange the envelopes on a grill stand so that when in the oven they will cook evenly top and bottom. Pre-heat a fairly hot oven (200°C/ 400°F/Gas Mark 6) for 15 minutes. Put in the fish and check the progress of cooking by watching the colour of the paper; it should not be allowed to burn.

Serve the fish still in their envelopes. This method avoids cooking smells and allows delays in serving without the fish drying out.

SAUMON EN PAPILLOTES
Salmon with mint

PREPARATION TIME: 20 minutes
COOKING TIME: 5 minutes
FOR SIX

6 salmon steaks each about 170 g (6 oz)	salt, pepper
450 g (1 lb) sorrel	1 lime
20 leaves of fresh mint	90 g (3 oz) butter

If sorrel is not available, use the same quantity of spinach with a squeeze of lemon juice.

Divide the vegetable and wash it in plenty of running water, also the leaves of mint. Dry them together, first in a salad-basket and then in a cloth. Chop the mixture finely.

Remove the skin and the spine from each piece of fish. Take six sheets of aluminium foil each large enough to enclose one piece of fish. On each sheet of foil, make a bed of chopped sorrel and mint, place a piece of fish on it, season, add another layer of sorrel and mint, a slice of lime and a knob of butter.

Bring the edges of the foil together to make an envelope, ensuring that there is a good tight seal but also that some space remains around the fish. Pre-heat an oven to its maximum temperature and cook the fish for 5 minutes. Serve with *beurre blanc*.

The chef of 'Le Petit Bedon' restuarant in Avignon from where this recipe comes, recommends serving a chilled still white wine from the Champagne region with the dish.

SAUMON AU BEURRE D'ANCHOIS
Salmon with anchovy butter

PREPARATION TIME: 10 minutes
COOKING TIME: 15 minutes
FOR SIX

6 salmon steaks each about 170 g (6 oz)	salt, freshly-ground pepper
oil	tube of anchovy paste
12 thin slices of smoked, streaky bacon	50 g (scant 2 oz) butter

Take 6 pieces of aluminium foil or greaseproof paper, each large enough to enclose a piece of fish, and lightly brush them with oil. Lay a slice of bacon on each one (rind removed), then a salmon steak, a light seasoning and finally a second slice of bacon. Close the edges of each envelope carefully and put them into a hot oven (220°C/425°F/Gas Mark 7) for 12–15 minutes, according to the thickness of the salmon.

During the cooking period, work the anchovy paste and the butter together with a fork into a smooth cream. Serve the fish with the envelope opened and with a knob of anchovy butter placed in the centre.

SAUMON EN RILLETTES
Terrine of salmon

PREPARATION TIME: 30 minutes
COOKING TIME: 8 minutes
TO MAKE 500 G (A GOOD LB) OF TERRINE:

250 g (about 8 oz) fresh salmon
200 ml (7 fl oz) dry white wine
50 ml (1¾ fl oz) olive oil
2 tablespoons brandy

salt, freshly-ground pepper
250 g (about 8 oz) smoked
  salmon
200 g (7 oz) butter

Skin and fillet the fresh salmon and cut the flesh into cubes. Put them in a saucepan, add the white wine and bring to the boil. As soon as the first bubbles appear, remove from the heat.

Warm the oil gently in a small pan and cook the cubes of salmon, removed with a perforated spoon from the wine in which they were poached, so that they do not take on any more colour. Add the brandy and seasoning, mix together and put to one side in a cool place.

Cut the smoked salmon into large pieces and cook it slowly in half the butter, again so that it does not take on any more colour. Allow it to cool and then pound it in a mortar, together with the rest of the butter, softened. Continue to work the mixture until a creamy paste results. Stir the cooked fresh salmon into this paste, check the seasoning, turn into a terrine dish and refrigerate overnight. Serve chilled.

The chef from the restaurant 'Julien' in Paris, from where this recipe comes, recommends that it be served with a cold bottle of Chablis.

SARDINES À L'AÏOLI
Sardines with garlic mayonnaise

PREPARATION TIME: 30 minutes
COOKING TIME: (POTATOES): 40–50 minutes
                    (SARDINES): 10 minutes
FOR SIX

6 large potatoes
24–30 fresh sardines
oil

1 egg yolk
250 ml (9 fl oz) olive oil
½ lemon
salt, pepper

For the aïoli
4 or 5 cloves of garlic

Begin by baking the potatoes. Wrap each in aluminium foil and put them in a very hot oven (230°C/450°F/Gas Mark 8). After 40 minutes, pierce each with a skewer – if it penetrates easily right through, they are done. Turn off the oven and keep the potatoes warm.

Make the garlic mayonnaise during this time. Crush the cloves of garlic into a fine paste and mix with the egg yolk in a bowl. Add the oil drop by drop, whipping all the time, as if making an ordinary mayonnaise. When it is stiff, fold in the juice of half a lemon and season. Keep in a cool place.

Gut the sardines but do not scale them. Brush them all over with oil and put them under a grill (or on a barbecue) for 4–5 minutes each side. Unwrap the potatoes and serve at once.

SARDINES AU FOUR
Baked sardines

PREPARATION TIME: 10 minutes
COOKING TIME: 15 minutes
FOR SIX

36 fresh sardines
twigs of dried fennel
fennel seeds

3 tablespoons olive oil
salt, pepper
lemons

Gut the sardines and remove the heads. Do not wash them but wipe them with a damp cloth.

Take an ovenproof dish and make a bed of fennel twigs on the bottom. Arrange the sardines in rows on this bed. Sprinkle fennel seeds and olive oil over them, and season. Mix 200 ml (7 fl oz) of water and the juice of one lemon and moisten the sardines with part of it.

Pre-heat a hot oven (220°C/425°F/Gas Mark 7) and cook for 15 minutes. Moisten the sardines frequently during the cooking with the water and lemon liquid. Serve with quarters of lemon.

Elle suggests that this quickly-prepared dish of sardines will go well with boiled potatoes.

COQUILLES SAINT-JACQUES
Scallops sautés

PREPARATION TIME: 15 minutes
COOKING TIME: 25 minutes
FOR SIX

24–30 scallops (according to size)
150 ml (5 fl oz) olive oil
flour

150 g (5 oz) butter
bunch of parsley
2 cloves of garlic
salt, pepper

Ask your fishmonger to open and trim the scallops for you. Only the white muscle and the red coral is eaten. Wash them quickly but well in running water, drain them and lightly sprinkle with salt.

Heat half the oil in a pan. Wipe the scallops and roll them in flour, shaking off any surplus. Cook them over a moderate heat until golden-brown, stirring frequently. If necessary, add a little more oil from time to time.

Clarify the butter by melting it in a saucepan over a low flame. When it foams, skim it off and then carefully decant the liquid butter into another saucepan, taking care that none of the deposit at the bottom of the pan goes with it.

Put the clarified butter back on the heat, and transfer the scallops to it using a perforated spoon so that any of their cooking oil drains off. Let them simmer gently over a very low heat until they are completely cooked. Chop parsley and garlic and put three-quarters of it in with the scallops to heat through. Remove the scallops and garnish to a warm serving dish, and sprinkle on the remaining chopped parsley.

COQUILLES AUX POIREAUX
Scallops with leeks

PREPARATION TIME: 20 minutes
COOKING TIME: 15–20 minutes
FOR SIX

2 kg (4½ lb) leeks (not large ones)
24 scallops
15 g (½ oz) butter
salt, freshly-ground pepper
cayenne pepper
300 ml (10½ fl oz) crème fraîche
grated nutmeg

Trim the leeks, keeping only the white parts, and tie them together in small bundles. Cook them in plenty of salted boiling water; when they are tender, remove and rinse them in cold water. They must be thoroughly drained of all water, squeezing them between the hands if necessary.

While the leeks are cooking, open and clean the scallops, retaining only the white muscle and the red coral. Rinse them under running water. Butter the insides of individual ovenproof dishes and line the bottom with round slices of leek 1 cm (about ¼–½ in) thick. Arrange the scallops on these beds of leeks so that the coral is uppermost. Season and sprinkle with a very little cayenne pepper. Cover the scallops with crème fraîche and dust with grated nutmeg.

Pre-heat a fairly hot oven (200°C/400°F/Gas Mark 6) and cook the scallops for about 10–15 minutes.

The chef of the restaurant 'L'Aquitaine' in Paris, from where this recipe comes, recommends serving a Chablis with this dish.

COQUILLES NEWBURG
Scallops Newburg

PREPARATION TIME: 10 minutes
COOKING TIME: 20–25 minutes
FOR SIX

4–6 scallops per person
flour
125 g (4½ oz) butter
salt, pepper
1 small glass of brandy
150 ml (5¼ fl oz) madeira
250 ml (9 fl oz) crème fraîche
3 egg yolks
1 small tin of truffles (if available)

Wash and wipe the scallops. Separate the coral from the white muscle and cut the latter into 2 or 3 pieces. Dust the scallops lightly with flour.

Melt 2 tablespoons of butter in a pan and, as it begins to foam, add the scallops. Cook gently so that they become firm without taking on any colour. Season, and pour over the brandy and madeira; increase the heat considerably and quickly reduce the liquid so as to cover the scallops completely in their sauce. Add half the crème fraîche. If truffles are available, add the liquid and any small pieces from the tin. Let everything simmer uncovered for 5–8 minutes, stirring occasionally.

Beat the egg yolks into the rest of the crème fraîche and add to the saucepan. Let the sauce thicken over a low heat, without it being allowed to boil, and then turn everything out on to a warmed serving dish. Garnish with slices of truffle if available.

Elle suggests that small button mushrooms, if necessary, can be substituted for the truffles. Slice them and cook them separately in a little butter and thereafter use them in the same manner prescribed for the truffles.

LOUP FLAMBÉ
Grilled sea bass

PREPARATION TIME: 10 minutes
COOKING TIME: 15–18 minutes per lb
FOR SIX

1 sea bass of about 2 kg (4½ lb)   2 large sprigs dried thyme
225 ml (8 fl oz) olive oil   2 tablespoons of Pernod
salt, pepper

Ask your fishmonger to gut the fish through its gills, but not to de-scale it. Brush the fish all over with oil, season and put it on a grid in a baking dish. Cook in a hot oven (220°C/425°F/Gas Mark 7) for 20 minutes, and then lower to a moderate heat (180°C/350°F/Gas Mark 4) so that the fish cooks through. Check the progress of cooking by running a blade of a knife along the backbone. The fish is cooked when the blade penetrates the whole length without resistance; put the fish on its grid to one side.

Clean and dry the baking dish and put in a sprig of dried thyme and 2 tablespoons of olive oil. In a bowl, put a tablespoon of crumbled leaves of dried thyme together with 2 tablespoons of Pernod; mix them well together. Put the grid with the fish back into the baking dish and pour the thyme and Pernod mixture over the fish. Light the dried thyme and flambé the fish. Take it to the table while still flaming making sure the fish flames all over.

As soon as the flames die down, transfer the fish to a warmed dish and serve at once. Have on the table a bottle of olive oil flavoured with fennel and with thyme, and some cut lemons.

Elle suggests that this dish can also be prepared on a barbecue grill.

RAIE AU BEURRE ROUGE
Skate in red butter

PREPARATION TIME: 30 minutes
COOKING TIME: 20 minutes
FOR SIX

2 kg (4½ lb) skate   For the red butter sauce
1 bay leaf   4 chopped shallots
1 sprig of thyme   2 glasses of red Loire wine
8 peppercorns   125 ml (4½ oz) crème fraîche
salt   300 g (10½ oz) salted butter
freshly-ground pepper

Remove any bloody parts from the skate and soak it in running cold water for 15 minutes. Cut the fish into pieces of about 350 g (¾ lb) in weight and arrange them in an oval casserole. Add the bay leaf, thyme, peppercorns and season with salt. Cover the fish with water and bring slowly to the boil; when the first bubbles appear, remove from the heat and put on one side. The fish will complete its cooking in this way.

In the meantime, prepare the sauce. Put the chopped shallots and the wine into a small saucepan and cook until all the wine has evaporated. At this point, add the crème fraîche and continue to reduce the sauce until it has a thick and almost syrupy consistency. Remove the pan from the heat and add the butter, cut into knobs, a little at a time, whipping constantly and occasionally returning the pan to the (very low) heat. Add a little pepper when the sauce is ready.

Take the skate out of its cooking liquid, drain and skin it, and arrange it on a warm serving dish. Cover it with the red butter sauce and serve with small boiled potatoes.

The chef of the Paris restaurant 'La Solonge', from where this recipe comes, recommends that a wine similar to the one used in cooking the dish should be drunk with it. Bourgeuil is especially good.

RAIE À LA CRÈME
Skate à la crème

PREPARATION TIME: 10 minutes
COOKING TIME: 25–30 minutes
FOR SIX

1200–1500 g (2¾–3¼ lb) skate, trimmed
1 sachet of powdered court-bouillon
60 g (2 oz) butter
400 ml (14 fl oz) double cream
salt, pepper
4 tablespoons of capers

Wash and drain tne skate and divide it into 6 even portions. Arrange them in a large saucepan, sprinkle the court-bouillon powder over them and amply cover them with water. Bring to the boil and as soon as the water bubbles, reduce the heat and let the fish simmer for 10–15 minutes, according to its thickness.

Take out the fish and remove its black skin. Arrange the portions on a warm serving dish (which should then be put with a cover on it over a pan of hot water, to keep the fish warm).

Melt the butter in a saucepan and add half the cream. Stir it over the heat until it thickens, remove from the heat and extend it with the remaining cream. Season and add the capers. Bring back to the boil and immediately pour it over the skate. Serve at once, with boiled potatoes.

LIMANDES À LA MOUTARDE
Lemon sole with mustard sauce

PREPARATION TIME: 30 minutes
COOKING TIME: 30 minutes
FOR SIX

2 large lemon soles, about 500 g (a generous lb) each, or 3 smaller ones
60 g (2 oz) butter
1 lemon
4 or 5 shallots
100 ml (3½ fl oz) white wine
200 ml (7 fl oz) single cream
tablespoon of Dijon mustard
salt, pepper

Ask your fishmonger to fillet the lemon sole. Wipe them and arrange them full-length in an ovenproof dish. Gently melt the butter and pour it over the fish, together with the lemon juice. Put into a fairly hot oven (200°C/400°F/Gas Mark 6).

Chop the shallots and put them into a saucepan along with the white wine. Bring to the boil; when the wine has evaporated, the shallots will be cooked and tender. Mix cream and mustard together and add to the shallots, season and thoroughly stir together. Pour the sauce over the fish and continue to cook in the oven until the dish is glazed but not browned.

Serve with boiled potatoes.

Elle advises that this recipe is equally good made with plaice.

FILETS DE SOLE PASTOURELLE
Fillets of sole in a cream and mussel sauce

PREPARATION TIME: 15 minutes
COOKING TIME: 30 minutes
FOR SIX

3 soles, each of about 700 g
  (1½ lb)
1½ litres (2½ pints) mussels
300 g (10½ oz) button
  mushrooms
2 lemons
50 g (scant 2 oz) butter

salt, pepper
100 ml (3½ fl oz) dry vermouth
75 ml (generous 2½ oz) crème
  fraîche
2 egg yolks
3 tablespoons chopped parsley

Ask your fishmonger to fillet the soles for you. Scrub and thoroughly wash the mussels in running water and put them in a pan with a glass (5 fl oz) of water. Put on a brisk heat until all the mussels open; reject any which do not open. Remove the mussels and discard the shells. Put the cooking liquid through a sieve and reserve it on one side.

Cut the stalks from the mushrooms, wash them in running water and toss them in the juice of 1 lemon. Chop them and put them into a saucepan with the butter, a small glass of water (3½ fl oz), the juice of the second lemon, and seasoning. Cook slowly for 10 minutes and then put on one side.

Butter an ovenproof dish and arrange the sole fillets in it, season and sprinkle on cooking liquid from the mussels, the liquid from the cooked mushrooms and the vermouth. Dot with knobs of butter. Cover the dish with aluminium foil and cook for 15–20 minutes in a hot oven (220°C/425°F/Gas Mark 7). When cooked, the fillets should be firm.

Remove and drain the fish well and put it on a warmed serving dish. Put the cooking liquids into a saucepan and reduce them by half over a brisk heat. Add the cream, remove the pan from the heat and, one by one, beat in the egg yolks. Finally, mix in the chopped parsley.

Arrange the mussels around the fillets, pour the sauce over them and serve.

The chef of the restaurant 'La Pastourelle' in Lyon, from where this recipe comes, recommends that a Pouilly-Fumé be drunk with it.

FILETS DE SOLE AUX ARACHIDES
Fillets of sole with peanuts

PREPARATION TIME: 10 minutes
COOKING TIME: 15 minutes
FOR SIX

3 medium-sized soles
100 g (3½ oz) unsalted peanuts
salt, freshly-ground pepper
150 g (5 oz) flour

100 ml (3½ fl oz) peanut oil
50 g (scant 2 oz) butter
1 lemon

Ask your fishmonger to fillet the soles for you. Thoroughly rinse and wipe the fillets.

Roughly break up the peanuts in a mortar. Season the fish, coat the fillets in flour and fry them in the peanut oil. Allow about 8–10 minutes' cooking time, turning them once. Remove and drain them, and arrange them on a hot serving-dish.

Brown the peanut pieces in a small pan in a little butter. When they are ready, sprinkle them over the fish, squeeze on the juice of a lemon, and serve.

Elle advises that salted peanuts can be used if unsalted ones cannot be found, but adjust the seasoning accordingly.

FILETS DE SOLE PRINTANIERS
Fillets of sole with spring vegetables

PREPARATION TIME: 45 minutes
COOKING TIME: 1 hour
FOR SIX TO EIGHT

2 soles about 500 g (a good lb) each	125 g (4½ oz) carrots
¾ bottle of Muscadet	125 g (4½ oz) young turnips
100 g (3½ oz) button mushrooms	salt, pepper
2 tomatoes	125 g (4½ oz) butter
1 leek	300 ml (10½ fl oz) crème fraîche
3 sticks celery	1 lemon
	sprig of chervil

Ask your fishmonger to fillet the soles for you. Keep the bones, and make a fish stock by simmering them for 20 minutes in three-quarters of the bottle of Muscadet. Strain and keep on one side.

Trim the stalks from the mushrooms, peel and seed the tomatoes and trim all the other vegetables. Cut all the vegetables into thin strips or slices and cook them in the fish stock for 8–10 minutes. Remove and drain.

Season the fillets of sole, fold them in two, smooth side inside, and arrange them in a lightly buttered fireproof dish. Set the cooked vegetables around them. Bring the fish stock to the boil, pour it over the fish and poach for 12 minutes over a very low heat.

Put the fish fillets into a warm serving dish, garnish with the various vegetables and moisten with a ladle of the cooking liquid. Keep it warm while preparing the sauce.

Melt the butter in a pan and, whipping vigorously, add the crème fraîche little by little. Season, stir in the juice of a lemon and the chopped chervil. Serve the sauce separately from the fish.

The chef of the famous 'Coq Hardy' restaurant at Bougival outside Paris from where this recipe comes, recommends that a white Burgundy, such as Chassagne-Montrachet, be drunk with this dish.

SOLES CHAMBERY
Fillets of sole in vermouth

PREPARATION TIME: 10 minutes
COOKING TIME: 20 minutes
FOR SIX

2 nice soles about 400 g (14 oz) each	30 g (1 oz) butter
2 shallots	salt, pepper
3 sprigs of tarragon	1 small glass of dry vermouth
1 sprig of chervil	100 ml (3½ fl oz) crème fraîche

Get your fishmonger to fillet the soles.

Finely chop the shallots, tarragon and chervil. Lavishly butter an ovenproof dish and sprinkle the chopped herbs over the bottom. Lay the fillets of sole on top, season, moisten with vermouth and pour the crème fraîche evenly over the fish. Cook for 20 minutes in a hot oven (200°C/400°F/Gas Mark 6).

The chef of the Paris restaurant 'Pauline' has provided this recipe and he recommends that a Sancerre be drunk with this dish.

TRUITES À L'OSEILLE
Trout with sorrel

PREPARATION TIME: 30 minutes
COOKING TIME: 30 minutes
FOR SIX

6 medium-sized trout	400 g (14 oz) sorrel
4 or 5 medium-sized onions	50 g (scant 2 oz) butter
1 tablespoon butter	2 tablespoons cornflour
salt, pepper	200 ml (7 fl oz) single cream
½ litre (18 fl oz) white wine, preferably from the Loire	2 egg yolks

Chop the onions finely and cook gently until transparent in the table-spoon of butter. Transfer them to an ovenproof dish in which the trout will be cooked. Spread out the cooked onion, lay the trout over them, head-to-tail, season and pour on the white wine. Put the dish in a fairly hot oven (200°C/400°F/Gas Mark 6). As soon as the cooking liquid bubbles, turn off the heat, cover the dish with a sheet of aluminium foil and leave it for 5 minutes in the oven with the door open.

Melt the 50 g (2 oz) butter and cook the sorrel, stirring constantly. If sorrel is not available, use the same quantity of spinach with a squeeze of lemon juice. Salt lightly and sprinkle the cornflour over it. When the vegetable is reduced to a creamy consistency, spread it over the bottom of a warmed serving dish.

Carefully remove the trout from their dish and skin them. Lay the fish head-to-tail on the sorrel and keep in a warm place; however, they should not be allowed to continue cooking.

Reduce the cooking liquid to a volume of about 150 ml (5½ fl oz) and add half the cream. Continue the reduction until a smooth and creamy texture is obtained. Then add the rest of the cream which should have been mixed with the beaten egg yolks. Heat the sauce without boiling it, check the seasoning, and pour it over the trout (leaving their heads exposed). Serve.

TRUITES VALENTRÉ
Trout in a red wine sauce

PREPARATION TIME: 20 minutes
COOKING TIME: 20 minutes
FOR SIX

6 good-sized trout	1 level tablespoon cornflour
200 g (7 oz) sole trimmings	300 ml (10½ fl oz) crème fraîche
1 sachet powdered court-bouillon	1 lemon
8 shallots	salt, pepper
75 g (generous 2½ oz) butter	350 g (¾ lb) button mushrooms
½ litre (18 fl oz) red wine (preferably Cahors)	

Make a fish stock with the sole trimmings, half of the powdered court-bouillon and a litre (1¾ pints) of water. Cook at boiling point with the pan uncovered for 20 minutes, strain it and put to one side.

Gut, wash and wipe the trout and chop the shallots. Butter an ovenproof pan, spread the chopped shallots over the bottom and lay the trout on top. Pour on the red wine and 200 ml (7 fl oz) of strained fish stock. Season and cover the pan with a sheet of aluminium foil.

Pre-heat a fairly hot oven (200°C/400°F/Gas Mark 6) and cook the trout for about 10 minutes. Remove the trout, skin them but leave the heads. Put them in a serving dish and keep them warm.

Put the oven-pan over a brisk heat and reduce the cooking liquid by half. Mix cornflour and crème fraîche together and stir them into the pan. Let the sauce just bubble; remove from the heat, put the sauce through a sieve and then cover the trout with it.

The button mushrooms should be tossed in butter and used to garnish the dish.

The chef of the 'Grand Hotel Palladium' in Alvignac-les-Eaux in the Lot, from where this recipe comes, recommends a vintage wine of the Cahors to go with the trout.

TRUITES AUX AMANDES
Trout with almonds

PREPARATION TIME: 12 minutes
COOKING TIME: 25 minutes
FOR SIX

6 trout each of 180–200 g (6–7 oz)	flour
	4 tablespoons oil
100 g (3½ oz) blanched whole almonds	200 g (7 oz) butter
	1 lemon
salt, pepper	

Lay the almonds out on a baking-sheet and roast them golden-brown in a slow oven, turning them from time to time.

Gut the trout through the gills, wash them, and wipe them very carefully so that their skin isn't broken. Half an hour before they are to be cooked, season them.

Roll the trout in flour and shake off any surplus. Put them into a pan with a tablespoon of oil and another of butter and let them cook slowly; it is important to retain the whole appearance of the fish. When the cooking fats go brown, discard them and remove the fish to an ovenproof serving dish where they may complete their cooking in a slow oven.

While this is going on, clarify the butter by heating it gently in a saucepan until it foams, then skimming off the froth and decanting the clear liquid, leaving the deposit in the bottom of the pan.

Sprinkle the trout with roasted almonds, then pour over the melted butter. Sprinkle with the juice of the lemon and serve very hot.

TURBOTINS À LA CRÈME
Young turbot in cream sauce

PREPARATION TIME: 40 minutes
COOKING TIME: 20 minutes
FOR SIX

3 young turbot	1 bouquet garni
1 leek (white part only)	125 g (4½ oz) mushrooms
3 sticks of celery	4 shallots
2 medium-sized carrots	60 g (2 oz) butter
1 onion	100 ml (3½ fl oz) dry white wine
salt, pepper	200 ml (7 fl oz) of single cream

Ask your fishmonger to skin and fillet the fish but make sure you take home the trimmings as well. Slice the leek, the celery, the carrots and the onions and, with the trimmings, seasoning and the bouquet garni, make a fish stock by simmering all the ingredients together with 250 ml (9 fl oz) of water for 20 minutes. Strain the stock and then reduce it over a brisk heat to a volume of 100 ml (3½ fl oz).

Finely chop the mushrooms and the shallots and put them in a cooking pan with the butter. Cook them very gently for 5–7 minutes over a low heat so that they do not discolour. Put the turbot fillets in another pan, pour in the wine and the fish stock and cover the pan with a sheet of aluminium foil. Cook for 20 minutes in a fairly hot oven (200°C/400°F/ Gas Mark 6).

Remove the fillets and arrange them on an ovenproof serving-dish. Keep it warm. Strain the cooking liquid into a saucepan and reduce it over a brisk heat until it has a syrupy consistency. Stir in the cream, bring to the boil for 3 minutes, season to taste and pour the sauce over the fish Return the dish to the fairly hot oven for 10–12 minutes when the surface should be lightly browned.

Serve with either rice or boiled potatoes.

TURBOT AUX ÉCHALOTES
Turbot with shallots

PREPARATION TIME: 10 minutes
COOKING TIME: 50 minutes
FOR SIX

1 turbot of 1¼–1½ kg (2¾–3¼ lb)
3 tablespoons of chopped
   shallots
80 g (scant 3 oz) butter
salt, pepper
300 ml (10½ fl oz) single cream
1 lemon

Ask your fishmonger to remove the spine from the black side of the fish and to separate the fillets so that they may be rolled back, as shown in the illustration.

Gently cook the chopped shallots in butter until they are transparent. Season them and spread them all around the inside of the fish; then press the fillets back into position.

Arrange the fish in an oval ovenproof dish and place in a fairly hot oven (200°C/400°F/Gas Mark 6). Keep a close eye on the progress of cooking and when liquid is given off and seen in the bottom of the dish, moisten the fish with half of the cream, which should have been seasoned and extended with the juice of the lemon.

Continue to add cream, 2 or 3 spoonfuls at a time, while the cooking continues. Watch the colour of the cooking liquid and when it just begins to darken, the fish will be done.

Adding the cream mixture little by little controls the rate of evaporation and allows the sauce to develop a creamy texture. If the cream were put in all at once, it would remain very liquid and the fats would tend to separate.

Serve the turbot in its cooking dish, with boiled potatoes sprinkled with parsley.

TURBOT HOLLANDIES
Turbot with hollandaise sauce

PREPARATION TIME: 30 minutes
COOKING TIME (FISH): 20 minutes
       (SAUCE): 10–12 minutes
FOR SIX TO EIGHT

1 turbot of about 2 kg (4½ lb)
2 sachets of powdered
   court-bouillon
6–8 big prawns

For the sauce
3 eggs
2 tablespoons of cider vinegar
pepper
250 g (scant 9 oz) slightly-salted
   butter
1 lemon

Ask your fishmonger to skin the fish and to divide it into portions. Lay them out in a large casserole or saucepan so that they do not overlap. Sprinkle on the powdered court-bouillon and pour in enough cold water to cover the fish completely.

Bring the pan to the boil and immediately lower the heat. Cover the pan and allow the fish just to simmer for 15 minutes. Remove from the heat and take the lid off the pan. (It is better that the fish should be slightly less hot than it should be overcooked.)

Make the hollandaise sauce while the fish is cooking. Beat the egg yolks, put them in the upper bowl of a double-boiler and mix them with the vinegar. Season with pepper. (The water in the double-boiler should *not* be boiling.) Add the butter knob by knob, constantly beating the sauce until it has the consistency of a mayonnaise. Add lemon juice little by little to taste and check the seasoning.

This sauce must be served immediately. At the most, it may be transferred to a warmed sauce-boat, itself standing in warm water.

Arrange the fish on a serving dish, garnished with the unpeeled prawns and serve with boiled potatoes.

POISSONS À LA MOUTARDE
Whiting in mustard sauce

PREPARATION TIME: 5 minutes
COOKING TIME: 25 minutes
FOR SIX

6 good fillets of whiting
25 g (scant 1 oz) butter
2 tablespoons of strong Dijon
  mustard

2 tablespoons of crème fraîche
1 heaped tablespoon chopped
  gherkins
salt, pepper

Butter a flat ovenproof dish and arrange the fish fillets in it. Put into a very hot oven (230°C/450°F/Gas Mark 8) for 15 minutes. Pour away the juices which the fish will have given off during the cooking.

Mix mustard, cream, chopped gherkins and seasoning together in a bowl and pour over the fish. Return to the oven for a further 10 minutes.

Serve with boiled potatoes or, better still, with chipped potatoes.

Elle suggests that it may be better to buy a whole fish and to get your fishmonger to fillet it for you. Lemon sole could also be used for this recipe.

(CONTINUED)

Peel the cucumber and cut into dice. Plunge them for 3 minutes in boiling salted water, remove and drain. Just before serving, whip the cream, season and stir in the chopped herbs.

Turn the terrine out on to its serving dish, surround it with cucumber dice and decorate the top with prawns. The sauce should be served separately.

The chef of the Paris restaurant 'Pauline' from where this recipe comes, recommends that a Sancerre Chavignol be drunk with this terrine.

TERRINE DE POISSON
Fish terrine

PREPARATION TIME: 40 minutes (the day before)
COOKING TIME: 1 hour (the day before)
FOR EIGHT

For the forcemeat
300 g (10½ oz) white bread
  without crusts
250 ml (9 fl oz) milk
500 g (a good lb) fillet of fish –
  whiting is suitable
150 g (5 oz) butter
1 egg yolk
2 eggs
500 ml (18 fl oz) crème fraîche
salt, pepper, nutmeg

The fish
3 filleted soles
1 kg (2¼ lb) fresh salmon steaks

The garnish
1 cucumber
8–10 good prawns

For the sauce
300 ml (10½ fl oz) crème fraîche
salt, pepper
sprigs of parsley, chervil and
  tarragon

Begin by making a panade. Soak the bread in boiling milk, mix very well together and dry off somewhat over a low heat, stirring frequently with a spatula.

Put the fillets of whiting through a blender and thoroughly mix them with the butter, 1 egg yolk, then the whole eggs. Put it all into a cold mixing bowl and gradually incorporate the cream, whipping constantly. Season with salt, pepper and grated nutmeg.

Lightly cook the fillets of sole and the salmon steaks in a little butter and then let them cool. Skin and fillet the salmon.

Butter the inside of an oblong cake-tin and line it alternately with a layer of forcemeat, a layer of sole fillets, another of forcemeat, a layer of salmon, finishing up with a layer of forcemeat. Press the filling well into the tin.

Put the tin into a large casserole, pour in water around it (making sure the tin does not float) and cook in a fairly hot oven (200°C/400°F/Gas Mark 6) for 1 hour. Remove and let it cool in its tin, place a weighted board on top and place in the refrigerator overnight.

(CONTINUED OPPOSITE)

CRABE EN SALADE
Crab salad

PREPARATION TIME (A FRESH CRAB): 1 hour
(TINNED CRAB): 30 minutes
COOKING TIME: 10 minutes
FOR SIX

1 crab of 1 kg (about 2¼ lb) or a   *1 lemon*
   large tin of crab (200 g, 7 oz,   *1 head of lettuce*
   size)   *2 hard-boiled eggs*
2 grapefruit   *bowl of mayonnaise*
2 avocado pears   *tabasco sauce*

Remove all the edible flesh from the crab. Peel and slice the grapefruit, using a sharp-pointed knife. Save any juice that is spilled.

Cut the avocado pears in half lengthways, remove the stones and take the flesh from the skins. Cut either in lengthways slices or in pieces, as preferred. Sprinkle with lemon juice to prevent discoloration. Line a salad bowl with lettuce and arrange all the ingredients including the peeled and sliced hard-boiled eggs.

Flavour the mayonnaise with some of the grapefruit juice and with a few drops of tabasco sauce. Put some mayonnaise onto the salad and serve the rest separately.

It is simpler and usually more pleasing to serve this salad in individual serving bowls.

FRUITS DE MER EN SALADE
Seafood salad

PREPARATION TIME: 40 minutes
COOKING TIME: 15–20 minutes
FOR SIX

500 g (generous 1 lb) potatoes   *2 tablespoons capers*
250 g (about 8 oz) mushrooms   *2 tablespoons chopped gherkins*
2 lemons   *4 tablespoons olive oil*
2 litres (3½ pints) mussels   *salt, pepper*
1 knob of butter   *1 head of lettuce*
15 langoustines   *bowl of mayonnaise*
200 g (7 oz) peeled prawns   *1 tablespoon of tomato ketchup*
2 onions   *chopped mixed herbs*

Cook the potatoes in their skins, let them cool, then peel them and cut them into dice. Quarter the mushrooms and sprinkle them with lemon juice to prevent discoloration.

Put the mussels in a saucepan with a knob of butter and cook them over a brisk flame until they open; discard any which remain closed. Take the mussels out of their shells. Cook the langoustines for 7 minutes in salted boiling water. Let them cool down in the cooking liquid and then shell the tails.

Put the potatoes, mushrooms and the shellfish into a bowl and mix with the finely-chopped onion, the capers, the chopped gherkins, the oil and 2 tablespoons of lemon juice. Season and leave to stand in a cool place for a few minutes.

Line a salad bowl with large lettuce leaves and add the heart cut into strips. Put the salad mixture into the bowl and serve.

Flavour the mayonnaise with ketchup and chopped mixed herbs and serve separately.

BOEUF À L'ANCIENNE
Traditional beef stew

PREPARATION TIME: 20 minutes (24 hours in advance)
COOKING TIME: 2¾–3 hours
FOR SIX

1 kg–1.2 kg (2¼–2¾ lb) stewing beef (rump for preference)
4 carrots
3 large onions
bouquet garni
1 clove of garlic
500 ml (18 fl oz) dry white wine
4 tablespoons brandy
2 tablespoons oil
a calf's foot (if available)
2 tomatoes
salt, pepper, nutmeg
200 g (7 oz) mushrooms
20 small onions

On the day before, cut the meat into cubes and marinate it with the carrots cut into strips, the whole but peeled large onions, the bouquet garni, the garlic, the wine, brandy and the oil. Stir it 2 or 3 times during the marination.

On the day of cooking, put the calf's foot, split in two, on the bottom of a casserole. Add the meat, the whole of the marinade and the peeled and seeded tomatoes. Season with salt, pepper and grated nutmeg. Bring the pot to the boil and let it simmer for 2 hours over a very low heat.

Add the sliced mushrooms and the small onions and simmer slowly for a further 30–45 minutes. Immediately before serving, take out the 3 large onions, the garlic and the bouquet garni.

Serve from the casserole with noodles or boiled potatoes.

DAUBE MÉRIDIONALE
Braised beef of the Midi

PREPARATION TIME: 15 minutes
COOKING TIME: 3 hours (at least)
FOR SIX

1½–2 kg (3¼–4½ lb) stewing beef (leg or shin for preference)
75 ml (2½ fl oz) olive oil
the rind of belly of pork
1 bottle of red wine
1 small tin of tomato purée
3 onions
3 cloves of garlic
sprig of thyme, bay leaf, parsley stalks
piece of orange peel
salt, pepper, nutmeg

Cut the meat into even-sized pieces and slowly seal them in the olive oil, taking care not to let the oil blacken. When they are done, lay the rind on the bottom of a casserole, pour in the wine, add the tomato purée, onions, the garlic (unpeeled) and the herbs and orange peel tied together in a bundle. Season with salt, pepper and grated nutmeg.

Bring to the boil and let the dish bubble, uncovered, for 10 minutes. Put the casserole lid on and simmer over a very low heat for 3 hours. The sauce should be smooth and quite thick but if it is too liquid, it can be reduced by removing the lid and raising to a brisk heat.

This dish is even more delicious if prepared in advance and re-heated before serving. It goes best with noodles or other large pasta, and with grated Gruyère cheese.

[63]

BOEUF À LA PAYSANNE
Country beef

PREPARATION TIME: 20 minutes (the day before)
COOKING TIME: 2 hours
FOR SIX

1.2 kg (2¾ lb) stewing beef
  (chuck steak for preference)
sprig of thyme, bay leaf
1 small sprig of rosemary
200 g (7 oz) onions
8 carrots
good pinch ground pepper
1 bottle red burgundy
6 baby turnips

150 g (5 oz) button mushrooms
1 lemon
2 tablespoons oil
20 g (¾ oz) butter
1 clove of garlic
10 g (scant ½ oz) flour
pinch of sea salt
400 g (14 oz) French beans
2 tablespoons crème fraîche

Cut the meat into large 5 cm (2 in) cubes. Make a marinade in a dish with the herbs, 2 of the onions, 2 sliced carrots, pepper and the wine. Add the meat and let all marinate overnight, turning it over several times.

Trim and dice the rest of the carrots and turnips, trim the stalks off the mushrooms, wipe them and sprinkle them with lemon juice.

Remove the pieces of meat from the marinade and dry them on kitchen paper. Strain the marinade and put aside. Heat the oil and butter in a casserole and seal the meat over a low heat. Add the remaining onions, chopped fine, and the crushed garlic. When the onion has begun to colour, pour off the fat, sprinkle the meat with flour, stir, moisten with the marinade, add the salt, and cover the casserole and cook for 1 hour over a low heat.

Cook the French beans separately for 15 minutes in salted boiling water. After the meat has been cooking for 1 hour, add the remaining carrots, then 15 minutes later add the drained beans, the turnips and the mushrooms.

Continue cooking for 15 minutes longer and then remove the meat to a warmed serving dish. Arrange the vegetables round it.

If the sauce in the casserole is too liquid, remove the lid and reduce over a brisk heat. Then whip in the cream and remove from the heat at the first sign of the sauce bubbling. Pour over the meat and serve hot.

RAGOÛT DE BOEUF
Beef ragoût

PREPARATION TIME: 30 minutes
COOKING TIME: 2½–3 hours
FOR SIX

1 kg (2¼ lb) stewing beef (rump
  for preference)
250 g (scant 9 oz) smoked
  streaky bacon
4 onions
flour
500 ml (18 fl oz) white wine

salt, pepper
bouquet garni
2 shallots
1 kg (2¼ lb) carrots
500 g (good lb) baby turnips
6–8 potatoes

Buy the bacon in thick slices and cut across the grain into thick strips and soften them slowly in a casserole over a very low heat. They should give out their fat and become golden without becoming crisp. Remove with a perforated spoon and put aside.

Cut the beef into cubes and put it with the onions, cut in half, into the same fat. Seal the meat on all sides, sprinkle on a heaped tablespoon of flour and when that has coloured, add the wine and enough extra water to completely cover the meat. Bring to the boil, season and add the bouquet garni and the shallots. Cover the casserole and continue cooking slowly; i.e. just very gently simmering.

After about 1 hour or so of slow cooking, add the sliced carrots and then, 20 minutes later, the young turnips cut into large pieces.

Peel the potatoes and, about 30 minutes before serving, arrange them with the bacon strips on the surface of the ragoût.

[64]

ESTOUFFADE DE BOEUF
Slow-cooked beef

PREPARATION TIME: 20 minutes
COOKING TIME: 3½–4 hours
FOR SIX

500 g (generous lb) chuck steak
600–800 g (21–28 oz) top rib of
   beef
250 g (about 9 oz) streaky bacon
2 tablespoons olive oil
flour
4 onions
salt, pepper

1 bottle of red wine
bouquet garni (with extra thyme)
2 cloves garlic
250 g (8 oz) button mushrooms
2 tablespoons tomato purée
   (optional)
100 g (3½ oz) black olives

Ask your butcher for lean meat and cut it into pieces each weighing about 80 g (3 oz). Buy the bacon in thick slices and cut into strips across the grain, blanch it in boiling water for 5 minutes, remove, drain and dry on kitchen paper. Put the bacon into a casserole with 1 tablespoon of oil and cook gently; remove before they take on any colour, and put aside.

Roll the pieces of beef in flour and brown in the bacon fat. Put in the onions, cut into quarters, at the same time. When brown, season and pour in the red wine; raise to a brisk heat and reduce by half the volume of the wine. Add enough water to cover the meat, add the bouquet garni and the garlic. Lay a sheet of aluminium foil over the casserole before replacing the lid. Cook in a moderate oven (180°C/350°F/Gas Mark 4) for 3 hours.

Quarter the mushrooms and brown them in a tablespoon of olive oil. After 3 hours' cooking, turn the casserole out through a sieve so that the cooking liquid (sauce) is transferred to a saucepan. Put the pieces of beef back in the casserole, together with the bacon strips and the mushrooms.

Skim the grease from the sauce, stir in the tomato purée and the stoned olives. Pour this over the meat and let the dish simmer for a further 20–25 minutes before serving.

Boiled or mashed potatoes, the larger pastas, gnocchi or polenta are the classic accompaniments to the dish.

BOEUF DES MARINIERS
Beef with anchovies

PREPARATION TIME: 30 minutes
COOKING TIME: 3–3½ hours
FOR SIX

1.2 kg (2¾ lb) beef, topside or
   silverside for preference
500 g (about 8 oz) peeled onions
7 tablespoons olive oil
salt, pepper

bay leaf
pinch of chopped thyme
100 g (3½ oz) anchovy fillets
1 tablespoon Dijon mustard
parsley

Ask your butcher to cut the meat into thin slices, about ½ cm (¼ in) thick; you should trim off any fat or gristle before cooking.

Slice the onions. Put 4 tablespoons of oil into a casserole and arrange a layer of meat, a layer of onion, another layer of meat and so on alternately, ending with a layer of onion. Season with pepper and a little salt, add the herbs and cover the dish. Cook over a very low heat so that the liquid just bubbles: do not stir during the cooking. When the upper layer of onion is soft and the liquid is visible on the surface, the dish will be cooked.

Drain the anchovies and pound them in a mortar to a smooth paste; add the mustard. Then, beating constantly, add 3 tablespoons olive oil, drop by drop, as if making a mayonnaise. Extend it with a spoonful of sauce from the meat and then add it to the contents of the casserole.

Sprinkle with parsley and serve from the casserole with boiled potatoes.

BOEUF DES LAVANDIÈRES
Sauté of beef with garlic

PREPARATION TIME: 10 minutes
COOKING TIME: 5 minutes
FOR SIX

1.8 kg (4 lb) rump or sirloin steak
12 cloves garlic
75 ml (2½ fl oz) olive oil
100 g (3½ oz) black olives,
   preserved in oil
1 tablespoon dried breadcrumbs
1 teaspoon chopped thyme
salt, pepper

Cut the steak into 2 cm (¾ in) cubes. Peel, but do not crush or break the cloves of garlic.

Heat the oil in a pan and when it is warm, add the cloves of garlic. Cook until golden-brown, stirring from time to time, then add the meat which should be briskly sealed on all sides. Add the olives, sprinkle the breadcrumbs and the thyme over the meat, and season. Moisten with 2 tablespoons of hot water and simmer for a minute or two when the breadcrumbs should have swollen. Serve immediately.

This quickly prepared dish goes well with chipped or sauté potatoes.

BOEUF AUX OLIVES
Beef with olives

PREPARATION TIME: 20 minutes
COOKING TIME: 3 hours
FOR SIX

1.2 kg (2¾ lb) stewing beef
100 g (3½ oz) streaky bacon
10 small onions
2 carrots
bouquet garni
nutmeg
salt, pepper
2 shallots
1 clove garlic
1 large glass Madeira or red wine
200 g (7 oz) green olives in brine
100 g (3½ oz) mushrooms

Buy the streaky bacon in thick slices and cut into strips across the grain and put them into a casserole. Cook them slowly over a very low heat so that they give off their fat without becoming crisp. Remove and put to one side.

Put the joint, the onions and the carrots into the same fat and slowly seal the meat on all sides. Take care not to let the fat burn. Lower the heat, add the bouquet garni and grated nutmeg, season (using very little salt because of the olives) and cover. Let the dish cook for 20 minutes, stirring once, then add the shallots, garlic, wine and bacon strips and simmer for 1½ hours.

During this time, stone the olives and blanch them briefly in boiling water to remove their saltiness. Drain them on kitchen paper. Trim and quarter the mushrooms and add them, together with the olives, to the casserole. Simmer for a further 45 minutes, then take out the bouquet garni and check the seasoning.

Remove and slice the joint and arrange on a warm serving dish with the sauce poured over it. Serve with noodles, leaf spinach, celery hearts or boiled potatoes.

Elle advises that if red wine, and not Madeira, is used in the cooking add a lump of sugar.

BOEUF STROGONOFF
Beef Strogonoff

PREPARATION TIME: 20 minutes
COOKING TIME: 40 minutes
FOR SIX

1.2 kg (2¾ lb) lean fillet steak
1 tablespoon dry mustard
1½ teaspoons caster sugar
8 medium-sized onions
500 g (generous lb) button
   mushrooms

5 tablespoons oil
1 lemon
500 ml (18 fl oz) crème fraîche
salt, pepper

Take a small mixing bowl and combine the dry mustard, sugar, a pinch of salt and enough drops of water to make a stiff paste. Leave to rest for at least 15 minutes before using.

Peel and finely chop the onions. Trim and slice the mushrooms and sprinkle them with lemon juice. Heat 2 tablespoons of oil in a large pan, add the onions and mushrooms, cover the pan, lower the heat and cook slowly for 20–30 minutes, stirring occasionally. Take the pan from the heat, remove the vegetables, pour off the cooking liquid and return the vegetables to the pan.

Cut the steak into ½ cm (¼ in) thick slices and then again into ½ cm (¼ in) wide strips. In a second pan, heat 2 tablespoons of oil over a brisk heat and when hot (but *not* smoking), put in a third of the strips of steak. Stir constantly with a wooden spoon: the strips should be lightly sealed all over after 2 minutes. Remove the cooked strips with a perforated spoon and add them to the onions and mushrooms.

Continue to cook the rest of the steak in batches, adding more oil as necessary and, as the meat is sealed, transfer it to the first pan. Then put this pan over a low heat and stir in the mustard paste. Season, cover the pan and simmer for 2 or 3 minutes.

Take out the contents of the pan and put to one side on a warm plate. Briskly stir the cream with the back of a fork into the juices in the pan and bring the sauce just to the boil. Return the meat etc. to the sauce and stir together. Serve immediately.

Elle says that although this is a simple dish, it must be remembered that the meat should be cooked quickly and at the last moment.

EMINCÉS DE BOEUF
Beef in a cream sauce

PREPARATION TIME: 15 minutes
COOKING TIME: 20 minutes
FOR SIX

1 kg (2¼ lb) rump steak
60 g (2 oz) butter
4 shallots

250 g (9 fl oz) single cream
teaspoon strong Dijon mustard
salt, white pepper

Trim all the fat from the meat. Cut it first into thin slices and then into strips.

Heat a small knob of butter in a pan and when transparent, put in half of the steak strips. Seal them quickly on all sides so that they remain rare in the middle. Remove, put to one side and continue with the second batch. Done in 2 halves, the meat is more likely to be evenly cooked. Keep the meat in a warm place.

Put the rest of the butter in the pan and, over a very low heat, slowly cook the finely-chopped shallots. Briskly stir in 4 tablespoons of cream with the back of a fork, increase the heat and, still stirring vigorously, reduce the mixture until the cream begins to colour. Add the rest of the cream and the mustard, season and bring to the boil.

Mix the meat, and any juices that have come out of it, with the sauce, heat just to the point of boiling once more and serve immediately.

If the sauce is too thin, before returning the meat to it, make a paste of a dessertspoon of cornflour and cold water and stir this into the sauce with the pan removed from the heat.

[67]

QUEUE DE BOEUF EN HOCHEPOT
Oxtail hotpot

PREPARATION TIME: 30 minutes
COOKING TIME: 3–3½ hours
FOR SIX TO EIGHT

1 oxtail	8 carrots
2 pig's trotters	6 baby turnips
1 pig's ear	1 small cabbage
4 onions	8 potatoes

Pig's ears and trotters are usually available if ordered in advance from your butcher.

Divide the oxtail into pieces about 7–8 cm (3 in) long. Cut the pig's trotters into quarters and put them and the oxtail, together with the pig's ear, into a saucepan or fireproof pot. Cover the meat with salt water, bring to the boil, and skim the surface.

Continue to cook slowly for 1½ hours, then add the onions, carrots and baby turnips. Cook for 45 minutes longer and then add the cabbage, cut into quarters. Go on cooking for a further 45 minutes with the liquid just bubbling.

Peel and boil the potatoes separately. To serve, arrange the pieces of meat around the edge of the serving dish, with the pig's ear cut into thick slices. Pile the vegetables in the centre but serve the boiled potatoes separately, together with mustard, sea-salt and pickled gherkins.

POT-AU-FEU
Boiled beef with vegetables

PREPARATION TIME: 30 minutes
COOKING TIME: 3 hours
FOR SIX

1 kg (2¼ lb) shoulder of beef, with bone in	4 cloves
	2 onions
600 g (generous 1¼ lb) chuck steak	8 carrots
	bouquet garni
2 bones (without marrow)	6 baby turnips
salt	peppercorns
4 leeks	6 slices of white bread
1 head of celery	Gruyère cheese

Put 4 litres (7 pints) of cold water into a saucepan or casserole, add the meat (both in the piece), the bones and a level tablespoon of salt. Bring to the boil, skim, lower the heat and cover the pan. Cook with the liquid just on the boil.

Meanwhile, tie the leeks and the celery sticks in bundles and stick the cloves into the onions.

Allow a cooking time of 3 hours: at the end of the first hour, put in the carrots, the onions and the bouquet garni. Half an hour later, add the leeks, the celery and the turnips, together with 10 peppercorns. Add more water if necessary and continue to cook at a slow boil.

When cooking is complete, pour off the liquid, strain it and serve it in cups. Float a round of toast piled with grated Gruyère cheese on each serving. Cut up the meat and arrange it and the vegetables alternately on a warmed serving dish. Have on the table both natural and aromatic mustards, sea-salt, pickled gherkins and tomato ketchup.

If you want to serve marrow bones with this dish, wrap them completely in aluminium foil and bake in the oven for 30 minutes.

GRILLADE DES MARINIERS
Beef Troisgros

PREPARATION TIME: 10 minutes
COOKING TIME: 2¼ hours
FOR SIX

2 sirloin steaks, each 500 g (generous lb)
50 g (scant 2 oz) butter
2 large onions
100 ml (3½ fl oz) wine vinegar
140 g (scant 5 oz) pickled gherkins
6 anchovy fillets in oil
100 g (3½ oz) streaky bacon
small sprig of parsley

Heat the butter in a pan and seal each steak successively. Put them into a casserole large enough to hold them side-by-side, and sprinkle the chopped onion over them. Cover the dish and cook over a very low heat for 10 minutes.

Pour in the vinegar and rapidly reduce it to half its volume. Add 200 ml (7 fl oz) water, the gherkins sliced thickly crossways, the anchovies, the thickly-sliced bacon cut into strips across the grain and the parsley. Cover the dish again and cook for 2 hours over a low heat.

Carve into portions and serve together with its garnish.

Les Frères Troisgros, from whose famous restaurant at Roanne this recipe comes, recommend that either a Gamay from the Loire or a white wine of the Rhône should be served with this dish.

GRILLADES NORMANDE
Normandy grill

PREPARATION TIME: 15–20 minutes
COOKING TIME (POTATOES): 45 minutes–1 hour (according to size)
(MEAT): 7–10 minutes
FOR SIX

2 sirloin steaks each of 400–500 g (around 1 lb)
cup of chopped parsley
4 tablespoons cream
salt, pepper
80 g (scant 3 oz) butter
2 tablespoons oil
1½ kg (3¼ lb) small new potatoes

Two hours before cooking, stir the chopped parsley into the cream. Lightly season.

Heat the butter and oil together in a pan and cook the whole potatoes slowly so that they become golden-brown and tender. The steaks may be either fried or grilled to whatever stage of rarity you prefer. Season them as they are turned over.

Put the potatoes into a warmed serving dish and arrange the steaks on top. Heat through the cream and parsley mixture but do not let it boil. Pour the sauce over the steaks.

This dish is at its best when arranged in this way. The flavour of the potatoes is much enhanced by the sauce which drips on them from the steaks.

STEAK AU POIVRE À LA CRÈME
Peppered steak in cream sauce

PREPARATION TIME: 40 minutes
COOKING TIME: 15 minutes
FOR SIX

1 kg (2¼ lb) fillet steak, cut into 2
   thick slices
2 tablespoons crushed
   peppercorns
50 g (scant 2 oz) butter

1 small glass of brandy
100 ml (3½ fl oz) double cream
teaspoon cornflour (or flour)
salt
strong Dijon mustard (optional)

Salt the steaks and cover them lavishly on each side with crushed peppercorns, pressing them with the palms of the hands to ensure the pepper adheres. Leave to stand for half an hour.

Melt the butter in a pan (begin with half the quantity and add more as necessary) and seal the steaks on each side. Complete the cooking to the degree of rareness preferred. Remove the steaks to a warmed serving dish kept over a pan of hot water.

Pour off any surplus fat from the pan and scrape the surface vigorously with the back of a fork in order to release the residues of cooking. Pour in the brandy, flame it and then add half of the cream, still stirring with the back of the fork. Bring the sauce to the boil and reduce its volume by a quarter.

Mix the cornflour with the rest of the cream and stir this into the sauce. Bring back to the boil and immediately pour over the steaks. Serve at once, with either game-chips or matchstick potatoes.

Occasionally, a little strong Dijon mustard is also added to the second batch of cream to heighten the taste.

HAMBURGERS AUX CACAHUÈTES
Hamburgers with peanuts

PREPARATION TIME: 10 minutes
COOKING TIME: 15–20 minutes
FOR SIX

For the sauce
2 tins of tomato purée, each
   140 g (5 oz)
140 ml (5 fl oz) white wine
1 pimento
1 onion
1 level teaspoon caster sugar
1 teaspoon chopped oregano
2 cloves of garlic
3 sprigs of thyme
salt
Tabasco sauce

For the hamburgers
1 kg (2¼ lb) minced lean steak
2 onions
2 cloves of garlic
salt, pepper
2 teaspoons Dijon mustard
1 egg
1 tablespoon chopped parsley
350 g (about 12 oz) salted
   peanuts
oil

Begin by making the sauce. Empty the tins of tomato purée into a saucepan, fill the tins with white wine and pour this into the pan. Add the chopped pimento, the sliced onion, sugar, oregano, crushed garlic and thyme. Season with salt, mix the ingredients together and simmer over a low heat for the time that it takes to prepare the hamburgers.

Into a mixing bowl, put the minced steak, the finely-chopped onions, crushed garlic, salt and freshly-ground pepper, mustard, a beaten egg and the chopped parsley. Work with a fork until everything is thoroughly mixed together; then divide it into 6 parts and form the usual hamburger shapes. Vary the thickness of the hamburgers according to the degree of rareness required.

Crush the peanuts coarsely (a blender can be used) and coat the hamburgers all over, pressing the nuts in with the fingers so that they adhere all over. Take a large frying pan, heat a little oil and cook the hamburgers over a gentle heat for 8 minutes each side. Arrange them on a warmed serving dish. Pass the sauce through a sieve, check the seasoning and add a few drops of tabasco sauce. Serve separately.

With this dish, the flavour of the peanuts tends to soften the piquancy of the sauce which otherwise would have a strong flavour.

ONGLET AUX ÉCHALOTES
Eye of fillet with shallots

PREPARATION TIME: 20 minutes
COOKING TIME: 5–8 minutes (according to degree of rareness)
FOR SIX

1 kg (2¼ lb) eye of fillet
100 g (3½ oz) peeled and
 chopped shallots
100 g (3½ oz) butter
salt, freshly-ground pepper

Eye of fillet is the tenderest part of the animal and it should be ordered in advance from your butcher. Ask him to open it along its length and slash it crossways.

Cook the meat, either under a grill or in a pan, to the degree of rareness required. Put the chopped shallots in 2 or 3 tablespoons of water and cook gently until the liquid has all evaporated. At this point, add the butter and continue to cook gently until the shallots are soft and transparent. Season.

Spread the shallots over the fillet and serve with chipped potatoes.

FILET DE BOEUF EN CROÛTE
Beef Wellington

PREPARATION TIME: 1 hour
COOKING TIME: 18–20 minutes per pound
FOR SIX TO EIGHT

1 kg (2¼ lb) brioche pastry
1.4 kg (3 lb) piece of fillet steak
salt, pepper
1 egg
Madeira sauce

Make the brioche pastry, without sugar, the day before: see page 175.

Two hours in advance, put the piece of meat in a pan without any other fat and seal it on all sides. Remove from the pan, season thoroughly and leave to cool.

Roll out the pastry to a thickness of ½ cm (¼ in) and lay it out on a greased baking-sheet. Fold the pastry around the fillet, sticking the edges together with beaten egg. Shape any pastry trimmings and stick them on, again with beaten egg, as decoration. Finally, brush all over with the rest of the egg.

If you are not yet ready to put the dish into the oven, keep it in a refrigerator so that the pastry does not rise.

Pre-heat a fairly hot oven (200°C/400°F/Gas Mark 6) for 20 minutes, put the dish in and cook until the pastry is golden-brown. Then cover it with aluminium foil and continue to cook to complete the length of time calculated according to the meat's weight. When this time is up, turn off the oven but leave the dish in it for a further 10 minutes.

Serve with Madeira sauce: see page 86.

[71]

BOEUF MODE
Casserole of beef and carrots

PREPARATION TIME: 15 minutes
COOKING TIME: 2½–3 hours
FOR SIX TO EIGHT

1.5 kg (3¼ lb) piece of beef,	*bouquet garni*
silverside for preference	*2 kg (4½ lb) carrots*
1 tablespoon of oil	*3 onions*
100 g (3½ oz) bacon rind,	*2 shallots*
without fat	*salt, pepper*
1 boned calf's foot	*200 ml (7 fl oz) white wine*

The calf's foot should be ordered in advance from your butcher. Buy a piece of topside or boned chuck steak. It should be lightly larded, edged with strips of fat bacon and tied into an even shape.

Heat the oil in a large casserole and seal the meat on all sides. Line the bottom of the casserole with bacon rinds and add the calf's foot, the bouquet garni, and the carrots sliced crossways, the onions and the shallots. Season, pour in the wine and the same amount of water and bring to the boil. Cover the casserole, lower the heat and simmer for at least 2½ hours.

This dish has even more flavour when re-heated and therefore it can be made the previous day. Furthermore, in cooling, the juices set as a jelly and the dish is delicious when eaten cold.

ROSBIF COCOTTE
Pot-roasted beef

PREPARATION TIME: 10 minutes
COOKING TIME: 10–12 minutes per pound
FOR SIX

1.5 kg (3¼ lb) piece of beef,	*3 medium-sized shallots*
rump or sirloin for preference	*bouquet garni*
fat bacon	*salt, pepper*

Trim off all the fat from the meat and tie it, with strips of fat bacon along one side, into an even shape.

Heat a casserole and put the joint into it, bacon side downwards, with no other cooking fats. Seal it on all sides and then add the shallots, the bouquet garni and 2 tablespoons of water. Season, cover the casserole and lower the heat to the very minimum.

After 15 minutes, turn the joint over, seasoning once more. Cook for 10 more minutes and then press the joint with the handle end of a wooden spoon: if it is still flabby, cook 5 minutes longer and then stick a sharp skewer into the centre of the roast. The juices coming out should be pink.

It is difficult to give a precise cooking time as so much depends upon the exact temperature within the casserole and the thickness and texture of the joint. In general, 10 minutes per pound of cooking time after sealing will give a roast which is hot through to the middle, tender and underdone.

If there is a delay in going to the table, take the casserole off the heat and slide open the lid.

Put the joint on a warm serving dish and cut a few slices. Skim off any fat from the cooking liquid, stir vigorously with the back of a fork, and add in the blood and juices coming from the sliced meat. Strain and serve separately in a sauceboat.

Serve the beef with either roast or sauté potatoes; a chard or leek tart is also delicious with beef cooked in this way.

HARICOT DE MOUTON
Mutton with beans

PREPARATION TIME: 15 minutes
COOKING TIME: 2½ hours
FOR SIX

1 shoulder of mutton, 1.2 kg (2¾ lb) boned weight	2 carrots
1 kg (2¼ lb) dried white haricot beans	2 onions
	2 cloves of garlic
	bouquet garni
60 g (2 oz) lard	

Use the current season's dried beans. Wash them but do not soak them. Put them in 5 litres (9 pints) of cold water and bring them slowly to the boil, taking at least half an hour to reach boiling point. Let the beans keep boiling for 10 more minutes, then drain them and pour in the same amount of salted boiling water. Check the progress of the cooking from time to time, but do not let the beans overcook or the skins will separate from the flesh.

While the beans are cooking, cut the mutton into chunks and heat the lard in a casserole. Seal the meat on all sides, then add the carrots sliced crossways, the onions, the garlic and the bouquet garni. Cover the casserole and cook over a very low heat (either on top of the stove or inside the oven) for 40 minutes.

Drain the cooked beans and add them to the meat. Moisten them with a few tablespoons of the liquid in which they were cooked, cover the casserole and simmer for at least another hour.

Serve direct from the cooking pot.

AGNEAU AU FOUR
Baked lamb

PREPARATION TIME: 20 minutes (½ hour in advance)
COOKING TIME: 1–1½ hours
FOR SIX

1.2 kg (2¾ lb) loin end of leg of lamb	salt, pepper, saffron
	100 ml (3½ fl oz) oil
1 kg (2¼ lb) potatoes	juice of 1 lemon

Peel the potatoes and cut them in 4 lengthways. Put them in a dish, season them and sprinkle with a good pinch of saffron; put aside for half an hour. Turn them from time to time.

Cut up the meat and season it. Take an ovenproof dish and arrange the pieces of meat and potato. Sprinkle the oil, 200 ml (7 fl oz) of water and the lemon juice over the dish, and cook in a moderate oven (180°C/350°F/Gas Mark 4) for about 1½ hours.

Elle advises that for this Tunisian recipe, a variety of potato should be used which is firm and will not break up while cooking: Desirée or Arran Pilot are recommended.

[73]

AGNEAU À LA ROMAINE
Lamb with rosemary

PREPARATION TIME: 15 minutes
COOKING TIME: 45 minutes
FOR SIX

1½ kg (3¼ lb) shoulder of lamb
200 ml (7 fl oz) oil
30 g (1 oz) butter
3 cloves of garlic

1 tablespoon rosemary
1 tin of flat anchovy fillets
250 ml (9 fl oz) wine vinegar
salt, pepper

Cut the lamb into even-sized pieces. Heat the oil and the butter together in a casserole and gently sweat 2 of the cloves of garlic for a few moments. Arrange the pieces of lamb in the casserole, cover it and cook over a very low flame for 30 minutes.

In the meantime, pound together in a mortar the rosemary, the third clove of garlic and 6 anchovy fillets until a smooth paste results. Mix the vinegar in with it, pour the mixture over the meat, stir and then simmer, with the lid off the casserole, for 15 minutes while the vinegar evaporates.

The chef of the restaurant 'Au Chateaubriant' in Paris, from where this recipe comes, recommends that a chilled rosé from Anjou be drunk with this lamb dish.

TARCARI D'AGNEAU
Venezuelan Lamb Tarcari

PREPARATION TIME: 20 minutes
COOKING TIME: 35–40 minutes
FOR SIX

1.7 kg (3¾ lb) lamb, chump
  chops for preference
100 g (3½ oz) butter
50 ml (1¾ fl oz) oil
1 tablespoon curry powder
1 kg (2¼ lb) tomatoes

750 g (good 1½ lb) onions
1 whole bulb of garlic
3 cubes of concentrated chicken
  stock
4 aubergines
1 small tin red peppers

Cut the lamb into even-sized pieces. Put the butter and oil into a casserole and slowly heat them. When the fats are hot, but not smoking, put in the pieces of lamb and seal them on all sides. Sprinkle the meat with curry powder.

Meanwhile peel, seed and chop the tomatoes; peel and slice the onions and peel and crush all the cloves of garlic. Put all these ingredients into the casserole, pour over the chicken stock cubes dissolved in 1 litre (1¾ pints) of hot water. Cover the dish, bring it to the boil and cook at the same temperature for 5 minutes.

Trim the aubergines and cut them into small dice. Take 2 of the red peppers from the tin, drain them and cut into thin strips. Add these vegetables to the casserole and cook, with the lid on, for a further 20 minutes.

Serve with boiled rice. If yellow rice is required, put a good pinch of powdered saffron into the cooking water.

AGNEAU AU CITRON
Lamb with lemon

PREPARATION TIME: 15 minutes
COOKING TIME: 1 hour
FOR SIX

1 shoulder of lamb about 1.2 kg
  (2¾ lb) boned weight
4 tablespoons olive oil
2 medium-sized onions
1 clove of garlic

2 tablespoons of paprika
2 tablespoons of chopped
  parsley
3 tablespoons of lemon juice
salt, pepper

Cut the shoulder into lean 2½ cm (1 in) cubes. Heat the oil in a casserole over a brisk flame and, as it begins to smoke, add the meat. Stir constantly until it is brown on all sides; then remove and put aside in a warm place.

Chop up the onions and the garlic and cook them gently in the juices from the meat until they are just transparent. Do not let them brown. Stir in the paprika, then add the meat, the chopped parsley and the lemon juice. Season.

Cover the casserole tightly (this can be done by placing a sheet of aluminium foil over the dish before the lid is put on). Simmer over a low heat for 1 hour; check the progress of cooking and remove from the heat when the meat is tender and when the point of a sharp knife will penetrate it easily. Check the seasoning and serve very hot.

Elle advises that the sauce for this Spanish dish should be thick when it is served, coating all the pieces of meat. If it is still too liquid, remove the meat and reduce the sauce over a brisk heat.

AGNEAU AU SAFRAN
Saffron lamb

PREPARATION TIME: 30 minutes
MARINADING TIME: 30 minutes
COOKING TIME: 50 minutes
FOR SIX

1.3 kg (generous 2¾ lb) boned
  shoulder of lamb
1 teaspoon dried saffron
500 ml (18 fl oz) natural yoghurt
2 teaspoons caraway seeds
salt
75 g (generous 2½ oz) blanched
  almonds
3 tablespoons of oil

4 medium-sized onions
4 cloves of garlic
1 stick of cinnamon
½ teaspoon cardamon seeds
6 cloves
1 root fresh ginger
½ teaspoon chilli powder
750 ml (27 fl oz) coconut milk

Soak the dried saffron for 10 minutes in 3 tablespoons of boiling water. Put it into a bowl with the yoghurt, caraway seeds and a pinch of salt. Mix together and add the meat, cut into large cubes, stirring until all the meat is covered. Leave to marinate for half an hour.

Soak the almonds for 10 minutes in 8 tablespoons of boiling water. Remove them, but do not discard the water. Chop up the nuts finely and put them and the soaking water into a blender. A runny paste should result.

Heat the oil in a thick-bottomed casserole, add the chopped onions and garlic, together with the cinnamon, the cardamon seeds, the cloves and 2 tablespoons of grated ginger. Cook gently for 7 or 8 minutes, stirring frequently. Add the lamb, the mixture in which it was marinated and also 8 tablespoons cold water. Finally, add the almond purée and the chilli powder. Mix together and cook for 10 minutes.

Add the coconut milk, bring everything to the boil and allow to simmer until the lamb is tender. This should be in about 20 minutes. Remove the cinnamon stick and the cloves, arrange the meat on a warmed serving dish and cover it with the sauce.

Serve with boiled rice and a variety of chutneys.

[75]

CARRÉ D'AGNEAU PRINTANIER
Rack of lamb with early vegetables

PREPARATION TIME: Nil
COOKING TIME: 25–30 minutes
FOR SIX

2 racks of lamb, giving 12 cutlets   a pinch of pepper
salt

The rack is the tenderest part of a lamb. If separated, tie the meat together as shown in the illustration.

Heat the oven up to its maximum. Put the meat fatty-side downwards on a grid above a drip-pan and put it in the oven. When the ends of the bones begin to blacken, turn the meat over on to its other side. Season and cook until the skin is golden-brown. Turn off the oven and let the meat rest inside for 5–8 minutes more.

To serve, remove the string and any parts of the backbone which remain. Separate the racks into individual cutlets; they should be pink in the centre, but not raw.

All the early vegetables go well with this lamb; small new potatoes tossed in butter, young peas cooked with lettuce hearts, french beans. Without doubt, it is the best of all roasts for spring.

CÔTES D'AGNEAU PROVENÇALE
Lamb chops with aubergines and tomatoes

PREPARATION TIME: 1 hour
COOKING TIME (CHOPS): 7 minutes
            (VEGETABLES): 30 minutes
FOR SIX

6 plump lamb chops   *2 tablespoons of chopped*
150 ml (5 fl oz) olive oil   *parsley*
1 tablespoon of dried thyme   *1 clove of garlic*
salt, pepper   *6 tomatoes*
6 medium-sized aubergines

The Chops: Put the oil and the thyme in a bowl and let them soak together for 1 hour. Brush each chop on both sides with the flavoured oil and put them under a grill at the last minute. Cook 3–4 minutes each side. Season.

The Aubergines: Trim them and cut them into thick slices. Sprinkle them with salt and let them sweat out their liquid for 20 minutes; then wipe them and cut into cubes. Brown them slowly in a pan in some of the oil and thyme and, before serving, sprinkle them with a mixture of chopped parsley and chopped garlic.

The Tomatoes: Cut them in half, remove the pips and sprinkle several drops of the remaining oil over the cut surface. Put them on a baking sheet into a very hot oven and, when they have softened, sprinkle them with chopped parsley, reduce the heat and leave them in the oven with the door open until the moment of serving.

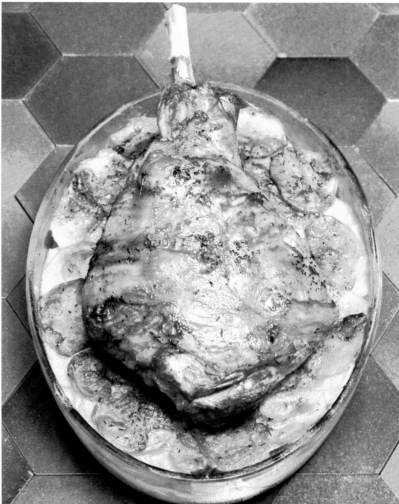

ÉPAULE D'AGNEAU FARCIE
Stuffed shoulder of lamb

PREPARATION TIME: 20 minutes
COOKING TIME: 40 minutes
FOR SIX

shoulder of lamb, about 1½ kg (3¼ lb)	1 sprig of parsley
120 g (scant 4½ oz) York ham	50 g (scant 2 oz) butter
shallot	2 small lamb's kidneys
2 sprigs of thyme	salt, pepper
	6 small tomatoes

Ask your butcher to remove the blade bone from the shoulder of lamb, but to leave the leg bone.

Chop the ham, the shallot and the herbs. Heat a tablespoon of butter in a pan and, when it begins to foam, put in the kidneys cut in half. Lightly season them. Take them out when they are about three-quarters cooked and before they have browned. Put in the chopped ham, shallot and herbs and lightly cook them over a gentle heat, at the same time deglazing the pan with the back of a fork.

Spread the chopped ingredients inside the shoulder of lamb and arrange the kidneys between the bone and the opening. Close by sewing up the opening in such a way that the joint retains its flat form. Weigh it.

Plunge the tomatoes into boiling water and peel them. Put the joint into an ovenproof dish and arrange the tomatoes around it. Season. Pre-heat a hot oven (220°C/425°F/Gas Mark 7).

Calculate the cooking time by allowing 20 minutes for the first pound and 15 minutes for each succeeding one. Turn the joint from time to time and when the cooking time is up, turn off the oven and leave the meat to rest for 8–10 minutes. Put a tablespoon of butter and several drops of water into the pan and deglaze it to make a sauce.

Cut in slices across the shoulder and serve with green beans.

GIGOT BOULANGÈRE
Leg of lamb baked with potatoes

PREPARATION TIME: 25 minutes
COOKING TIME (POTATOES): 1¾–2 hours
      (LAMB): 15–18 minutes per pound
FOR SIX TO EIGHT

1½ kg (3¼ lb) leg of lamb	1 onion
2 kg (4½ lb) potatoes	salt, pepper
thyme	100 g (3½ oz) butter
2 bay leaves	2 cloves of garlic

Peel the potatoes and cut them into thin round slices. Crumble a heaped teaspoon of dried thyme and the 2 bayleaves and finely chop the onion; mix all together with a teaspoon of salt and a good pinch of ground pepper.

Butter the inside of an ovenproof dish and put half the potatoes in as a bottom layer. Sprinkle half the onion and herb mixture over them and repeat with the rest of the potatoes and the second half of the mixture. Dot with half the butter and just cover the potatoes with warm water.

Pre-heat a very hot oven (230°C/450°F/Gas Mark 8) for 10 minutes and put in the potatoes. They will be cooked when very little liquid remains in the bottom of the dish (about 1¾ hours).

Work ¾ of a teaspoon of mixed salt and pepper into the rest of the butter and spread it over the joint; stick the sliced garlic under the skin. Weigh the joint and calculate the cooking time. Lay it on top of the potatoes in the oven and, when the skin is golden-brown, turn the joint over. Turn off the oven at the end of the calculated time, open the door and leave the joint to rest.

Take the dish to the table and remove the joint to a warmed carving dish which will collect the juices coming from the joint. Serve these juices with the meat.

The complete success of this dish depends upon the potatoes being properly cooked when the joint goes into the oven.

ÉPAULE D'AGNEAU EN GIGOT
Shoulder of lamb with garlic

PREPARATION TIME: 10 minutes
COOKING TIME: 20 minutes per pound
FOR SIX

1 shoulder of lamb, about 1½ kg   salt, pepper
  (3¼ lb)   50 g (scant 2 oz) butter
1 clove of garlic

Ask your butcher to remove the blade bone from the joint, but to leave the leg bone.

Slice the garlic and stick the pieces into the lamb. Work salt and pepper into a small knob of butter and spread it over the joint.

Pre-heat the oven for 15 minutes to its highest temperature. Put the joint into the oven on to the grid of a drip-pan and let it cook for 15 minutes, then reduce the heat to 200°C/400°F/Gas Mark 6 and continue cooking for 40 minutes. Turn off the oven and light the grill: put the joint under it and turn the lamb over until the skin is golden-brown on all sides. Turn off the grill and return the joint to the oven to rest for about 8 minutes.

Carve the joint on a dish which will collect the juices coming from the meat. Put a tablespoon of boiling water and the rest of the butter into the drip-pan and deglaze it with the back of a fork. Pour the sauce into a warmed sauceboat and mix with the juices from the meat.

Serve flageolet or white haricot beans with the lamb.

GIGOT FARCI A L'AIL
Leg of lamb stuffed with garlic

PREPARATION TIME: 20 minutes (in advance)
COOKING TIME: 18–20 minutes per pound
FOR SIX

1½ kg (3¼ lb) leg of lamb   2 tablespoons chopped parsley
3 cloves of garlic   salt, pepper
100 g (3½ oz) butter

Ask your butcher to take the bone out from the top, without cutting the joint right open.

Chop the garlic finely and work it into the butter, together with the chopped parsley. Season. Form into a sausage shape, wrap it in aluminium foil and put it into the refrigerator. When it is firm, unwrap it and slip it into the bone-cavity of the joint; sew up the openings at each end. Tie the joint with string to maintain its shape and place it in a drip-pan.

Pre-heat a very hot oven (230°C/450°F/Gas Mark 8) and put in the joint. Turn it so that it seals on all sides and then reduce the heat (200°C/400°F/Gas Mark 6). Continue cooking for the calculated time, turning the joint over 2 or 3 times, and then turn off the oven, open the door a little and let the lamb rest for several minutes.

Carve in slices across the joint while it is still in its drip-pan. Remove the meat to a warmed serving dish; put 1 or 2 tablespoons of boiling water into the pan and deglaze with the back of a fork. Pour the contents into a warmed sauceboat.

SAUTÉ DE PORC
Sauté of pork with onions

PREPARATION TIME: 10 minutes
COOKING TIME: 1 hour
FOR SIX

1.2 kg (2¾ lb) boned shoulder of pork	salt, pepper
	bouquet garni
lard	1 clove of garlic
6 onions	

Cut the boned meat into pieces as if for a stew. Heat a large knob of lard in a pan and gently seal the meat, stirring so that all the sides are done. Remove the meat and put the onions in the same cooking fat until they are browned. Return the meat to the pan, season, add the bouquet garni, the garlic and 4 tablespoons of water.

Cover the pan and simmer until the onions are cooked: they should be soft without having begun to break up. The meat should be cooked in the same time.

Serve together with a purée of cabbage, with noodles or with boiled or sauté potatoes.

PORC SAUTÉ AU CHOU CHINOIS
Sauté of pork with Chinese cabbage

PREPARATION TIME: 20 minutes (2 hours in advance)
COOKING TIME: 20 minutes
FOR SIX

600 g (generous 1¼ lb) pork fillet	For the sauce
2 Chinese cabbages	2 teaspoons of cornflour
50 ml (1¾ fl oz) oil	pinch of salt
salt	1 teaspoon of freshly-grated ginger
	2 tablespoons of soya sauce
For the marinade	
1 tablespoon of soya sauce	
2 teaspoons of cornflour	
2 egg whites	

Begin by putting the pork fillet in the freezing compartment of your refrigerator for an hour so that it will stiffen and make cutting it up easier.

Cut the fillet first lengthways, then across in thin slices. Mix the marinade in a dish from the ingredients given (the whites should be from freshly-cracked eggs) and 3 tablespoons of water. Leave the pork pieces in it for 30 minutes, turning the meat from time to time.

Make the sauce in a bowl with the ingredients shown and 4 table-spoons of water. Wash the Chinese cabbage and shake dry. Slice into very thin strips crossways.

Using, if possible, a wok, stir-fry the slices of pork in a little oil, removing them as they are done to a warm place. When all the pork is cooked, add a little more oil and stir-cook the chopped cabbage, half at a time. Each batch should take about 5 minutes, and should then be kept warm with the pork.

Put more oil in the wok and return pork and cabbage to it, turning and stirring over a brisk heat for a further 5 minutes. Season with salt and rapidly mix in the sauce and any juices given off by the pork while being kept warm.

Season to taste and serve at once.

[79]

PORC BRAISÉ AU CITRON
Braised pork with lemon

PREPARATION TIME: 10 minutes
COOKING TIME: 1½ hours
FOR SIX

1 ½ kg (3 ¼ lb) boned shoulder of
  pork
1 tablespoon of lard
200 ml (7 fl oz) dry white wine
2 cloves of garlic

2 teaspoons of powdered cumin
2 teaspoons of coriander seeds
salt, pepper
1 lemon

Cut the boned meat into small chunks. Heat the lard in a large pan and put in the meat, turning it so that it seals on all sides. When this is done, transfer it to a casserole.

Pour the fat from the pan and add the white wine. Deglaze the pan by vigorously scraping the bottom with the back of a fork. Transfer the liquid to the casserole and add the chopped garlic and the spices. Season, cover the dish and cook over a medium heat for 45 minutes.

Cut the lemon into thin round slices, add them to the casserole and continue to cook with the lid on for another 30 minutes.

This Portuguese dish can be served either with rice or boiled potatoes.

RÔTI DE PORC À LA MOUTARDE
Roast pork in mustard

PREPARATION TIME: 10 minutes
COOKING TIME: 16–20 minutes per pound
FOR SIX

1 ½ kg (3 ¼ lb) fillet or boned
  shoulder of pork
150 ml (5 fl oz) strong Dijon
  mustard

1 pig's caul
150 ml (5 fl oz) white wine

Tie the boned meat into an even shape, without any extra larding fat. Spread it thickly with mustard and enclose it in the pig's caul: you can usually obtain a pig's caul from your butcher if you order it in advance. Weigh the joint and calculate the cooking time.

Pre-heat a hot oven (200°C/400°F/Gas Mark 6) for 20 minutes. As the meat becomes golden-brown in the oven, moisten it occasionally with the wine. When the cooking time is up, turn off the oven and let the meat prove for between 5 and 10 minutes.

Take the joint from its roasting pan, add a tablespoon of boiling water and deglaze the pan with the back of a fork. Be sure to get all the small pieces into the sauce which should be served in a warmed sauceboat.

As this dish is equally delicious cold, it would be sensible to buy a piece of meat big enough for 2 meals.

CHOUCROUTE FARCIE
Cabbage stuffed with pork

PREPARATION TIME: 30 minutes
COOKING TIME: 2¾ hours
FOR SIX

1 cabbage
3 onions
50 g (scant 2 oz) lard
350 g (about ¾ lb) boned and
  minced shoulder of pork
100 g (3½ oz) cooked rice
2 eggs

2 teaspoons of paprika
1 kg (2¼ lb) cooked sauerkraut
1 bottle dry white wine
salt, pepper
250 ml (9 fl oz) crème fraîche
8 boned pork chops

Wash the cabbage in running water and blanch it in salted boiling water for 5–6 minutes. Remove and drain. Chop the onions and cook them slowly in about a third of the lard until transparent. Mix together in a bowl the minced pork, cooked rice, the beaten eggs, paprika and chopped onion.

Take off the cabbage leaves one by one and place 3 of them together on the work-surface. Put ⅙ of the minced pork mixture, rolled into a ball, into the middle of the cabbage leaves; wrap the leaves around the mixture and tie into a packet. Make 5 more stuffed cabbages in the same way.

Put the rest of the lard into a large casserole. Wash and blanch the sauerkraut and put half of it in the casserole as a bed. Arrange the stuffed cabbages on top and cover with the rest of the sauerkraut. Pour in the wine, season, put the lid on the casserole and cook in a fairly hot oven (200°C/400°F/Gas Mark 6) for 2½ hours. Towards the end of this time, cook the pork chops in a frying pan.

Remove the stuffed cabbages and put them aside in a warm place. Thoroughly stir the cream into the sauerkraut. Place the sauerkraut on a large serving dish and arrange stuffed cabbage and pork chops alternately on top.

Elle advises that this very filling Hungarian dish makes a complete meal for a winter's evening.

POTÉE AUX LENTILLES
Lentil hotpot

PREPARATION TIME: 45 minutes
COOKING TIME: 2½–3 hours
FOR EIGHT

500 g (generous 1 lb) smoked
  streaky bacon, in a piece
1 gammon hock
4 leeks
300 g (10½ oz) carrots
2 small turnips
2 onions
4 cloves

2 cloves of garlic
bouquet garni
10 black peppercorns
1 cervelas sausage
250 g (9 oz) green lentils
3 sticks of celery
500 g (generous 1 lb) potatoes
salt, pepper

Put 4 litres (7 pints) of water into a large saucepan and put in the bacon and the gammon. Bring to the boil, skim and surface and simmer for 1½ hours.

Then tie the leeks in a bundle and put them into the saucepan with the carrots, turnips, the onions stuck with cloves, the garlic, the bouquet garni and the peppercorns. Continue cooking at a slow boil for 45 minutes longer, then add the cabbage, cut into quarters, and the cervelas. Remember to prick the sausage to prevent it bursting. Cook for 30 minutes more; do not add salt before seasoning has been checked.

In the meantime, cook the lentils and the chopped celery together over a low heat, taking care that they do not disintegrate. Season lightly. Boil the potatoes.

To serve, slice the bacon and carve the gammon and arrange the slices on a large warmed serving plate. Put the vegetables and lentils in groups around the meat.

Skim any fat from the cooking juices and serve separately in soup cups.

Elle advises that a good method of skimming fat is to soak a linen cloth in warm water then squeeze it out well. Fold it in 4 and pass the edges of the cloth over the surface of the boiling liquid.

CÔTES DE PORC AUX PRUNEAUX
Pork chops with prunes

PREPARATION TIME: 30 minutes
COOKING TIME: 15 minutes
FOR SIX

6 boned pork chops
400 g (14 oz) prunes
600 ml (21 fl oz) dry white wine
salt, pepper

butter, oil
75 ml (2½ fl oz) crème fraîche
redcurrant jelly

Stone the prunes and put them to soak for 10 minutes in a small saucepan with 400 ml (14 fl oz) of wine, 2 good pinches of salt and freshly-ground pepper.

Heat some butter and oil half-and-half in a pan and seal the chops on each side (to save time, 2 pans could be used). Remove the chops to an ovenproof dish and continue the cooking in a pre-heated oven (200°C/400°F/Gas Mark 6).

Bring the wine and prunes to the boil; cover the pan, reduce the heat and gently poach the prunes for 10 minutes.

Pour off the surplus fat from the pan in which the chops were sealed, and deglaze it by pouring in the rest of the wine and scraping the bottom of the pan with the back of a fork. Reduce the sauce by half, remove from the heat and stir in the crème fraîche. Season and mix in a tablespoon of redcurrant jelly.

Remove and drain the prunes and put them in the centre of a warmed serving dish. Arrange the chops around the edge and pour the sauce over them.

CÔTES DE PORC AUX HERBES
Pork chops with herbs

PREPARATION TIME: 15 minutes (1 hour in advance)
COOKING TIME: 30 minutes
FOR SIX

6 pork chops, each about 180 g
  (about 6½ oz)
salt, pepper

dried mixed herbs
1 tablespoon of lard
60 g (2 oz) butter

Season the chops and sparingly sprinkle herbs on to both sides of each chop. Press with the palms of the hands to ensure that the herbs adhere to the meat, and leave to stand in a cool place for 45 minutes.

Gently melt the lard in a pan and cook the chops until they are golden-brown on each side. Remove to a covered ovenproof serving-dish and complete the cooking for a further 10 minutes in a pre-heated fairly hot oven (200°C/400°F/Gas Mark 6). Just before serving, put a knob of butter on each chop.

To go with the pork, prepare a dish of haricot beans. Butter them and sprinkle them with chopped parsley lightly flavoured with garlic.

Elle advises that the success of this dish depends on using the herbs with a very light hand.

CÔTES DE PORC AU MUSCADET
Pork chops in Muscadet

PREPARATION TIME: 30 minutes
COOKING TIME: 40–60 minutes
FOR SIX

6 pork chops, each weighing about 180 g (6½ oz)	1 bay leaf
2 tablespoons of flour	60 g (2 oz) butter
salt, pepper	500 ml (18 fl oz) Muscadet
1 teaspoon dried thyme	150 g (5 fl oz) single cream
	2 sprigs of tarragon

Put the flour on a wooden board, season it and mix thoroughly with the dried thyme and the crumbled bay leaf. Coat both sides of each chop in the mixture.

Gently heat the butter in a large pan and slowly seal each chop to a golden-brown colour. Do not heat the butter to the point where it darkens. Remove the chops when they are sealed and keep warm.

Deglaze the pan by pouring in the wine and vigorously scraping the pan with the back of a fork. Be sure to detach all the residual particles from the bottom of the pan. Reduce the wine to about half its volume, stir in the cream and add the tarragon. Check the seasoning, bring the sauce to the boil and put the chops back into the pan. Cover and reduce to a very low heat; cook the chops for at least 20 minutes more.

To serve, arrange the chops in a warm dish and pour the sauce over them. They can be accompanied by a pilaff or by boiled rice or sauté potatoes.

CÔTES DE PORC SAINT-HUBERT
St Hubert's pork chops

PREPARATION TIME: 5 minutes (the day before)
COOKING TIME: 25 minutes
FOR SIX

6 boned pork chops, each weighing about 180 g (6½ oz)	30 g (1 oz) butter
1 tablespoon of lard	For the marinade
salt, pepper	½ bottle of good red wine
1 tablespoon of Dijon mustard	1 tablespoon olive oil
1 tablespoon of redcurrant jelly	1 clove of garlic
1 tablespoon of tarragon vinegar	bouquet garni
1 level dessertspoon of cornflour	freshly-ground pepper, nutmeg

Make the marinade in an earthenware dish with wine, oil, sliced garlic, the bouquet garni, pepper and nutmeg. Mix well together and put in the chops which must be completely covered by the marinade. Cover the dish with aluminium foil and put in a cool place for 24 hours.

Take out the chops and dry them on kitchen paper. Melt the lard in a pan and cook the chops slowly on both sides, for about 20 minutes altogether. Season the cooked chops and keep them warm.

Pour the marinade into the pan and deglaze it with the back of a fork. Bring to the boil and reduce the sauce by half. Stir in the mustard, redcurrant jelly and the vinegar and reduce the heat; let the sauce simmer for a good 5 minutes.

Mix the cornflour to a paste with a little water and stir it vigorously into the sauce which should be allowed to thicken. Pass it through a fine sieve, put it back on a low heat and check the seasoning. Then, off the heat, beat in the butter, knob by knob. This should produce a smooth and velvety sauce.

Pour the sauce over the chops and serve either with a dish of green lentils or a chestnut purée.

Elle advises that the importance of thorough marination cannot be overstressed. Done properly, the meat has the flavour of game (St Hubert is the patron saint of hunters).

CÔTES DE PORC AU POIVRE VERT
Pork chops and green peppercorns

PREPARATION TIME: 20 minutes
COOKING TIME: 30 minutes
FOR SIX

6 pork chops, each weighing about 180 g (6½ oz)
50 g (scant 2 oz) butter
9 tablespoons of green peppercorn vinegar (if unobtainable, use wine vinegar and crushed green peppercorns)
100 g (3½ oz) grated Gruyère cheese
125 ml (4½ fl oz) single cream
salt

Melt the butter in a pan and without letting it burn, seal the chops to a golden-brown on each side. Remove from the pan, and the pan from the stove and, with the back of a fork, vigorously incorporate the vinegar with the cooking fats. Put the liquid on one side.

Mix the grated cheese and 2 tablespoons of cream together into a paste and spread it on to one side of each of the chops. Put them into an ovenproof dish and in a moderate oven (170°C/325°F/Gas Mark 3) continue cooking slowly until the chops are done and the cheese paste has formed a crust. Carefully arrange the chops in a serving dish, taking care not to disturb the crust, and keep in a warm place.

Take the vinegar mixture which was kept aside and add to the fats in the dish in which the chops were cooked in the oven. Stir in 2 tablespoons of cream, bring to the boil, still stirring, and then pass through a sieve into a small saucepan. Add a little salt to taste, and then more cream, spoonful by spoonful, until the flavour is to your taste.

Warm the sauce through without boiling it and pour over the chops. Serve with sautéed new potatoes.

PORC EN PAPILLOTES
Pork chops in foil

PREPARATION TIME: 30 minutes
COOKING TIME: 40 minutes
FOR SIX

6 boned pork chops
50 g (scant 2 oz) lard
salt, pepper
250 g (about 8 oz) button mushrooms
2 shallots
6 tablespoons dry vermouth
3 thin slices of smoked ham
100 ml (3½ fl oz) crème fraîche
tablespoon chopped parsley

Use only boned chops. Seal them in lard until golden-brown, season and remove to one side. Chop up the mushrooms and the shallots and add them to the pan in which the chops were cooked. With the back of a fork, vigorously scrape the bottom of the pan in order to release any particles of meat. When the liquid from the mushrooms has evaporated, add the vermouth, and the ham chopped up small. Season lightly and cook with the pan uncovered until the mixture begins to look dry.

Cut pieces of aluminium foil large enough to wrap each chop individually. Put in first a spread spoonful of the chopped mushroom mixture, then a chop and a further spread of mushroom. A dab of cream should be added before the envelopes are closed. Seal the edges of the foil well but do not make the envelope too tight a fit around the meat.

Complete the cooking in a fairly hot oven (200°C/400°F/Gas Mark 6) for about 20–25 minutes. The chops can also finish cooking on a barbecue grill.

This dish can be prepared in advance and the final cooking completed at the last moment. If serving is delayed, the meat will not dry out so long as the envelopes remain closed.

Sprinkle each chop with parsley as it is served.

CARRÉ DE PORC À L'ANANAS
Loin of pork with pineapple

PREPARATION TIME: 30 minutes
COOKING TIME: 1–1¼ hours
FOR SIX

1½ kg (3¼ lb) boned loin joint
  of pork
brown sugar
salt, pepper
100 ml (3½ fl oz) rum

6 cooking apples
200 g (7 oz) butter
6 bananas
½ tin pineapple slices, or a fresh
  pineapple

Mix together a heaped teaspoon of dark brown sugar with a half-teaspoon of salt and a little freshly-ground pepper, and sprinkle it over the joint. Put it into a pre-heated very hot oven (230°C/450°F/Gas Mark 8) and quickly seal it on all sides. Reduce the oven to fairly hot (190°C/375°F/Gas Mark 5) as soon as the meat is a golden-brown colour all over. Pour 3 tablespoons of rum over the joint and continue the cooking for a total period of 20 minutes per pound. Sprinkle on a little more rum from time to time.

Peel and quarter the apples, sprinkle with a level tablespoon of brown sugar mixed with a little salt and cook them in a pan with three tablespoons of butter until they are soft. Peel the bananas (which should be ripe but firm) and cook them whole in 2 tablespoons of butter and a little sugar until they are soft and golden. Cook the pineapple rings similarly.

When the joint is cooked, bring all the fruit together into the same pan, pour four tablespoons of rum over and increase the heat. Flame off the rum.

Slice the joint and put it on a warmed serving dish; arrange the fruit around it and serve in a sauce made from the juices of the meat extended with a tablespoon of boiling water.

PORCELET AUX HERBES
Suckling-pig in herbs

PREPARATION TIME: 30 minutes
COOKING TIME: 25 minutes per pound
FOR SIX

2½–3 kg (5½–6¾ lb)
  hind-quarters of a suckling-pig
2 tablespoons mixed herbs

2 tablespoons lard
salt, pepper
1¼ kg (2¾ lb) small potatoes

Knead the herbs into the lard and season. Score the rind of the pork into diamonds and coat the joint with the herb paste, keeping some of it aside. This will be spread into the gaps in the skin as they open up during the cooking.

Weigh the joint and place it on a trivet in an oven pan. Par-boil the potatoes in their skins, peel them and arrange them whole around the joint in the pan. Put into a cold oven and heat to 200°C/400°F/Gas Mark 6.

Cook at 25 minutes per pound, turning the joint occasionally so that the rind crisps all round. When this has been done, cover the pan with aluminium foil, reduce the heat if necessary and let the joint cook through. Check progress with a long fine skewer: when withdrawn, the point should be at the same temperature as the part near the surface.

To serve, remove the crackling and carve the joint as for a leg of lamb.

Those who like garlic can stick cloves into the meat before cooking: two will be quite sufficient.

Elle advises that this method of cooking is equally delicious for other joints of pork.

JAMBON À LA BOURGUIGNONNE
Burgundy ham

PREPARATION TIME: 15 minutes
COOKING TIME: 25 minutes
FOR SIX

6 good slices of cooked ham
60 g (2 oz) butter
2 tablespoons of chopped
  shallots
200 ml (7 fl oz) dry white
  Burgundy, preferably Chablis

2 tablespoons wine vinegar
250 ml (9 fl oz) single cream
level tablespoon tomato purée
salt, pepper, nutmeg
1 egg yolk

Arrange the ham slices in a fireproof serving dish.

Put the butter and the chopped shallots into a saucepan and cook slowly until the vegetables are just beginning to colour. Add the wine and the vinegar and reduce until about 3 tablespoons of liquid remain. Stir in the cream and the tomato purée, heat together without boiling, season, grate on some nutmeg and then beat in the egg yolk.

Pass the mixture through a fine sieve directly on to the ham. Put the dish over a low heat for 20 minutes, again taking care that the liquid does not boil, until all the flavours have mingled together. Serve at once.

(CONTINUED)

The Madeira Sauce
Roughly chop the ham rind. Slice the onion and the carrots and cook them slowly in half the butter. Add the ham rind, the bouquet garni, tomato purée, a litre (1¾ pints) of water and the chicken cube. Season and cook in a covered pan for 2 hours over a low heat. Pass through a fine sieve.

In another saucepan, make a brown roux with the rest of the butter and the flour. Mix the sieved sauce into it, add the Madeira and cook without boiling for 15 minutes.

JAMBON EN CROÛTE
Ham in pastry

PREPARATION TIME: 40 minutes, spread over 2 days
COOKING TIME (THE HAM): 30 minutes per kg
         (THE SAUCE): 2¼ hours
FOR TWELVE

A whole York ham weighing·
  about 4½ kg (10 lb)
1 bottle of dry white wine
4 onions
3 carrots
6 shallots
bouquet garni
freshly-ground pepper
4 cloves
1 kg (scant 2¼ lb) frozen puff
  pastry
1 egg

For the sauce
100 g (3½ oz) rind from the ham
1 onion
1 carrot
100 g (3½ oz) butter
bouquet garni
1 small tin tomato purée
1 cube chicken stock
salt, pepper
60 g (2 oz) flour
250 ml (9 fl oz) Madeira

Soak the uncooked ham overnight. Then replace the water and bring it slowly to the boil. As soon as boiling point is reached, pour off the water and replace it with new boiling water; add the cut vegetables, bouquet garni and some freshly-ground pepper. Calculate the cooking time from when the ham comes back to the boil and allow 30 minutes per kg (roughly 14 minutes per pound). Let the ham stand overnight in its cooking water.

Remove the ham. With a sharp skinning knife, remove the rind and put aside 100 g (3½ oz). Carefully carve 12 slices from the upper part of the ham and then replace them in order. Stick in the 4 cloves.

Roll out the puff pastry and completely envelope the ham, sealing the edges by dampening them with a little water and smoothing them together. Decorate the ham with patterns made from trimmings of pastry, and brush it all over with beaten egg.

Heat a fairly hot oven (200°C/400°F/Gas Mark 6) and cook the ham for a good hour. Cut the lid from the pastry and serve the pre-carved slices together with a Madeira sauce.
(CONTINUED OPPOSITE)

CÔTES DE VEAU AU CERFEUIL
Veal chops with chervil

PREPARATION TIME: 5 minutes
COOKING TIME: 20 minutes
FOR SIX

6 veal chops, each weighing
   about 180 g (6½ oz)
125 g (4½ oz) butter

tablespoon of flour
100 ml (3½ fl oz) crème fraîche
2 large sprigs of chervil

Melt 60 g (2 oz) butter in a pan and seal the chops on both sides over a moderate heat. When they are golden-brown, remove and arrange on an ovenproof serving-dish.

Work the flour and the rest of the butter together. Scrape the bottom of the pan in which the chops were sealed with the back of a fork and then add, bit by bit, the flour/butter mixture to these cooking juices; also add the crème fraîche and the finely chopped chervil. Cover the chops with this sauce and put the dish into a pre-heated fairly hot oven (190°C/375°F/Gas Mark 5) for a further 10 minutes to complete the cooking of the meat.

When the chops are cooked, leave them in the oven, with the heat turned well down, until serving time.

CÔTES DE VEAU FLAMBÉES
Veal chops flambé

PREPARATION TIME: 10 minutes
COOKING TIME: 35 minutes
FOR SIX

6 veal chops, each weighing
   about 180 g (6½ oz)
2 tablespoons of oil
400 g (14 oz) button mushrooms
lemon juice

60 g (2 oz) butter
100 ml (3½ fl oz) brandy
200 ml (7 fl oz) single cream
salt, pepper
½ teaspoon flour

Bone and trim the veal chops so that they are roughly equal in size. Take a large pan and seal them to a golden colour, 3 at a time, using a tablespoon of oil for each batch. Arrange them in a fireproof serving-dish, and keep in a warm place.

Trim the mushroom stalks, wipe them in a solution of water and lemon juice, and slice them, keeping the best six as a garnish. Melt 2 tablespoons of butter and gently cook all the mushrooms, sliced and whole.

Put a knob of butter into the chop dish and put it back on the heat. When the chops are heated through, pour on the brandy and flame it off. Add the sliced mushrooms and their cooking liquid and arrange the chops on top. Stir in half the cream, bring to the boil and continue to simmer until the liquid takes a little colour. Season.

Thoroughly mix the flour with the rest of the cream and add it to the chops. Let it all simmer for a few minutes. Decorate with the 6 whole mushrooms.

The dish is best served with sauté potatoes, peas or leaf spinach.

CÔTES DE VEAU FOYOT
Gratin of veal chops

PREPARATION TIME: 10 minutes
COOKING TIME: 55 minutes
FOR SIX

3 large veal chops cut from the
  fillet, each weighing about
  350–400 g (12–14 oz)
150 g (5 oz) butter
400 g (14 oz) chopped
  onion

100 g (3½ oz) grated Parmesan
  cheese
50 g (scant 2 oz) white
  breadcrumbs
150 ml (5 fl oz) dry white wine
150 ml (5 fl oz) chicken stock

Bone the chops. Take a third of the butter and slowly cook the chopped onion until it is transparent. In another pan, quickly seal the chops in another third of the butter until they are golden-brown.

Mix the cheese and breadcrumbs together. In a shallow ovenproof dish, arrange first a thin layer of cooked onion, then the chops, the rest of the onion and finally the grated cheese mixture. Pour in the wine and the chicken stock, the rest of the butter (melted) and cook for 45 minutes in a fairly hot oven (200°C/400°F/Gas Mark 6).

Elle advises that the preparatory steps can, if necessary, be done well in advance. Cut the chops in half before serving.

CÔTES DE VEAU AUX ENDIVES
Veal chops with chicory

PREPARATION TIME: 5 minutes
COOKING TIME: 25 minutes
FOR SIX

6 veal chops each weighing
  about 180 g (6½ oz) after
  trimming
2½ kg (5½ lb) chicory
175 g (6 oz) butter

tablespoon of sugar
salt, pepper
100 ml (3½ fl oz) dry white wine
75 ml (generous 2½ fl oz) crème
  fraîche

Trim off any brown or torn outer leaves from the chicory, take off the vestigial stalk and cut them lengthways into 8 pieces. Melt 70 g (2½ oz) butter in a pan and add the chicory, sprinkle in the sugar and a little salt. Let it cook uncovered and over a fair heat for 15 minutes, turning constantly.

Take 2 pans so that all the chops cook at the same time. Melt 60 g (scant 2 oz) butter in each and seal the chops to a golden-brown colour: lower the heat and let the chops cook through for up to 15 minutes. Season.

When the chops are cooked, keep them warm until the chicory is ready. Use the wine to deglaze each pan, vigorously stirring with the back of a fork. Add the cream and boil at least once, stirring well. Put the sauce into a warmed sauceboat.

Take a warmed serving dish and arrange a bed of chicory, put the chops on top and serve the sauce separately.

GRENADINS AU POIVRE VERT
Medallions of veal with peppercorns

PREPARATION TIME: 20 minutes
COOKING TIME: 20–30 minutes
FOR SIX

6 boned and trimmed veal chops,
   weighing about 180 g (6½ oz)
flour
100 g (3½ oz) butter
1 liqueur glass of brandy
200 ml (7 fl oz) dry white wine

3 or 4 teaspoons of green
   peppercorns
teaspoon cornflour
250 ml (9 fl oz) double cream
½ teaspoon tomato purée
salt

Wrap and tie bacon fat around the boned and trimmed chops. Powder the chops lightly with flour and cook them gently to a golden-brown on each side in a good tablespoon of butter. Do not let the butter burn. Put them in a fireproof serving-dish, pour the brandy over them, cover the dish and leave them to steep.

Pour the white wine into the pan in which the chops were cooked and deglaze vigorously with the back of a fork. Add the coarsely crushed peppercorns. Bring to the boil and pour the liquid over the veal.

Thoroughly mix the cornflour and the cream together with the tomato purée to give it a pinkish colour. Pour into the meat dish, season with salt and cook for a further 20 minutes over a very low heat, turning the chops over once.

This dish can be served with rice or chipped potatoes, french beans or peas.

GRENADINS SAUCE AVOCAT
Medallions of veal in avocado sauce

PREPARATION TIME: 10 minutes
COOKING TIME: 15 minutes
FOR SIX

6 boned and trimmed veal chops,
   each weighing about 180 g
   (6½ oz)
salt, pepper
1 onion

1 clove of garlic
60 g (2 oz) butter
250 ml (9 fl oz) crème fraîche
1 avocado pear

Wrap and tie bacon fat around the boned and trimmed chops. Season the pieces of veal on both sides. Chop the onion and garlic. Take a large and heavy pan and cook the meat, onion and garlic in the butter for about 4 minutes, turning the meat once. Remove the veal to a serving dish and keep in a warm place.

Pour the cooking butter from the pan and replace it with the crème fraîche. Bring it to the boil, and let it reduce for 3 minutes. Remove from the heat.

Put the flesh of the avocado through a blender and mix it in with the sauce in the pan. Season and pass through a fine sieve over the veal. Serve at once.

The chef of the 'L'Archestrate' restaurant in Paris, from where this recipe comes, suggests a St Emilion to accompany it.

GRENADINS À L'ORANGE
Medallions of veal in orange sauce

PREPARATION TIME: 30 minutes
COOKING TIME: 30 minutes
FOR SIX

6 boned and trimmed veal chops, each weighing about 180 g (6½ oz)	salt, pepper
	heaped tablespoon flour
	100 g (3½ oz) butter
3 oranges	1 onion
tablespoon of brandy	1 carrot
tablespoon of orange liqueur	

Take the peel of 2 of the oranges and cut into thin strips. Steep them in a mixture of the brandy and orange liqueur.

Season the flour and coat the veal chops on both sides, shaking off any surplus. Heat the butter over a moderate heat and, without letting it brown, seal the chops to a golden-brown colour. Chop the onion and slice the carrot and add these vegetables to the meat, letting them all cook together for 15 minutes. Remove the chops and keep them in a warm place.

Take the juice of the 2 peeled oranges and pour it, together with 4 tablespoons of water and the liquor in which the peel has been steeped, into the pan. Deglaze the pan vigorously with the back of a fork. Bring the sauce to the boil and pass through a sieve.

Peel the third orange and divide it into slices. Put the veal chops back into the pan, pour the sauce over them and decorate with the steeped strips of orange peel and slices of orange. Gently re-heat and serve at once.

POITRINE AUX ÉPINARDS
Stuffed breast of veal

PREPARATION TIME: 30 minutes
COOKING TIME: 1½ hours
FOR SIX

1½ kg (3¼ lb) breast of veal	2 cloves of garlic
2 packets of frozen chopped spinach	1 egg
	salt, pepper, nutmeg
400 g (14 oz) blade of pork	5 hard-boiled eggs
250 g (about 9 oz) back bacon	30 g (1 oz) lard
6 onions	200 ml (7 fl oz) white wine

Have the breast of veal boned and trimmed into an oblong shape so that it can be more easily rolled.

Boil a large saucepan of salted water, plunge in the spinach and cook for 10 minutes. Remove and thoroughly drain it. Mince all the ingredients going into the stuffing: pork, bacon, spinach, 2 of the onions and the garlic. Mix them all together with the beaten egg and season with salt, pepper and grated nutmeg.

Lay out the veal and spread a layer of half the stuffing in the middle of the meat. Trim the ends of the hard-boiled egg just back to the yolks and lay them end to end in the middle of the stuffing. Cover them with the rest of the stuffing and roll up the meat so that the two ends overlap. Tie firmly to prevent it unrolling during the cooking.

Heat the lard in a casserole and seal the rolled meat on all sides. Chop the remaining onions and add them to the dish; pour in the wine, together with an equal quantity of hot water. Season, cover the casserole and cook slowly for 1½ hours.

During cooking, be sure to moisten the joint frequently with its own juices.

Slice before serving. This dish also makes a delicous cold main course for a picnic.

RÔTI DE VEAU A L'ESTRAGON
Roast veal with tarragon

PREPARATION TIME: 5 minutes
COOKING TIME: 1¼ hours
FOR SIX

¼ kg (2¾ lb) boned fillet of veal
50 g (scant 2 oz) butter
1 liqueur glass of brandy
400 ml (14 fl oz) dry white wine
salt, pepper
sprig of tarragon
125 ml (4½ fl oz) crème fraîche

Melt the butter in an iron casserole and gently seal and brown the joint. Take care not to let the butter burn. When the meat has a good even colour, pour off any surplus cooking fats, pour on the brandy and flame it. Warm the white wine and pour this also over the meat. Season, cover the joint with tarragon leaves, cover the casserole and cook for 1–1¼ hours, turning the meat over frequently.

When cooked, remove the joint and cut it into slices. Arrange them on a warm serving dish. If a lot of liquid remains in the casserole, reduce it over a brisk heat, then stir in the crème fraîche and bring the sauce to a quick boil. As soon as it has bubbled, pass it through a fine sieve and pour it over the meat. Serve immediately.

The chef of the 'La Boule d'Or' restaurant in Barbezieux in the Charente, from where this recipe comes, recommends the good dark red wine of Cahors to go with it.

RÔTI DE VEAU AUX OLIVES
Roast veal with olives

PREPARATION TIME: 15 minutes (an hour in advance)
COOKING TIME: 1½ hours
FOR SIX

1½ kg (3¼ lb) boned fillet of veal
thyme and rosemary
salt, pepper
olive oil
2 cloves of garlic
100 ml (3½ fl oz) dry white wine
250 g (about 8 oz) black olives
500 g (generous 1 lb) button
    mushrooms
1 lemon

Put the herbs and seasoning into a dish and cover them with two tablespoons of olive oil. Let the meat stand in this marinade for at least an hour, turning it frequently.

Put the joint into a large pan and seal it on all sides (adding extra oil if necessary) until it is a golden-brown colour. Remove it to a casserole, add the crushed garlic and a little extra thyme. Pour in the white wine, cover the dish and cook in a fairly hot oven (200°C/400°F/Gas Mark 6) for about 1½ hours.

In the meantime, stone the olives and plunge them for 2 minutes into boiling water. Put to one side. Trim the stalks of the mushrooms, wipe them under running water and sprinkle them with lemon juice. Slice them and cook in 2 tablespoons of olive oil. Ten minutes before the veal is cooked, add mushrooms and olives to the casserole.

The dish on which the joint is served should be garnished with the olives and the mushrooms. Tomatoes provençales go very well with this dish.

LONGE DE VEAU JARDINIÈRE
Loin of veal with spring vegetables

PREPARATION TIME: 45 minutes
COOKING TIME: 1½–1¾ hours
FOR SIX TO EIGHT

1¾–2 kg (4–4½ lb) boned loin of
  veal
fat bacon
olive oil
25–30 small white onions
6 small young carrots
head of celery
4 tomatoes

bouquet garni
2 cloves of garlic
tin of artichoke hearts
salt, pepper
1½ kg (3¼ lb) peas, to make
  700 g (1½ lb) shelled peas
60 g (2 oz) butter

Trim and tie the joint with a slice of fat bacon each side. Heat a little oil in a casserole over a brisk flame and seal the meat on all sides. Add the peeled onions, the whole carrots, the inner and tender sticks of celery (cut up, three tablespoons at the most), the peeled and seeded tomatoes, the bouquet garni, whole garlic and the drained artichoke hearts.

Season, cover the casserole and cook over a very low heat, turning the joint from time to time. After an hour of cooking, add the peas together with half a glass of hot water. Keeping the casserole covered, simmer for a further 30 minutes.

Carve the veal into slices and put it on to a warmed serving-dish. Remove the vegetables with a perforated spoon and put them on to a separate serving dish. Bring the juices in the casserole to the boil, remove from the heat and mix in the butter knob by knob. When the sauce is thoroughly blended, serve it separately.

VEAU AUX PISTACHES
Veal with pistachio nuts

PREPARATION TIME: 30 minutes
COOKING TIME: 20 minutes per pound
FOR EIGHT TO TEN

2 kg (4½ lb) boned leg of veal
150 g (5 oz) shelled pistachio
  nuts
tablespoon of lard
1 carrot

4 onions
4 shallots
bouquet garni
salt, pepper
60 g (2 oz) butter

Have the leg of veal boned but be sure to retain the bone. Put the pistachio nuts in warm water which will facilitate the peeling of the inner skin; then stick the nuts into the joint right through to the middle. Tie the meat up so that it keeps its shape during cooking.

Heat the lard in a casserole and seal the joint all over; the sliced vegetables, bouquet garni and the bone should then be put in. Season and add 4 tablespoons of water. Cover the dish and cook over a very moderate heat.

Turn the joint frequently and check to see that it does not cook too quickly. If necessary, add a spoonful of cold water and reduce the heat.

When the joint is cooked, remove from the casserole and carve into slices. Put on a serving dish and keep warm. Strain the cooking liquid, bring to the boil in a saucepan, remove from the heat and stir in the butter, knob by knob, beating vigorously until a smooth sauce results.

Meat and sauce should be served separately; button mushrooms tossed in butter and sprinkled with chopped parsley are an excellent accompaniment.

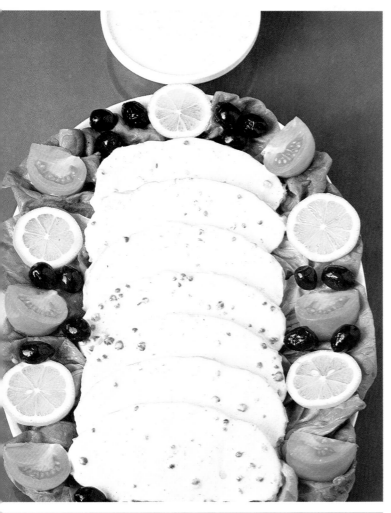

VEAU AU THON
Veal with tunny fish

PREPARATION TIME: 30 minutes
COOKING TIME: 1½ hours (the day before)
FOR SIX

1 ¾ kg (3¾ lb) boned loin or fillet
  of veal
4 cloves of garlic
4 anchovy fillets
1 sachet of court-bouillon
300 ml (10 fl oz) dry white wine
3 onions
2 carrots
3 sticks of celery
bouquet garni

For the sauce
cup of veal liquor
6 anchovy fillets
small tin of tunny fish
1 egg yolk
salt, pepper
250 ml (9 fl oz) olive oil
1 lemon
tablespoon of crème fraîche
2 tablespoons of capers

Stick the joint with the garlic cloves and the anchovy fillets and put it into a large pan of boiling water. When it comes back to the boil, leave it there for 1 minute and then remove the joint. Put it into an oval casserole, sprinkle on the court-bouillon powder and add the wine and 2 litres (3½ pints) of water. Put in the onions, carrots, celery and the bouquet garni.

Cover the dish, bring to the boil and cook over a moderate heat for about 1 hour 20 minutes to 1½ hours. The joint is cooked when the point of a knife penetrates easily into the centre of the meat. Leave it to cool in its own juices, but put a cupful of the liquid aside for the sauce.

To make the sauce, put the anchovy fillets and the tuna through a blender. Add the egg yolk, season and then pour in the oil, drop by drop as though making a mayonnaise. Skim the grease from the cup of meat juices and add 2 tablespoons of the liquid to the tuna sauce, together with the juice of a lemon, the crème fraîche and the capers.

Carve the veal into thin slices. Take a large flat dish and cover the bottom with a thin layer of sauce. Lay out the slices of veal so that they do not overlap, and cover them with the rest of the sauce. Use a spatula to ensure an even coating, and then refrigerate overnight.

Lift the slices carefully on to a serving dish and decorate the edges with lettuce, slices of tomato and of lemon, and black olives.

VEAU FOURRÉ
Stuffed veal

PREPARATION TIME: 30 minutes
COOKING TIME: 1 hour
FOR SIX

1 kg (2¼ lb) boned loin or fillet of
  veal
125 g (4½ oz) sliced gammon
200 g (7 oz) Gruyère cheese
1 pig's caul

2 tablespoons strong Dijon
  mustard
3 onions
2 sprigs of thyme
1 bay leaf
12 tablespoons of Madeira

Ask your butcher to cut the joint into slices 1 cm (under ½ in) thick, that do not go right through the meat. The gammon and the cheese should both be cut into thin slices and the pig's caul soaked in cold water. Order the pig's caul from your butcher in advance.

The faces of each cut in the joint should be lightly spread with mustard and then a slice of cheese and one of gammon put into each cut. Use a long skewer to maintain the shape of the joint as you proceed, and when the last slices are in, tie the joint, envelope it in the caul and tie with string to keep it in place. Remove the skewer and trim off any surplus ends of caul.

Put the joint in an uncovered ovenproof dish, together with the onions (cut in half) and the herbs, and cook in a fairly hot oven (200°C/400°F/Gas Mark 6).

When the joint begins to brown, baste it with its own juices but do not turn the joint: the aim is to achieve a golden-brown crust on the meat. As this develops, pour a few tablespoons of Madeira over the meat.

When the joint is cooked, remove it to a warm serving dish. Skim the grease from the pan and add the rest of the Madeira. Bring the juices to the boil, stirring vigorously with the back of a fork so that all the meat juices are incorporated. Pass through a fine sieve.

The sauce can either be poured over the joint before it is carved, or served separately.

AILLADE DE VEAU
Veal with garlic

PREPARATION TIME: 15 minutes
COOKING TIME: 1 hour
FOR SIX

1.3 kg (good 2¾ lb) shoulder of
 veal
50 g (scant 2 oz) goose fat or lard
3 heaped tablespoons fresh
 breadcrumbs

2 cloves of garlic
1 large tin of peeled tomatoes
500 ml (18 fl oz) dry white wine
salt, pepper

Cut the veal into cubes 3–4 cm (about 1½ in) in size. Heat the fat in a casserole and briskly seal the meat all over. When it has a good colour, sprinkle it with the breadcrumbs and finely chopped garlic.

The tomatoes should be put through the fine mesh of a vegetable mill and then sieved so a purée without pips results. Add this to the dish, together with the white wine: season. Cook uncovered over a low heat for about an hour.

The sauce should be thick and completely cover the meat. If at the end of cooking, it is still too thin and liquid, remove the meat with a perforated spoon and reduce the sauce by rapid boiling. Serve this dish from Gascony very hot.

Elle suggests that you can, if you prefer, use fresh tomatoes when in season. Peel and seed them, and cook them slowly with a chopped shallot in 2 or 3 tablespoons of oil. Finish the purée, of which you will need about 300–400 g (12 oz), in the blender.

VEAU VERT
Veal with green herbs

PREPARATION TIME: 20 minutes
COOKING TIME: 1–1¼ hours
FOR SIX

1.2 kg (2¾ lb) of boned shoulder
 of veal
100 g (3½ oz) butter
4 tablespoons of chopped fresh
 parsley, chervil and tarragon

200 ml (7 fl oz) dry white wine
1 lemon
2 tablespoons of single cream
salt, pepper

Cut the meat into 4 cm (1½ in) cubes. Season well.

Melt the butter in a casserole and add the meat and the chopped herbs. Stir well so that herbs and butter are thoroughly distributed. Cover the dish and cook in a fairly hot oven (200°C/400°F/Gas Mark 6) for an hour, stirring the meat 2 or 3 times. Watch that the herbs do not burn and, if necessary, reduce the heat to 180°C/350°F/Gas Mark 4.

When the meat is cooked, add the wine, the juice of half a lemon and the cream. Stir well together and bring quickly to the boil for 5 minutes.

Serve with a dish of leaf spinach cooked in butter.

SAUTÉ DE VEAU AU CITRON
Sauté of veal with lemon

PREPARATION TIME: 30 minutes
COOKING TIME: 50 minutes
FOR SIX

1.2 kg (2¾ lb) boned shoulder of veal
1 large onion
80 g (scant 3 oz) butter
1 tablespoon flour
1 bottle of dry white wine
1 tablespoon tomato purée
salt, pepper
bunch of chervil
7 lemons
250 ml (9 fl oz) crème fraîche
6 egg yolks

Cut the meat into 5 cm (2 inch) cubes. Peel and slice the onion.

Melt the butter in a casserole and add the meat and sliced onion. Cook until the meat is sealed on all sides, and the onion transparent, adding additional butter if necessary.

Pour off the cooking fats and sprinkle the meat with flour, stirring at the same time. Add the wine and the tomato purée, season and simmer with the casserole covered for 15 minutes. Then add the chopped chervil and continue cooking over a moderate heat.

When the meat is done, remove it and put it on its serving plate and keep warm.

Put the casserole back on the heat and stir in the juice of 5 lemons. Let the sauce boil for 10 minutes in the uncovered dish. In the meantime, carefully peel the final 2 lemons and cut them into small pieces.

Stir the crème fraîche into the sauce, bring back to the boil and immediately remove from the heat. Briskly whip the egg yolks into the sauce and pour it over the meat. Garnish with the small pieces of lemon.

The chef of the Paris restaurant 'Le Petit Pre', from where this recipe comes, recommends a Brouilly or a red Sancerre as the ideal accompaniment.

VEAU VAPEUR
Provençale veal stew

PREPARATION TIME: 20 minutes
COOKING TIME: 2 hours
FOR SIX

1 kg (2¼ lb) boned shoulder of veal
salt, pepper
cube of chicken stock
2 sprigs of thyme
1 bay leaf
1 sprig of basil
2 bunches of spring onions

For the sauce
2 cloves of garlic
1 sprig of basil
6 individual pots of natural yoghurt, 150 g (5 oz) size
1 lemon
teaspoon of olive oil
salt, pepper

In this recipe, the meat is cooked in a steamer. Remove all fat and gristle from the veal and cut it into large chunks. Season.

Put 2½ litres (4 pints) of water in the steamer together with the chicken cube, the thyme, bay leaf and basil. Bring to the boil, arrange the meat above it and cover the steamer. Trim the stems from the onions and, after an hour's cooking, add the white onions to the meat and steam for a further hour. Retain the onion stems.

In the meantime, prepare the sauce. Empty the yoghurt into a mixing bowl, add the finely-chopped garlic and basil, the chopped onion stems, juice of a lemon, and season. Stir all together and put in the blender for a final mixing.

The meat can be accompanied by boiled rice, with the cold sauce served separately.

PAUPIETTES AUX ANCHOIS
Veal birds with anchovy paste

PREPARATION TIME: 30 minutes
COOKING TIME: 40 minutes
FOR SIX

6 escalopes of veal
18 black olives
3 hard-boiled eggs
anchovy paste
salt, pepper
6 slices of smoked ham
pork fat for larding
chopped thyme

crushed bay leaf
goose fat or lard
cube of chicken stock
200 ml (7 fl oz) dry white wine
30 small white onions
clove of garlic
liqueur glass of armagnac or
    brandy

Stone and chop the olives, chop up the hard-boiled eggs and put them into a bowl. Add 3 tablespoons of anchovy paste, season lightly and work everything together into a smooth mixture.

Beat the escalopes out with a wooden rolling pin. Lay them out, put a slice of ham on each one, spread on a layer of olive and anchovy stuffing and roll up the escalopes.

Cut the pork fat into thin rectangles the size of the rolled veal, sprinkle them with the chopped thyme and crushed bay leaf. Wrap the veal 'birds' in them and tie into shape.

Heat the fat in a casserole and, when hot, put in the veal birds to brown. Dissolve the chicken cube in 250 ml (9 fl oz) of boiling water. Take 150 ml (5 fl oz) and pour, together with the wine, over the meat. Add the onions, garlic; season and cover the casserole and cook slowly over a low heat for the given time.

Put the armagnac into a metal ladle, heat it and when it is flaming, pour it over the veal. Remove the veal birds, cut their string ties and take the string and pieces of cooking fat away. Put the birds into a warmed serving dish and cover with a sauce made from the skimmed and strained meat juices.

Elle advises that, to remove the grease from the cooking juices, heat one end of the casserole to boiling point. The grease will migrate to the other end of the dish and can be removed carefully with a spatula.

BOCCONCINI
Veal stuffed with ham and cheese

PREPARATION TIME: 20 minutes
COOKING TIME: 30 minutes
FOR SIX

6 tender escalopes of veal
6 slices of York ham
300 g (10½ oz) Emmanthaler
    cheese
50 g (scant 2 oz) flour
150 ml (5 fl oz) olive oil

500 g (good 1 lb) button
    mushrooms
sage
350 g (about 12 oz) frozen peas
6 thick slices of white bread
25 g (scant 1 oz) butter
salt, pepper

Beat the escalopes with a wooden rolling pin. Lay them out and first put a slice of ham on each one, followed by the Emmenthaler cheese cut into thin strips. Roll the meat, making sure that the ends overlap and tie firmly. Cover the veal rolls with flour and brown them over a brisk flame in 100 ml (3½ fl oz) of oil for 10 minutes, turning them often so that they brown evenly. Season and remove to a sauté pan o fireproof dish.

Quickly deglaze the pan with ½ a glass of boiling water, briskly stirring with the back of a fork. Pour the liquid over the veal rolls.

Trim the stalks of the mushrooms, wipe and slice them. Add them to the veal together with 2 crushed sage leaves. Cover and cook slowly Ten minutes before the end of cooking, add the frozen peas which should already have been blanched in boiling salted water.

Trim the crusts from 6 thick slices of bread and fry them on both sides in the butter and the rest of the oil. Remove the string ties arrange the veal rolls on the croutons on a warmed serving dish surround them with their vegetables and serve at once.

The chef of the Marseille restaurant 'Chez Caruso' from where this recipe comes, recommends a light and fruity red wine, such as a Beaujolais, to go with the dish.

SAUCISSE AU COULIS	CHIPOLATAS AU VIN BLANC
Sausage in tomato sauce	Chipolatas in white wine

SAUCISSE AU COULIS
Sausage in tomato sauce

PREPARATION TIME: 15 minutes
COOKING TIME: 35 minutes
FOR SIX

1 metre (about 1 yard) of Cumberland sausage (or 6 good pork sausages)	3 tablespoons olive oil
500 g (good lb) small or spring onions	750 g (good 1½ lb) tomatoes
	5 cloves of garlic
	salt, pepper
	25 g (scant 2 oz) butter

Peel and chop half the onions and cook gently in 2 tablespoons of olive oil until transparent. Add the skinned, seeded and chopped tomatoes, and the crushed garlic. Season and allow to simmer for 25 minutes over a low heat. Strain the sauce through a sieve.

Cut the remaining onions in half and cook slowly in the butter for 15–20 minutes. Season.

Heat the rest of the oil in a large frying pan and put in the sausage. Cook for about 15 minutes over a moderate heat, turning from time to time so it browns evenly. Five minutes before cooking is completed, put in the onions and the juice in which they have been cooked.

Take out the sausage and stir its fat into the tomato sauce. The sausage should be served with the onions and with the tomato sauce poured over it. A dish of mashed potatoes makes an excellent accompaniment to this dish which comes from the Languedoc.

Elle reminds you to prick the sausage so that it does not burst during cooking.

CHIPOLATAS AU VIN BLANC
Chipolatas in white wine

PREPARATION TIME: 15 minutes
COOKING TIME (SAUSAGES): 10 minutes
(SAUCE): 15 minutes
FOR SIX

12 chipolata sausages	2 egg yolks
100 g (3½ oz) butter	tablespoon crème fraîche
2 shallots	oil
250 ml (9 fl oz) dry white wine	6 slices of white bread without crusts
salt, pepper	chopped parsley
teaspoon tomato purée	

Try to buy the French chipolatas for this dish. They are longer and may well be meatier. If only English ones are available, buy double the quantity.

Melt a tablespoon of butter in a thick-bottomed pan. When it foams, put in the sausages (which should have been pricked to prevent them bursting), cook on both sides for 10 minutes. Remove to a warm place.

Finely chop the shallots. If the sausages have given off much fat, pour half of it away and cook the shallots gently until they are transparent. Add the white wine and reduce by a third, season and stir in the tomato purée little by little to give colour to the sauce. Beat the egg yolks and the cream together and fold them into the sauce just before serving; it should be allowed to thicken without boiling.

Lightly fry the bread in half butter, half oil, arrange on a serving dish with the sausages on top. The sauce should be served separately; chopped parsley should also be served. Other side dishes which go well with the sausages are mashed potatoes, purée of peas, purée of chestnut or a rice pilaff.

CERVELLES DE VEAU POULETTE
Calves' brains with sauce poulette

PREPARATION TIME: 1 hour
COOKING TIME (BRAINS): 20–25 minutes
(SAUCE): 10 minutes
FOR SIX

2 calves' brains, with (if possible)
  the spinal marrow
wine vinegar
bouquet garni
1 onion
salt, pepper

For the sauce
200 g (7 oz) button mushrooms

2 lemons
60 g (2 oz) butter
300 ml (10½ fl oz) of the cooking
  liquid
tablespoon of flour
2 egg yolks
150 ml (5 fl oz) double cream
salt, pepper
tablespoon of chopped parsley

Ask your butcher to give you the spinal marrow with the brains. Clean the brains thoroughly under running water and remove any skin or membranes and any traces of blood.

Put 4 tablespoons of vinegar, the bouquet garni and the onion cut into quarters into 2 litres (3½ pints) of water. Season, boil for 15 minutes and allow to cool. Cut the brains and the marrow in 4–5 cm (2 in) pieces, put them into the water, bring back to the boil and then, with the pan covered and over a very low heat, keep them just on the boil for 20–25 minutes. Then remove the brains and marrow and let them cool. Retain the cooking liquid.

Trim, wipe and slice the mushrooms and sprinkle them with lemon juice. Soften them gently in butter for 15 minutes.

To make the sauce, strain 300 ml (10½ fl oz) of the liquid in which the brains were cooked into a saucepan. Using a little of the liquid, make a paste of the cornflour and stir it in to the contents of the saucepan. Bring to the boil, stirring constantly. Add the mushrooms and their juices, remove from the heat and add the egg yolks and cream beaten together with a frew drops of lemon juice. Check the seasoning.

Cut the pieces of brain into slices 1 cm (½ in) thick, pour on the sauce, warm over a low heat and serve sprinkled with parsley.

RIS DE VEAU AU CHAMPAGNE
Calves' sweetbreads in champagne

PREPARATION TIME: 25 minutes
COOKING TIME: 25 minutes
FOR SIX

3 good-sized calves'
  sweetbreads
200 g (7 oz) button mushrooms
1 lemon
salt, pepper

flour
100 g (3½ oz) unsalted butter
¼ bottle of champagne
200 ml (7 fl oz) crème fraîche

Put the sweetbreads into a large saucepan of cold water and bring to the boil. Let them blanch for 2 minutes. Remove into a sieve and run them under cold water until they are quite cool. Carefully remove any skin and membranes and cut the sweetbreads into 1 cm (½ inch) thick slices. Put to one side.

Trim the stalks of the mushrooms, wash them in a solution of water and lemon juice, wipe them dry, slice them and sprinkle them with lemon juice to prevent discoloration.

Season the slices of sweetbread, roll them in flour and shake off any surplus. Melt the butter in a large pan over a low heat and gently cook the sweetbreads. When they are golden-brown on both sides, put the sliced mushrooms on top and pour on the champagne; increase the heat and reduce the volume of liquid by a quarter. Stir in the crème fraîche, reduce the heat and continue to reduce down to half-volume. Remove the sweetbreads to a deep, very hot serving dish and cover them with the sauce.

A purée of celery is excellent with this dish.

The chef of 'La Sologne' restaurant in Paris, from where this recipe comes, suggests that the dish be accompanied by the same marque of champagne in which it was cooked.

ROGNONS DE BOEUF AU BORDEAUX
Beef kidneys in red wine

PREPARATION TIME: 30 minutes
COOKING TIME: 30 minutes
FOR SIX

2 whole beef kidneys
2 large onions
4 shallots
2 tablespoons of lard
300 ml (10½ fl oz) red Bordeaux
flour
60 g (2 oz) butter

sprig of thyme
clove of garlic
salt, pepper, nutmeg
bay leaf
chopped parsley, chervil and
   chives

Chop the onions and shallots finely and cook them in a casserole slowly with a tablespoon of lard. When done, they will be soft and transparent. Pour on the red wine and 150 ml (5 fl oz) water and keep at a slow boil for 20 minutes. Remove from the heat and thicken the sauce by stirring in 2 tablespoons of flour which have been worked into a paste with a tablespoon of butter.

Add the leaves of thyme, the crushed garlic and bay leaf and bring back to the boil, stirring constantly. The sauce should be fairly thick. Season with salt, pepper and grated nutmeg and put to one side.

Cut the kidneys into pieces about the size of a walnut, removing any fat or veins. Heat a tablespoon each of lard and butter in a large pan and quickly seal the kidneys all over. When no raw patches remain and they are giving out their own juices, empty the contents of the pan into the casserole. Simmer for 4–5 minutes, but no longer since over-cooked kidneys become tough. Check the seasoning.

To accompany the kidneys, sauté some potatoes, cut into small cubes, in lard. Sprinkle with chopped mixed herbs before serving.

ROGNONS AUX TROIS MOUTARDES
Kidneys in three mustards

PREPARATION TIME: 10 minutes
COOKING TIME: 18–20 minutes
FOR SIX

3 whole veal kidneys
400 g (15 oz) button mushrooms
1 lemon
60 g (2 oz) butter
50 ml (1¾ fl oz) brandy

3 mustards: Meaux, Dijon and
   green peppercorn
250 ml (9 fl oz) crème fraîche
salt, pepper

Remove any fat, veins, etc. from the kidneys and cut them up. Trim the stalks of the mushrooms and wipe them in a solution of lemon juice and water.

Heat 30 g (1 oz) butter in a large pan and, over a brisk heat, quickly seal the kidneys so that they remain pink at the centre. Remove and keep warm. Discard the fat in the pan and in its place put the mushrooms, cut into quarters, and the rest of the butter. Cook with the pan covered for 5–6 minutes. Then remove the mushrooms and add to the kidneys in a warm place.

Deglaze the pan with the brandy, stirring vigorously with the back of a fork.

Put 2 teaspoons of each of the mustards into a bowl with the crème fraîche and mix them all together. Put this mixture into the pan, and stirring vigorously, let it boil for a second or two. Put the kidneys and the mushrooms into the sauce and let the whole dish warm through over a low heat.

The chef of the Paris restaurant 'Le Ciel de Paris' from where this recipe comes, recommends a good Beaujolais, preferably a Morgon, with these kidneys.

ROGNONS BONNE FEMME
Kidneys with bacon and mushrooms

PREPARATION TIME: 15 minutes
COOKING TIME: 20 minutes
FOR SIX

3 whole veal kidneys	*50 g (scant 2 oz) butter*
250 g (9 oz) streaky bacon	*salt, pepper*
150 g (5 oz) button mushrooms	*chopped parsley*
1 lemon	

Put the bacon into a saucepan with cold water, bring to the boil and let it blanch for 5 minutes. Drain and cut into dice.

Trim the stalks of the mushrooms and wipe them in lemon juice. Cut them also into dice.

Heat half the butter in a pan and briskly cook the bacon and mushrooms together. Remove to a warm place.

Heat the remainder of the butter and seal the whole kidneys on all sides. Transfer them to an ovenproof dish, season, add the bacon and mushrooms and put into a slow oven (150°C/300°F/Gas Mark 2) for 15 minutes. Turn on to a hot serving dish and sprinkle with chopped parsley.

Small new potatoes, par-boiled and then browned in butter, make a delicious accompaniment to this dish.

ROGNONS DE VEAU AU CURRY
Curried kidneys

PREPARATION TIME: 20 minutes
COOKING TIME: 50 minutes
FOR SIX

3 whole veal kidneys	*flour*
2 onions	*salt, pepper*
60 g (2 oz) butter	*tablespoon of oil*
2 crisp eating apples	*dessertspoon of brandy*
2 tablespoons curry powder	*100 ml (3½ fl oz) crème fraîche*

Trim all the fat and veins from the kidneys and cut them into small pieces.

Peel and chop up the onions and cook gently in half the butter. Peel and core the apples, cut into dice and add them to the onions. Cook together for 10 minutes, sprinkle on the curry powder and the flour. Vary the amount of curry powder according to taste. Stir everything together quickly, add enough water to cover the ingredients, season and cook slowly for 30 minutes. Then pass everything through the fine disc of a vegetable mill and put the sauce to one side.

Heat the oil and the rest of the butter in a pan and cook the kidneys for 5 minutes over a brisk heat. Pour in the brandy and flame it. Remove the kidneys and keep in a warm place.

Add the curry sauce and the crème fraîche to the juices in the pan, stir all together, raise the heat and reduce the volume of the sauce by a quarter. Return the kidneys to the pan and serve, with wild or brown rice, as soon as they are heated through.

The chef of the 'La Salle à Manger' restaurant in Paris from where this recipe comes, suggests a red wine of Cahors to go with the dish.

BROCHETTES DE FOIE
Liver kebabs

PREPARATION TIME: 10 minutes
COOKING TIME: 25 minutes
FOR SIX

1.2 kg (2¾ lb) calves' or lambs'
   liver
3 packets of frozen leaf spinach,
   each about 225 g (8 oz) size
150 g (5 oz) butter
3 onions
2 cloves of garlic

30 dried leaves of sage
15 thin slices of smoked streaky
   bacon
6 tablespoons of oil
150 ml (5 fl oz) dry white wine
salt, freshly-ground pepper

Do not defrost the spinach but plunge it still frozen into a large pan of boiling salted water. Cook for about 5–8 minutes, drain thoroughly and roughly chop it up.

Melt half the butter in a pan and gently cook the chopped onions and garlic. When they are transparent, mix in the spinach and simmer with the pan covered for about a further 5 minutes.

During this time, cut up the liver into 2–3 cm (1 in) squares and put each one on to a dried sage leaf. Wrap each piece of meat and herb in half a slice of bacon and pass a kebab skewer through them: 5 to each skewer, making 6 kebabs in all.

Take a large pan and heat the rest of the butter and the oil; when it begins to sizzle, put in the kebabs and cook for 10–12 minutes, turning them over once or twice. The bacon should be golden and crisp when the kebabs are cooked.

Arrange the spinach in the bottom of a warmed serving dish and put the kebabs, still on their skewers, on top.

Quickly pour the fat from the pan and replace it with the white wine. Season, bring to the boil, stir vigorously with the back of a fork and pour the sauce immediately over the kebabs.

Elle advises that it is best to buy the bacon pre-packed in order to get it in the required thickness. These kebabs can, if necessary, be prepared well in advance and kept in the refrigerator.

FOIE DE VEAU AU VIN BLANC
Calves' liver in white wine

PREPARATION TIME: 10 minutes
COOKING TIME: 10 minutes
FOR SIX

6 slices of calves' liver
3 shallots
2 tablespoons of goose fat (or
   lard)

250 ml (9 fl oz) dry white wine
salt, pepper
chives

Chop the shallots and gently cook them until transparent in a tablespoon of fat. Remove and put to one side.

Take a large pan and with all the remaining fat, cook the liver over a low heat, turning it from time to time. When it is done (it will still be pink at the centre), put it onto a serving dish and keep warm. Pour off all the fat from the pan.

Raise the heat and add the white wine. Deglaze the pan by vigorously stirring with the back of a fork and then put in the cooked shallots. Reduce the sauce by half, season and pour over the liver. Serve sprinkled with chopped chives.

FOIES DE VOLAILLE EN ASPICS
Chicken livers in aspic

PREPARATION TIME: 20 minutes
COOKING TIME: 8 minutes
COOLING TIME: 6 hours
FOR SIX

500 g (generous 1 lb) chicken   *salt, pepper*
livers   *tablespoon of brandy*
1 small shallot   *3 tablespoons powdered*
40 g (scant 1½ oz) butter   *gelatine*
sprig of thyme

Chop the shallot very finely and cook it gently in the butter, together with the leaves of the thyme. When it is quite softened, separate the pieces of liver and add them to the pan. Raise the heat and stir the contents of the pan so that the livers become firm but are still pink at the centre. Season and pour on the brandy.

Take the pan from the heat, cover it and let the livers steep for a few minutes. Remove the pan to a cool place until the livers are quite cold; make sure they are covered with their cooking juices.

Make the aspic according to the instructions on the packet and leave it to cool. Put the livers into aspic moulds or ramekins and cover them with the aspic just as it is on the point of setting. Refrigerate for several hours.

Turn each mould out by beating it sharply into the palm of the hand, arrange them on a serving dish, garnish with chopped lettuce and quarters of tomatoes.

<u>Elle advises</u> that the secret of a really clear aspic is to make sure that the livers are really cold and that the gelatine is on the point of setting when it is poured over them.

FOIE DE VEAU À L'ORANGE
Liver with orange sauce

PREPARATION TIME: 15 minutes
COOKING TIME: 8–10 minutes
FOR SIX

6 slices of calves' liver   *salt, pepper*
100 g (3½ oz) butter   *3 oranges*

Melt ¾ of the butter over a moderate heat and when it begins to foam, put in the liver. When properly cooked, the liver should be slightly pink in the middle while the outer skin should still be soft. Season, and put to one side on a serving dish, kept warm over a saucepan of simmering water.

Squeeze the juice of 1 orange into the pan and deglaze it by vigorously stirring with the back of a fork. Season and bring to the boil, adding the peeled slices of the 2 remaining oranges. Shake the pan until the orange is warmed through, then remove the slices and decorate the serving dish.

Take the pan off the heat and melt the rest of the butter in the sauce, whisking with a fork into a smooth sauce. Pour over the liver and serve.

POULE AU POT
Chicken in the pot

PREPARATION TIME: 25 minutes
COOKING TIME: 1½–2 hours
FOR SIX TO EIGHT

1 chicken of 2 kg (4½ lb)
900 kg (2 lb) veal bones
2 onions
cloves
4 small leeks

2 heads of celery
6 good-sized carrots
bouquet garni
salt

Buy a plump and meaty chicken and ask your butcher for 900 g (2 lb) of veal bones (without the marrow).

Truss and trim the chicken as if for roasting and put it together with its giblets and the veal bones into a saucepan. Pour in cold water until the contents are well covered, and bring to the boil, skimming from time to time.

In the meantime, peel the onions and put them in a very hot oven until they are brown. Remove and stick them with cloves. Quarter the leeks and the celery lengthways, then tie them back together. When the cooking liquid has developed into a good broth, add all the vegetables (whole carrots, leeks, celery, onions) and the bouquet garni. Season.

When the pan comes back to the boil, lower the heat and simmer for about 1½ hours.

Serve the chicken surrounded by the vegetables with which it was cooked, together with the customary accompaniments of sea-salt, mustard, gherkins, etc. Skim the fat from the chicken broth and pour a cup of the broth over the serving dish.

Elle says that if preferred, the chicken can be cooked stuffed. to prepare the stuffing, chop the liver and heart of the chicken, 100 g (3½ oz) of ham, 2 shallots, and mix together with half a cup of fresh breadcrumbs moistened with milk. Season and thoroughly mix a beaten egg into the stuffing. Ensure that the bird is trussed tightly before going into the pot.

POULET AU WHISKY
Chicken in a whisky sauce

PREPARATION TIME: 15 minutes
COOKING TIME: 30 minutes
FOR SIX

2 young chickens, each of 900 g
  (2 lb)
100 g (3½ oz) butter
150 ml (5 fl oz) whisky
150 g (5 oz) button mushrooms

1 lemon
1 shallot
100 g (3½ fl oz) double cream
teaspoon of cornflour

Divide each chicken into 4 pieces. Melt a third of the butter in a casserole and seal the chicken pieces, making sure that the butter does not go brown. Pour the whisky over them, remove the casserole from the heat, cover it and allow the contents to steep for 10 minutes.

In the meantime, cut the mushrooms in quarters, sprinkle them with lemon juice to prevent discoloration. Chop the shallot.

Melt the rest of the butter in a saucepan and gently cook the mushrooms until their liquid has evaporated. Add the chopped shallot and continue cooking until it is transparent. Add the contents of the pan to the chicken in the casserole, together with half the cream. Season, cover the dish and put back over a moderate heat for about 30 minutes until the chicken is completely cooked.

Blend the cornflour into the remaining cream. Remove the chicken to a warmed serving dish and bring the sauce to the boil. Remove it at once from the heat, and stir in the cream/cornflour mixture until a smooth sauce results. Check the seasoning, add a few drops of lemon juice to taste and pour over the chicken.

Serve with French beans, peas or matchstick potatoes.

POULET AU CÉLERI
Chicken with celery

PREPARATION TIME: 20 minutes
COOKING TIME: 1 hour
FOR SIX

2 chickens, each of 900 g (2 lb)	500 g (good lb) onions
4 tablespoons of goose fat (or lard)	2 heads of celery
	4 cloves of garlic
salt, pepper	500 g (good lb) tomatoes

Divide the chickens into pieces. Heat the cooking fat in a casserole until it is hot, but not smoking, season it and cook the chicken pieces for about 3 minutes on each side until they are golden-brown. Remove and put on one side in a warm place.

Peel and slice the onions, divide the celery into sticks and cut them up into 5 cm (2 in) lengths. Peel the garlic and leave in whole cloves. Put all the ingredients into the casserole in which the chicken was cooked, cover the dish and cook over a low heat for about half an hour, stirring from time to time.

Then peel and remove the seeds from the tomatoes and add them to the casserole. Arrange the chicken pieces on this bed of vegetables, cover the dish and continue cooking over a low heat for a further 30 minutes.

The chef of the Paris restaurant 'Lous Landes', from where this recipe comes, suggests a red Bordeaux or Cahors to go with the dish.

POULET BASQUAISE
Chicken Basque

PREPARATION TIME: 30 minutes
COOKING TIME: 1–1¼ hours
FOR SIX

1 chicken of about 1½ kg (3¼ lb)	bouquet garni
	2 large red peppers
olive oil	2 large green peppers
100 ml (3½ fl oz) dry white wine	4 tomatoes
salt, pepper	6 large spring onions

Divide the chickens into pieces. Heat some olive oil in a pan and gently cook the chicken until the pieces are golden-brown all over. Remove to a casserole, pour in the white wine, season, add the bouquet garni and cook, covered, over a moderate heat.

Grill the peppers whole and when the skin has bubbled and blackened, wrap them separately in damp kitchen paper. Peel and seed the tomatoes. Peel and slice the onions, and cook them gently in olive oil until they are soft and transparent.

Unwrap the peppers, when their skins should peel off like a glove. Slice into strips, taking care to discard all seeds and inner membranes. Add them to the onions and, after 10 minutes of cooking together, add the tomatoes. Season and continue to cook gently until the vegetables are reduced to a pulp. Pour them over the chicken and keep over a very low heat for a further 20 minutes.

Elle says this method of preparation brings out all the flavour of the ingredients without making a chicken stew of the dish

POULE AU POT EN GELÉE
Poached chicken in aspic

PREPARATION TIME: 1 hour (2 days in advance)
COOKING TIME: 4 hours
FOR SIX TO EIGHT

2 chickens each weighing 900 g
  (2 lb)
1 kg (2¼ lb) carrots
500 g (generous 1 lb) young
  turnips
6 leeks (white parts only)
2 heads of celery
½ sachet gelatine powder, 7 g
  (¼ oz)
For the stock
1 calf's foot
500 g (good 1 lb) carrots
2 leeks
300 g (10½ oz) young turnips
4 sticks of celery

2 onions
bouquet garni
salt, pepper
1 egg

For the forcemeat
250 g (9 oz) chicken livers
250 g (9 oz) smoked ham
125 g (4½ oz) fat bacon
100 g (3½ oz) fresh white
  breadcrumbs moistened with
  milk
1 egg
tablespoon chopped mixed
  parsley, chervil and chives

Two days before, make a stock with the giblets, the calf's foot (which should be ordered in advance from the butcher), the vegetables, bouquet garni and 3 litres (5 pints) of water. Skim off any fat, bring the stock to the boil, season and break in a whole egg, shell and all. Let it boil once more, then pass it through a fine sieve.

The day before, make a forcemeat by mixing together in a blender the ingredients shown. Form it into a thick sausage, roll it in some clean muslin and tie the ends.

Trim the other vegetables shown at the beginning of the list of ingredients and cut them into strips. Tie the leeks into small bundles and blanch all the vegetables in boiling water for 5 minutes. Remove and drain.

Cook the chickens and the forcemeat sausage in the stock for 50–60 minutes. Remove and leave to cool. Put the vegetables in the stock and cook until tender. Remove and put to one side. Skim the fat from

(CONTINUED OPPOSITE)

POULET AU VERJUS
Chicken in grape juice

PREPARATION TIME: 10 minutes
COOKING TIME: 30 minutes
FOR SIX

2 chickens, each of 900 g (2 lb)
70 ml (2½ fl oz) oil
500 g (good lb) green (unripe)
  grapes

4 cloves of garlic
sprig of parsley
30 g (1 oz) butter
salt, pepper

Divide the chickens into portions. Heat the oil in a pan and gently seal the chicken pieces to a pale golden colour. Remove and keep warm.

Press the juice from the grapes; about 200 ml (7 fl oz) should result. Crush the garlic and chop the parsley.

Melt the butter in a casserole and arrange the pieces of chicken in it. Sprinkle on the garlic and parsley, pour in the grape juice, season, and cover the dish. Cook over a moderate heat for 20–25 minutes when the sauce should have the consistency of a thin syrup. Serve with sauté potatoes.

Elle advises that verjus is, strictly speaking, the rather sharp juice of unripe grapes. Unsweetened grape juice could be substituted, cut with the juice of half a lemon.

(CONTINUED)

the stock once more and, if necessary, clarify it with an egg. Strain it and add the gelatine which should have been soaked in fresh water. Mix well together.

Skin the chickens, remove the meat and cut into pieces. Put ½ cm (¼ in) of stock in the bottom of the required number of soup bowls and refrigerate until set. Then fill the bowls with pieces of chicken, strips of vegetables and the forcemeat removed from its muslin and cut into slices. Top up with stock. Return to the refrigerator to set.

Turn out each bowl on to a plate garnished with lettuce, spring onions and gherkins.

COQUELETS AU CITRON VERT
Spring chicken in lime sauce

PREPARATION TIME: 45 minutes (partly in advance)
COOKING TIME: 40 minutes
FOR SIX

*3 spring chickens each of 700 g
  (1½ lb)
chopped tarragon, parsley,
  basil, chervil, chives and sage
500 ml (18 fl oz) dry white wine
6 limes*

*2 tablespoons olive oil
salt, pepper
2 carrots
2 onions
50 ml (scant 2 fl oz) double
  cream*

Two or three hours in advance, split the chickens in half lengthways
and press the pieces between two boards under a heavy weight.

Arrange the flattened chicken pieces on a large earthenware plate
and sprinkle them with a little of each of the chopped herbs, no single
one being dominant. Prepare a marinade from the white wine, juice of
4 limes, a tablespoon of oil and seasoning, and pour it over the
chicken. Turn the pieces frequently. Peel the other 2 limes and divide
them into segments.

Grate the carrots and chop the onions and put them into a saucepan, together with a pinch of each of the herbs and a tablespoon of oil;
cook gently until the onion is transparent. Spread the vegetables over
the bottom of an ovenproof dish and arrange the chicken pieces, skin
side upwards, on top. Put this dish into a pre-heated hot oven (220°C/
425°F/Gas Mark 7) for 20–25 minutes. Turn the chicken once or twice;
the pieces should not brown too much.

Pour the marinade into a small saucepan and reduce it to a third of
its volume over a brisk heat. Skim the surface frequently.

When the chicken is cooked, arrange the pieces in a warmed
serving dish. Skim the juices remaining in the oven dish and pour in
the reduced marinade, deglazing it by stirring vigorously with the
back of a fork. Let the sauce simmer for a few minutes. Strain, stir in the
cream and the lime segments, heat the sauce through without allowing it to boil and pour it over the chicken.

POULET AU VINAIGRE
Chicken in vinegar sauce

PREPARATION TIME: 30 minutes
COOKING TIME: 45 minutes–1 hour
FOR SIX

*1 chicken of about 1.8 kg (4 lb)
125 g (4½ oz) butter
salt, pepper
1 carrot
2 onions*

*1 good stick of celery
bouquet garni
100 ml (3½ fl oz) tarragon
  vinegar
100 ml (3½ fl oz) chicken stock*

Remove the giblets and strip the breasts, thighs and legs from the
bird.

Melt half the butter in a casserole and seal the chicken pieces
gently, without letting the butter darken. Remove, season and keep in
a warm place.

Grate the carrot and chop the onions and celery and put them into
the casserole. Cook gently in the butter for a few minutes and then
add the bouquet garni, the vinegar and the stock. Bring to the boil and
add the chicken and any juices it has given off while standing; cover
the dish and cook over a very low heat for a further 30 minutes. Stir from
time to time.

Remove the chicken pieces to a warmed serving dish and strain the
juices into a saucepan. Check the seasoning, bring to the boil, remove
from the heat and whisk in the rest of the butter, knob by knob. Pour
over the chicken and serve with sauté potatoes and French beans.

[106]

POULET À L'ESTRAGON
Chicken in tarragon sauce

PREPARATION TIME: 5 minutes
COOKING TIME: 30 minutes
FOR SIX

1 chicken of about 1.8 kg (4 lb)	2 sprigs of tarragon
3 tablespoons of oil	salt, pepper
100 g (3½ oz) butter	1 egg yolk
6 shallots	200 ml (7 fl oz) single cream
1 carrot	level teaspoon of flour
1 liqueur glass of brandy	2 tablespoons chopped tarragon
200 ml (7 fl oz) white wine	1 tablespoon chopped chervil

Divide the chicken into pieces. Heat the oil and 3 tablespoons of butter in a casserole and brown the chicken. Do not let the fats burn. Remove the chicken and keep in a warm place.

Add another tablespoon of butter to the casserole. Slice the shallots and cut the carrots into thin rounds, and cook them gently for 5 minutes, stirring frequently. Return the chicken to the dish and, when everything is hot, add the brandy and flame it.

Pour on the white wine and enough water just to cover the chicken. Add the sprigs of tarragon, season and bring the dish to the boil. Cover and let it simmer over a low heat for 30 minutes.

Remove the pieces of chicken and arrange them on a warmed serving dish. Beat the egg yolk and blend it with the cream and the flour; stir into the cooking juices. Bring just to the boil and immediately remove it from the heat: pass the sauce through a strainer and pour over the chicken.

Serve sprinkled with chopped tarragon and chervil.

POULET À L'AIL
Chicken with garlic

PREPARATION TIME: 30 minutes
COOKING TIME: 2 hours
FOR SIX

1 chicken of about 1.4 kg (good 3 lb)	1 bulb of garlic
6 small slices of white bread	salt, pepper
olive oil	sprig of dried thyme
	flour

For this dish, a chicken-brick (a covered, unglazed earthenware pot) is ideal. If unavailable, use a casserole with a tightly fitting lid in which the chicken just fits.

Remove the crusts and cut the bread into small cubes. Fry them in the oil and then rub them in some crushed garlic. Season the inside of the bird and stuff it with the garlic croûtons.

Put the thyme into the bottom of the chicken-brick or casserole, add 2 tablespoons of olive oil and the remaining cloves of garlic, unpeeled. Put in the chicken and seal the lid carefully with a flour and water paste. (If using a casserole, place a piece of aluminium foil over the casserole before covering with the lid.)

Put into a very hot oven (230°C/450°F/Gas Mark 8) for 2 hours. When the lid of the pot is lifted, the chicken will have been browned and will be giving off a most delicious aromas.

COQ AU VIN ET AUX MORILLES
Chicken with wine and morels

POULET PRINTANIER
Chicken with spring vegetables

PREPARATION TIME: 20 minutes
COOKING TIME: 50 minutes–1 hour (according to size of bird)
FOR SIX

1 cockerel of about 2 kg (4½ lb)	100 g (3½ oz) morels
180 g (scant 6½ oz) green streaky bacon	1 bottle of red wine of Cahors
	salt, pepper
20 small white onions	sugar, nutmeg
1 small glass of brandy	3 tablespoons of flour
4 shallots	2 tablespoons of butter
bouquet garni	chopped parsley
clove of garlic	

Morels (*morilles*) may be bought dried in packets. Reconstitute them according to the instructions given. If fresh ones are available, soak them in water for an hour and then drain them well before using.

Ask your poultry dealer to joint the cockerel for you. Buy thick 6 mm (¼ in) slices of bacon, trim the rind and cut into strips across the slice. Chop the onions and put them and the bacon, without any other fats, into a large casserole. Cook gently until the onion is soft and transparent. Remove the bacon and onion and put to one side.

Put the pieces of chicken in the casserole and slowly seal them to a golden-brown colour. Pour the brandy over and flame it. Add the chopped shallots, the bouquet garni, the garlic and the morels, cover the dish and simmer over a low heat for 20 minutes.

During this time, put the bacon and onions into a saucepan, warm them through and pour in ¾ of the bottle of wine. Bring to the boil and pour over the chicken. If there is not enough liquid to cover the meat, add more wine. Season, and sprinkle in a little sugar and grated nutmeg. Cover the dish and simmer for another 30 minutes.

Remove the chicken to a warmed serving dish. Blend flour and butter together and mix the paste into the cooking juices, with the casserole removed from the heat. Bring the sauce back to the boil, then remove once more. The sauce should be smooth without being thick. Serve the chicken, sprinkled with chopped parsley, with sauté or boiled potatoes, and serve the sauce separately.

PREPARATION TIME: 25 minutes
COOKING TIME: 1 hour
FOR SIX

1 chicken of 1½ kg (3¼ lb)	1½ kg (3¼ lb) peas in pod
salt, pepper	6 spring onions
50 g (scant 2 oz) butter	bouquet garni
small lettuce heart	sugar
1 kg (2¼ lb) small carrots	

Truss the chicken as if for roasting. Season it inside. Melt a tablespoon of butter in a casserole and when it begins to foam, put in the chicken and seal it on all sides to a golden-brown. Add the lettuce heart, sliced in half, the carrots (cut up if small ones were not obtainable), the shelled peas, the onions and the bouquet garni. Season very lightly and put in 2 lumps of sugar.

Pour in enough cold water just to cover the vegetables, cover the dish and bring it to the boil; then immediately reduce the heat and simmer gently, without stirring, for 1 hour.

Carve the chicken into portions. Remove the vegetables with a perforated spoon and arrange them on a warmed serving dish, with the pieces of chicken on top.

Reduce the cooking juices in the casserole over a brisk heat, remove from the stove and whisk in the rest of the butter. Pour the sauce over the chicken.

COQ AUX CACAHUÈTES
Chicken in peanut sauce

PREPARATION TIME: 40 minutes
COOKING TIME: 3 hours
FOR EIGHT

1 cockerel about 2½ kg (5½ lb)
150 ml (5 fl oz) peanut oil
3 onions
3 tomatoes
1 litre (36 fl oz) coconut milk,
* tinned*
4 tablespoons coconut extract
4 tablespoons curry powder
coriander seed
ground ginger (or a grated root of
* ginger)*

2 sweet chillies
smooth peanut butter

For the side dishes
4 bananas
1 cucumber
3 tomatoes
1 tin (190 g 6¾ oz size) red
* peppers*
4–6 hard-boiled eggs
roasted peanuts

Cut the bird up into pieces, heat the oil in a pan and gently cook the chicken to a golden-brown colour. Remove to a casserole and put the chopped onions in the pan in its place. Peel the tomatoes, remove their seeds and, when the onion is almost transparent, add them to the pan; cook, stirring continuously, for a few minutes.

Pour the contents of the pan into the casserole and then add the coconut milk (which can usually be obtained from shops selling Indian spices), the coconut extract prepared according to the packet's instructions, the curry powder (according to taste), 2 tea-spoons of coriander seed, the ground ginger, chopped chillies and 4 tablespoons of peanut butter. Cover with salted boiling water, put the lid on the casserole and simmer over a very low heat for 3 hours or more.

Serve with boiled rice and a variety of side dishes. These should be fried bananas, diced cucumber, wedges of tomato (to cut the heat of the sauce) and strips of red peppers, sliced hard-boiled eggs and roasted, unsalted, peanuts.

POULET CONFIT
Jellied chicken

PREPARATION TIME: 40 minutes (in advance)
COOKING TIME: 1 hour (in advance)
FOR SIX

1 chicken of about 2½ kg (5½ lb)
1 kg (2¼ lb) lean streaky bacon
1½ bottles of good red wine
sprigs of tarragon, parsley and
* chervil*
5 shallots
1 clove of garlic

25 g (scant oz) crushed
* peppercorns*
250 g (9 oz) small white onions
75 g (good 2½ oz) butter
250 g (9 oz) carrots
chives
salt, pepper

Joint the chicken and put the pieces into a casserole with the gizzard. Keep the chicken liver and heart to one side. Buy the bacon in thick slices, remove the rind and cut in strips across the slice. Add these, together with 20 g (¾ oz) of salt and a bottle of wine, to the casserole.

Take the leaves from the herbs and reserve them; put the stalks into a clean cloth with 4 of the shallots, peeled and halved, the garlic and the crushed peppercorns, fold and tie into a bundle; add to the casserole. Cover the dish and put over a low flame for an hour to 1 hour 10 minutes.

Put the onions into a saucepan with a knob of butter, just cover them with wine and cook until the liquid has almost entirely evaporated.

Peel and cut the carrots into thick strips and trim them so that each has a good shape. Cook gently in a tablespoon of butter, add a chopped shallot and pour in the rest of the wine. Cover the dish and continue the cooking.

Melt the rest of the butter in a pan and cook the chicken liver and heart. Cut into pieces.

When the chicken is cooked, bone it and break the flesh into pieces, each as large as possible. Lay them out on a large shallow dish together with the bacon strips, the carrots, the onions, and the liver and heart. Sprinkle chopped chives over everything.

Strain the cooking juices and reduce them to a syrupy consistency. Pour into the dish and leave to set overnight in the refrigerator.

POULARDE MEXICAINE
Mexican chicken

PREPARATION TIME: 40 minutes
COOKING TIME: 1½–1¾ hours
FOR SIX

1 roasting chicken of 2–2¼ kg (4½–5 lb)	tablespoon of oil
1 large tin of sweetcorn, 325 g (11½ oz) size	3 carrots
	2 leeks
1 packet frozen peas (petits-pois), 300 g (10½ oz) size	2 sticks of celery
	2 onions
2 onions	clove of garlic
3 or 4 tinned red peppers	bouquet garni
salt, pepper, cayenne pepper	500 ml (18 fl oz) chicken stock
	60 g (2 oz) butter

Drain the sweetcorn and plunge the frozen peas into salted boiling water for 10 minutes. Chop up the onions and cut the peppers into small pieces. Mix together, season and add a pinch of cayenne pepper. Add this mixture to the sweetcorn, reserve 2 cups and put the rest aside. Chop up the chicken liver and gizzard and add them; stuff the bird with the mixture, sewing up all the openings afterwards.

Heat the oil in a casserole until it is hot, but not smoking, and seal the chicken all over. Add the carrots, leeks, celery and onions, all cut in half, and the garlic and bouquet garni. Pour in the chicken stock. The level of the liquid should be about halfway up the sides of the casserole; if necessary, add a little water. Season, using very little salt. Bring the dish to the boil, then cover it and put into a moderate oven (180°C/350°F/Gas Mark 4). Cook gently for 1½ hours.

Thirty minutes before the chicken is ready to serve, very gently warm through the remaining sweetcorn in butter in a covered saucepan. When the chicken is done, draw off half its juices, strain them and degrease them by passing them through a cloth that has been soaked in water and well squeezed out. Briskly reduce the juices to a syrupy consistency and brush the chicken all over with this sauce.

Remove the stuffing. Put the chicken on to a warmed serving dish and garnish it with its stuffing. Serve the rest of the sweetcorn mixture and sauce separately.

FONDUE DE POULARDE
Poached chicken with garlic sauce

PREPARATION TIME: 30 minutes
COOKING TIME: 2 hours
FOR SIX TO EIGHT

2 roasting chickens, each 900 g (2 lbs)	75 ml (2½ fl oz) Pernod
	50 g (scant 2 oz) butter
300 ml (10½ fl oz) olive oil	salt, pepper
2 onions	16 small boiled potatoes
4 carrots	
2 leeks (white parts only)	For the stock
bulb of fennel	2 carrots
6 peeled and seeded tomatoes	1 leek
bulb of garlic	2 onions
2 sticks of celery	bouquet garni
saffron	salt, pepper
thyme, basil, a bay leaf	

Cut off the wings, legs, thighs and breasts from the chickens. Cook the carcasses and the peeled and halved stock vegetables in 2 litres (3½ pints) of water for an hour with the bouquet garni and seasoning. Strain and put to one side.

Heat the olive oil in a heavy saucepan and seal the chicken pieces to a golden-brown colour. Add the stock and cook for 30 minutes. Remove and skin the chickens; take the meat from the bones and cut into large pieces. Reduce the stock to half its volume, skim the fat and strain it once more

Slice the onions, carrots, leeks and fennel into strips and cook gently for a few minutes in a little oil, then add the stock, the tomatoes, peeled garlic and a pinch of saffron. Cover the pan and cook slowly for 20 minutes. At this point, add the pieces of chicken, chopped herbs, bay leaf, boiled potatoes and the Pernod and bring back to the boil. Remove the pan immediately from the heat, and using a perforated spoon, transfer the chicken meat and the vegetables to a warmed soup tureen.

Whisk the butter into the stock knob by knob and pour into the tureen. Serve a small dish of rouille separately (see page 147).

MAGRETS AU BEURRE ROUGE
Breast of duck in butter and wine sauce

PREPARATION TIME: 15 minutes
COOKING TIME: 20 minutes
FOR SIX

6 boned breasts of duck
6 shallots
400 ml (14 fl oz) strong red wine
  (preferably Madiran)

125 ml (4½ fl oz) crème fraîche
350 g (12½ oz) slightly-salted
  butter
salt, freshly-ground pepper

The skin and the layer of fat beneath it should not be removed from the breasts of duck.

Begin by making the sauce. Finely chop the shallots and put them with 300 ml (10½ fl oz) of red wine (Rioja can be substituted if Madiran is unobtainable) into a small saucepan. Cook until all the wine has been evaporated. Add the cream, stir and continue to reduce until the sauce obtains the consistency of syrup.

Reduce the heat, take the pan off the stove and whip the butter into the sauce knob by knob. Put the pan back on the heat from time to time, just for a few moments. When all the butter is absorbed, and a smooth creamy sauce results, keep it warm in a double-boiler.

Put the breasts of duck skinside downwards into a dry pan and seal them over a brisk heat, turning the breasts occasionally. Reduce the heat, season and cook the duck through for about another 15 minutes. Remove and arrange on a warmed serving dish.

Pour off the cooking fats and deglaze the pan with the rest of the red wine, scraping the pan vigorously with the back of a fork. Remove from the heat and stir in, little by little, a tablespoon of the creamy sauce. Pour the contents of the pan over the duck and serve the rest of the sauce separately.

The chef of the Hotel de France in Auch, from where this recipe comes, recommends that the wine drunk with this dish should be similar to the one used in the sauce.

CANARD AUX OIGNONS
Duck with onions

PREPARATION TIME: 30 minutes
COOKING TIME: 1½–1¾ hours
FOR SIX

1 plump duck of about 2 kg
  (4–4½ lb)
salt, pepper
5 tablespoons of armagnac or
  brandy
500 g (generous 1 lb) small
  onions

6 tinned artichoke bottoms
1 lemon
300 g (10½ oz) shelled peas
60 g (2 oz) butter
200 g (7 oz) ham

If dressing your own duck, be sure to remove the fat glands from the back of the tail, or the bird will have a strong flavour.

Season the cavity, put the duck's liver and gizzard inside and sew it up; then truss the bird. Put it on a grid in an oven pan and cook in an oven pre-heated to its maximum, for a time sufficient to brown the bird all over and for its fat to begin to exude.

Remove the duck to a casserole, together with a tablespoon of its own fat, the armagnac and the onions. Season, cover the dish and simmer for 50 minutes to an hour.

During this time, heat through the artichoke bottoms in a solution of salted water and lemon juice and cook the peas in butter. Cut the ham into strips and fry gently. Fill the artichoke bottoms with a mixture of ham and peas. Keep them warm in a greased covered pan, over a very low heat, so that the bases are lightly browned.

Serve the duck whole, surrounded by the onions and artichoke bottoms.

CANARD AU POIVRE VERT
Duck with green peppercorns

PREPARATION TIME: 1 hour
COOKING TIME: 1 hour
FOR SIX

2 ducks each of 1 kg (2¼ lb)
60 g (2 oz) butter
2 shallots
150 ml (5 fl oz) dry white wine
4 tablespoons of brandy

1 small tin of green peppercorns
100 ml (3½ fl oz) single cream
level tablespoon cornflour
salt

Roast the birds in a hot oven (220°C/425°F/Gas Mark 7) for 30 minutes. Do not add any other cooking fats and turn the birds 2 or 3 times so that they brown all over.

As soon as they are cooked, carve them in a dish which will retain their juices. First remove the legs, then the wings. Remove the remaining skin and carve the breasts in slices parallel to the backbone. The meat should be pink with traces of blood: put aside in a warm place but one not so hot as will allow cooking to continue.

Strip the carcasses of any remaining pieces of lean meat and chop them up. Heat a tablespoon of butter and cook the chopped shallots until soft. Add the chopped duck, let it sizzle and then add the white wine and the brandy. Cover the pan and let it bubble for 20–25 minutes. Then pass the contents of the pan through a sieve into a small saucepan. Press the pieces of meat to extract as much juice as possible. Deglaze the pan by vigorously scraping the bottom with the back of a fork, add a tablespoon of boiling water and then add the contents to the rest of the sauce.

Leave the sauce for a few minutes so that the fat rises to the surface, then skim it off. Crush the green peppercorns roughly and put them into the sauce together with 4 or 5 tablespoons of cream and the cornflour, made into a paste with a little cold water. Stir, simmer for 10–15 minutes and again skim the fat should it be necessary. Season.

Arrange the slices of breast and their juices on a warmed serving dish. Bring the sauce to the boil and pour it over the meat. Complete the dish by crisping the skin of the legs and wings under a grill. Serve all together.

[112]

CANARD AU BOURGOGNE
Duck in burgundy

PREPARATION TIME: 20 minutes
COOKING TIME: 2 hours
FOR SIX TO EIGHT

1 duck of about 3 kg (6¾ lb)
250 g (9 oz) pork belly
bottle of red Burgundy
salt, pepper, nutmeg
bouquet garni
2 shallots
clove of garlic
12 small onions

125 g (4½ oz) butter
sugar
vinegar
150 g (5 oz) button mushrooms
lemon
60 g (2 oz) flour
small glass of brandy
3–4 slices of white bread

Divide up the duck into pieces. Cut the pork belly into oblong strips and blanch them for 5 minutes in boiling water. Drain and dry them and put them into a casserole where they should be sweated over a low heat so that their fat is given off. Remove and put to one side.

Seal the pieces of duck in the hot pork fat. Pour in the wine and if the meat is not completely covered, add sufficient water. Season with salt, pepper and grated nutmeg, add the bouquet garni and the chopped shallots and garlic. Cover the casserole and cook slowly over a very low heat for 1¼ hours. Add the pork belly strips and cook for a further 30 minutes, when the duck should be cooked.

In the meantime, blanch the onions in a little boiling water, dry them and continue the cooking in 15 g (½ oz) butter in an open pan, over a very low heat. Sprinkle on a level tablespoon of sugar, add a few drops of vinegar and this should glaze the onions while they finish cooking.

Slice the mushrooms and blanch them in a boiling solution of water and lemon juice.

Put the juices from the casserole into a saucepan. Work the flour into 60 g (2 oz) butter, bring the sauce to the boil, remove from the heat and whisk in the butter and flour knob by knob. Mince the duck's liver, bring the sauce back to the boil, stir in the minced liver and the brandy but do not let the sauce boil again.

Pour the sauce over the duck and serve with triangles of bread crisply fried in the rest of the butter.

PINTADE AU CHOU
Guinea-fowl with cabbage

PREPARATION TIME: 30 minutes
COOKING TIME: 1½–2 hours
FOR SIX

2 young guinea-fowl	300 g (10½ oz) streaky bacon
1 firm cabbage	salt, pepper

If not already so prepared, wrap and tie barding fat around the birds and season the cavities.

Cut the cabbage into quarters and blanch in salted boiling water for 5 minutes. Drain, remove stalk and coarse outer leaves.

Buy the bacon in thick slices. Remove the rind and cut into strips of equal thickness across the slice. Put them into a dry casserole and cook gently so that they give off their fat without becoming crisp and brown. Remove the bacon with a perforated spoon and replace with the well-drained cabbage. Soften gently in the bacon fat and then put back the bacon, season, cover the pan and let its contents simmer.

In the meantime, put the guinea-fowl into a very hot oven (230°C/450°F/Gas Mark 8). As soon as the birds become a light golden colour, transfer them into the casserole with the cabbage and complete cooking slowly. The cabbage will be soft and melting.

Remove the birds, carve into portions and arrange on a warmed serving dish on a bed of cabbage and bacon. If necessary, reduce the cooking juices rapidly over a brisk heat and then pour over the dish.

Serve with a dish of boiled potatoes.

PINTADES FARCIES
Stuffed guinea-fowl

PREPARATION TIME: 30 minutes
COOKING TIME: 20 minutes per lb of stuffed weight
FOR SIX

2 young guinea-fowl	1 small tin (100 g), 3½ oz)
150 g (5 oz) of trimmings of fat	mousse de foie gras
ham or unsmoked bacon	sprig of thyme
250 g (9 oz) chicken livers	salt, pepper, nutmeg
1 shallot	oil
1 cup of fresh white breadcrumbs	50 g (scant 2 oz) butter
1 egg	

Ask your poultry dealer to dress, but not to truss, the 2 birds. Retain their livers.

Chop up the ham or bacon and slice the shallot and put them into a pan over a medium heat. When the ham-fat becomes transparent, add the livers and stiffen them without letting them cook through.

Soak the breadcrumbs in milk, squeeze them well out and put into a bowl with the beaten egg, the mousse de foie gras, the liver and all the rest of the contents of the pan and a stalk of thyme. Mix together with a fork, mashing the livers at the same time. Season with salt, pepper and grated nutmeg. This stuffing should be light, not compounded too densely together. Divide in half, stuff both fowl, sew up their openings, and truss them. Wipe them over with a little oil; finally, weigh the birds and calculate the cooking time.

Pre-heat the oven for 20 minutes to 200°–220°C/400°–425°F/Gas Mark 6–7. Arrange the fowl on a grid of an oven-pan and put them into the oven, turning them from time to time so that they brown evenly.

Halfway through the cooking time, add half a glass of water to the pan. When the birds are cooked, turn off the oven and leave them to prove for 10 minutes.

Joint and carve the birds and arrange on a serving dish with their stuffing. Add the juice given off during carving to the oven-pan and deglaze it with a little boiling water. Stir in the butter, check the seasoning and serve separately in a sauceboat.

[113]

OIE EN CIVET
Civet of goose

PREPARATION TIME: 30 minutes
COOKING TIME: 1½–2 hours
FOR EIGHT TO TEN

1 young goose weighing about
   3 kg (6½ lb)
3 level tablespoons of flour
1 bottle of red Burgundy
3 onions
4 shallots

1 clove of garlic
bouquet garni
salt, pepper
100 ml (3½ fl oz) goose or pig's
   blood, if available.

Ask your poultry dealer to divide the bird into pieces and to give you the gizzard, the liver and the bird's fat.

Gently cook the pieces of goose in a dry pan, beginning with the ones with most fat. As they are sealed, remove to a casserole. Strain the goose fat given off into the rest of the bird's fat which should have been melted down; retain it for other cooking purposes.

When all the goose is in the casserole, heat it through, powder it with flour and brown each piece. Add the wine and enough water to cover the meat; add the peeled and halved onions and shallots, the gizzard, the garlic and bouquet garni. Season and cover the dish. Let it simmer for 1½ hours, checking its progress occasionally.

Ten minutes before serving, remove the bouquet garni and add the liver. Skim off any excess fat there might be on the surface of the cooking liquid. Check the seasoning and bring to the boil for 5 minutes.

Mix a few tablespoons of the cooking liquid with the blood. Remove the casserole from the heat and slowly add the blood, stirring well. Reduce to a very low heat and cook for 5 minutes more, without allowing the sauce to boil.

This dish can be served with pasta, with boiled potatoes or with potatoes sautéed in goose fat and sprinkled with chopped parsley.

OIE RÔTIE AUX POMMES
Roast goose with apples

PREPARATION TIME: 25 minutes
COOKING TIME: 15 minutes per lb of stuffed weight
FOR SIX TO EIGHT

1 young goose of about 3 kg
   (6½ lb)
2 chicken livers
60 g (2 oz) ham fat
1 onion
2 shallots
small sprig of parsley

3 sage leaves
2 cooking apples
60 g (2 oz) butter
cup of fresh white breadcrumbs
1 egg
salt, pepper

Mince well together the livers, ham fat, onion, shallots and the herbs. Peel core and chop the apples separately and soften in a pan with a knobs of butter. Remove and put to one side.

Put the minced stuffing into the same pan with a knob of butter and cook gently until the pieces of liver are undistinguishable from the rest of the mixture (about 10 minutes).

Soak the breadcrumbs in milk and squeeze them out well. Put into a bowl and mix in apples, stuffing and beaten egg. Mix so a light stuffing results.

Cut off the parson's-nose and the wing tips from the bird, stuff it, sew up the openings and truss it. Then weigh it and calculate the cooking time. Beat salt and pepper into the rest of the butter and smear it over the bird; then arrange it on the grid of an oven-pan and put into a cold oven.

Cook at a fairly hot temperature (190°–200°C/375°–400°F/Gas Mark 5–6), turning the bird occasionally to brown it all over. Halfway through the cooking, add a glass of water to the pan. When the cooking time is up, remove the bird, wrap it in aluminium foil and leave to prove in a warm place for at least 15 minutes.

Joint and carve the bird, adding the juices which escape to those in the oven-pan. Deglaze and serve this sauce separately.

Serve with peeled and cored whole baked apples, which can have been cooked in the oven at the same time as the goose. Top the apples with redcurrant preserve. For wine, a claret is recommended.

FONDUE DE DINDE
Turkey with prunes

PREPARATION TIME: 30 minutes
COOKING TIME: 40–45 minutes
FOR SIX

50 g (1¾ lb) breasts or
  escalopes of turkey
tea-bag
00 g (3½ oz) stoned dried
  prunes
medium-sized aubergines

salt, pepper
75 g (good 2½ oz) butter
large pack of dried cèpes, or
  tinned cèpes
several leaves of tarragon
100 ml (3½ fl oz) chicken stock

Pour boiling water over the tea-bag and, when it has steeped, remove and put the prunes in to soak for about 15 minutes.

Trim the aubergines, cut them into large cubes, sprinkle with salt and leave to sweat for 10 minutes. Then rinse, drain and dry the cubes; soften them in a pan with ⅔ of the butter. Rinse and drain the reconstituted (or tinned) cèpes, cut them into quarters and add them to the aubergines in the pan. Cook for a few minutes, then sprinkle on the chopped tarragon, cover the pan and cook for 15–20 minutes.

Cut the turkey into cubes. Melt a little butter in a pan, add the turkey and stir so that it seals on all sides. Season and add to the vegetables in the first pan. Moisten with 3 tablespoons of chicken stock and continue to cook, taking care not to overcook the meat.

Drain the prunes and cook them gently in the rest of the butter.

Arrange turkey and vegetables in the middle of a warmed serving dish and surround them with the prunes.

The chef of the restaurant 'Le Parc' in Villemomble on the outskirts of Paris, from where this recipe comes, suggests a claret to go with this dish.

ESCALOPES DE DINDE NORMANDE
Turkey escalopes with
tarragon mustard

PREPARATION TIME: 15 minutes
COOKING TIME: 30 minutes
FOR SIX

6 turkey escalopes
70 g (2½ oz) butter
150 ml (5 fl oz) dry white wine
2 teaspoons of tarragon mustard
salt, pepper

150 g (5 oz) button mushrooms
1 lemon
125 ml (4½ fl oz) single cream
2 egg yolks

Melt 40 g (1½ oz) butter in a sauté pan and when it begins to foam, put in the escalopes and seal them on both sides. Remove and keep warm.

Pour in the white wine, bring it to the boil and stir in the mustard. When it is thoroughly mixed, reduce the heat and put in the escalopes. Season.

Trim off the mushroom stalks and wipe them in a solution of lemon juice and water. Slice the mushrooms and add them, with the cream, to the pan. Cook all together for 10–15 minutes. Remove the escalopes and arrange them on a warmed serving dish.

Beat the egg yolks and slowly mix in 2 or 3 tablespoons of sauce from the pan. Remove the pan from the heat and stir in the extended beaten eggs. If the sauce is not hot enough, gently re-warm it but do not let it boil. Pour over the escalopes.

Any green vegetables and sauté potatoes go well with this delicious dish.

FILETS DE DINDE AU CERVEUIL
Turkey breasts with chervil

PREPARATION TIME: 15 minutes
COOKING TIME: 10 minutes
FOR SIX

6 turkey breasts
1 tablespoon of flour
125 g (4½ oz) butter

100 ml (3½ fl oz) crème fraîche
2 good sprigs of chervil

Work the flour into half the butter. Melt the rest of the butter in a pan and, over a moderate heat, seal the turkey breasts on both sides. They should be light-golden in colour. Remove to an ovenproof serving-dish.

Deglaze the pan by adding, little by little, the flour and butter mixture, the cream and the chopped chervil, scraping the bottom of the pan vigorously with the back of a fork.

Pour this sauce over the turkey breasts and put the dish into a pre-heated fairly hot oven (190°C/375°F/Gas Mark 5) for 10 minutes to complete the cooking of the meat.

Elle advises that this dish may, if necessary, be kept in the oven, which should be turned off, for a few minutes before serving.

CHOUCROUTE
Sauerkraut

PREPARATION TIME: 20 minutes, plus overnight soaking
COOKING TIME: 4–5 hours
FOR EIGHT TO TEN

2 kg (4½ lb) uncooked
    sauerkraut
piece of bacon (collar)
700 g (1½ lb) smoked pork belly
2 onions
3 tablespoons of goose fat (or
    lard)

15 juniper berries
1 bottle of Riesling
1 ham sausage
12 frankfurter sausages
12 boiled potatoes
pepper

Soak the collar and pork belly overnight in plenty of cold water.

Wash the sauerkraut (probably bought tinned) in cold water and then plunge it into a very large pan of boiling water. Remove immediately, drain, and separate it.

Coarsely chop the onions and put them in a very large casserole. Gently cook in the lard until transparent, then add the sauerkraut and the juniper berries. Slowly warm through, lifting and separating the sauerkraut, then add ¾ of the bottle of wine. Season with pepper.

Drain the piece of bacon and the pork belly and put them into the middle of the sauerkraut, cover the dish and simmer over a very low flame. Check from time to time that the cabbage is not sticking to the bottom of the pan; add more wine if necessary.

After about 3 hours of slow cooking, add the ham sausage. Twenty minutes before the end of cooking, put the frankfurters on top.

Carve the bacon and the pork belly into thick slices, and slice the ham sausage. To serve, heap up the sauerkraut, pile the sliced meat around it, surmount with frankfurters and surround by boiled potatoes.

This is a substantial dish.

RÂBLE DE LIÈVRE À LA PIRON
Saddle of hare with grapes

PREPARATION TIME: 10 minutes, plus 12 hours of marinating
COOKING TIME: 30 minutes
FOR SIX

the saddle of a good-sized hare
50 ml (1¾ fl oz) dry white wine
3 tablespoons olive oil
tablespoon wine vinegar
salt, pepper
a bunch of grapes (washed and deseeded)

100 ml (3½ fl oz) grape juice
dessertspoon of Marc de Bourgogne (or brandy)
4 tablespoons crème fraîche
25 g (scant 1 oz) flour
25 g (scant 1 oz) butter

Make a marinade in a dish by mixing together the white wine, a tablespoon of oil and the vinegar. Rub the saddle of hare with salt and pepper and leave it for 12 hours in the marinade, turning as frequently as possible.

When ready to begin cooking, remove and drain the saddle and dry it on kitchen paper. Put it into an ovenproof dish with the rest of the oil and cook for 20 minutes in a very hot oven (230°C/450°F/Gas Mark 8): baste regularly.

Remove the saddle from the dish and keep it warm on its serving dish in the oven, which should have been turned off, while the sauce is being prepared.

Pour off the cooking fat and deglaze the pan with the grape juice, the Marc de Bourgogne and the marinade, scraping and stirring vigorously with the back of a fork. Bring to the boil and reduce to half its volume; remove from the heat and stir in the crème fraîche. Return to the heat and once more reduce to half-volume.

Meanwhile, work flour and butter together into a paste and, away from the heat, whip it little by little into the sauce until a creamy mixture results. Add the seeded grapes, heat up for a few minutes, season, and pour the sauce over the saddle before serving.

CIVET DE LIÈVRE
Civet of hare

PREPARATION TIME: 30 minutes, plus 2–3 hours marinating time
COOKING TIME: 2½–3 hours
FOR SIX

1 hare of 2 kg (4½ lb) when skinned and dressed
tablespoon of vinegar
70 ml (2½ fl oz) brandy
2 tablespoons olive oil
2 onions
salt, pepper
125 g (4½ oz) butter
2 heaped tablespoons of flour

1 bottle of red wine
bouquet garni (with thyme)
clove of garlic
200 g (7 oz) thick unsmoked streaky bacon
20 small onions
teaspoon of sugar
200 g (7 oz) button mushrooms

Remember to ask your butcher or game dealer to let you have the blood and liver of the hare. Mix the blood with a tablespoon of vinegar.

Joint the hare. Make the marinade with the brandy, the olive oil, an onion finely sliced and seasoning. Steep the pieces of hare in it for several hours.

Make a white roux in a casserole using 2 tablespoons of butter and the flour. Put in the pieces of hare, turning them so that they seal on all sides, then pour in the wine and the marinade. Add the bouquet garni, the second onion and the garlic, cover the casserole and simmer over a very low heat for at least 2½ hours.

Cut the bacon into thick strips across the grain and blanch them for 3 minutes in boiling water. Drain and dry them and then cook gently in a dry pan until the fat is just transparent. Remove and put to one side.

Add a tablespoon of butter to the bacon fat in the pan. Blanch the small onions and then put them in the pan, sprinkle with sugar and lightly brown them. Trim and slice the mushrooms and cook them in the rest of the butter.

Remove the pieces of hare from the casserole and put them on a warmed serving dish. Mince the hare's liver into its blood. Add the onions, bacon and mushrooms to the sauce in the casserole, bring it to the boil, then remove from the heat and stir the blood and liver mixture well in. Pour over the hare.

LAPIN À LA CAUCHOISE
Rabbit in mustard sauce

PREPARATION TIME: 10 minutes
COOKING TIME: 45–50 minutes
FOR SIX

a plump rabbit
50 g (scant 2 oz) butter
5 tablespoons single cream
salt, pepper

2 shallots
3 tablespoons strong Dijon
  mustard
200 ml (7 fl oz) dry white wine

Cut up the rabbit, taking care to separate rather than chop the joints so that little splinters of bone are avoided.

Melt the butter in a deep casserole and when it begins to foam, put in the rabbit pieces, turning them so that they seal on all sides. As soon as they are a light golden colour, remove and pour off the cooking fat, replacing it with 2 tablespoons of cream. Put back the rabbit and stir well so that each piece becomes coated with cream. Season, cover the casserole and cook gently. Add a tablespoon of cream each 10 minutes.

Chop the shallots finely. Mix mustard and wine together well in a bowl, add the shallots. Pour the mixture over the rabbit, together with the last tablespoon of cream. Allow to simmer for a further 15–20 minutes. Serve this Normandy dish very hot, with chipped or sauté potatoes.

LAPIN AUX POIVRONS
Rabbit with green peppers

PREPARATION TIME: 15 minutes
COOKING TIME: 1 hour
FOR SIX

2 young rabbits
flour
olive oil
750 g (good 1½ lb) green
  peppers
2 onions

small tin of peeled tomatoes
  (225 g, 8 oz size)
150 g (5 oz) stoned green olives
2 cloves of garlic
basil
150 ml (5 fl oz) dry white wine
salt, pepper

Joint the rabbits, roll them in flour and lightly brown them in a pan with 3 tablespoons of olive oil. Remove the rabbit when each piece is sealed on each side; put to one side.

Halve the peppers, remove the seeds and inner membranes and cut the pods into slices. Soften them in 3 tablespoons of oil in a deep casserole, together with the peeled and sliced onions. Cook slowly: it should take 30 minutes to soften the peppers and make the onion transparent.

Add the pieces of rabbit, the tomatoes (passed through a sieve to remove the seeds), the stoned olives, the whole garlic, the basil and the white wine. Season, using very little salt, cover and cook for a further 30 minutes.

Elle says that this Italian rabbit dish is excellent served with boiled rice which has been coloured with saffron and sprinkled with grated Parmesan cheese.

PERDREAUX À L'ARMAGNAC
Partridge in armagnac

PREPARATION TIME: 30 minutes
COOKING TIME: 40 minutes
FOR SIX

3 partridge
100 g (3½ oz) butter
salt, pepper
4 tablespoons of armagnac (or
  brandy)

small tin of black truffles
  (optional)
125 ml (4½ fl oz) single cream
6 slices of white bread

Truss the partridge as for roasting, but do not tie on any barding fat or bacon. Save the birds' livers or, if not available, use a small chicken liver.

Melt 2 tablespoons of butter in a large sauté pan and seal the birds to a light golden-brown, turning frequently. Cook slowly, being sure not to let the butter burn. Season and pour the brandy over them; cover the pan, remove from the heat and leave the birds to rest for 5 minutes.

Pass the livers through a fine sieve so a smooth pulp results. Remove the birds from the pan and stir the liver pulp into the cooking juices. Add the truffles, cut into thin slices, and the cream. Stir together.

Divide the partridge in half lengthways and return them to the sauce in the pan. Keep warm over a low heat, not letting the sauce boil, for 15 minutes.

Cut the crusts from the bread and fry the slices in butter until lightly crisp. Arrange a half-bird on each croûton, decorate with pieces of truffle and a little sauce, and serve the rest of the sauce in a warmed sauceboat.

FAISAN EN COCOTTE
Casseroled pheasant

PREPARATION TIME: 25 minutes
COOKING TIME: 30–35 minutes
FOR SIX

2 young pheasants (or one large
  but tender bird)
2 chicken livers
60 g (2 oz) fat ham
salt, pepper

sprig of thyme
2 or 3 sage leaves
125 g (4½ oz) butter
5 tablespoons of brandy
6 slices of white bread

Mince the livers of the pheasants together with the chicken livers and the fat ham. Season and mix in the leaves of thyme and the crushed sage. Stuff the birds with the mixture and truss them as if for roasting.

Melt a tablespoon of butter in a casserole and when it foams, put in the birds, turning them so that they lightly brown on all sides. Take care not to let the butter burn. Pour over the brandy (but do not flame it), cover the dish, remove from the heat and let the birds rest for a few minutes. Then return the casserole to a low heat and cook for 30–35 minutes, turning the pheasants from time to time.

Cut the crusts from the bread and lightly fry them in butter. Keep in a warm place.

Joint and carve the pheasants, pouring any juice that comes from the birds into the sauce in the casserole. Spread the croûtons with the stuffing and arrange the pieces of bird on them before serving.

If too thin, the sauce may be quickly reduced over a brisk heat. Serve separately, together with a purée of green peas.

Elle advises that if you prefer to cook your pheasants in the oven, prepare in the same way except that all the openings should be sewn up and barding fat and bacon tied to the breasts to prevent the birds drying out. Cook for the same length of time.

PIGEONS À LA SARRIETTE
Pigeons in a herb sauce

PREPARATION TIME: 20 minutes
COOKING TIME: 45 minutes–1 hour
FOR SIX

6 young pigeons
125 g (4½ oz) butter
tablespoon of dried savory or of
    chopped fresh savory
6 sage leaves
500 ml (18 fl oz) dry white wine
4 tablespoons single cream
2 egg yolks (or 2 level teaspoons
    of cornflour)
salt, pepper
1 lemon

Work half the butter and the crushed herbs together and put a good knob of the mixture into the cavity of each pigeon.

Melt the rest of the butter in a casserole and gently seal the pigeons on each side. Do not let the butter burn. When a light golden colour, pour in the wine, cover the dish and allow to simmer.

When the pigeons are cooked, arrange them on a serving dish and put aside in a warm place. Bring the cooking juices to the boil and reduce their volume to about 250 ml (9 fl oz). Beat the eggs and stir into the cream; remove the casserole from the heat and stir in the mixture. Return the dish to a low heat but do not let it boil. Check the seasoning, and add a few drops of lemon juice to taste. Pour a little sauce over each pigeon and serve the rest separately.

Elle advises that if you prefer to thicken your sauces with cornflour rather than egg yolk, mix the cornflour with a little cream and bring the sauce to the boil after the paste has been stirred in.

SALMIS DE PIGEONS
Salmis of pigeon

PREPARATION TIME: 20 minutes
COOKING TIME: 2 hours 10 minutes
FOR SIX

3 plump pigeons
150 g (5 oz) butter
50 ml (1¾ fl oz) armagnac or
    brandy
2 shallots
30 g (1 oz) flour
1 bottle of red wine
salt, pepper
slice of smoked ham
200 g (7 oz) button mushrooms
20 small onions

Cut the pigeons in half lengthways. Melt 50 g (scant 2 oz) butter in a sauté pan and seal the birds. When they have taken colour, pour off the cooking fat, sprinkle on the brandy and flame it. Cover the pan and leave on one side.

Chop the shallots finely and cook gently in 30 g (1 oz) butter in a casserole until soft and transparent. Sprinkle in the flour, stir and cook for a few seconds, then pour in the wine. Put in the halved pigeons and the juice from the sauté pan, season, cover and cook slowly for 2 hours.

During this time, cut the ham into dice and lightly brown the pieces in 30 g (1 oz) butter. Trim the stalks of the mushrooms, wipe and slice them and put them in a saucepan, just covered in water. Add 20 g (¾ oz) of butter, cover the pan and cook for about 5–8 minutes. Cook the onions (whole) in the same way.

After the birds have been cooking for 2 hours, remove them to a warmed serving dish and keep warm. Put the edge of the casserole back on the heat, remove any scum or surplus grease from the surface of the sauce and then pass through a fine sieve.

Pour the sauce over the pigeons and serve surrounded by the onions, the diced ham and the mushrooms.

The chef of the Relais de la Poste in Magesq in the Landes, from where this recipe comes, recommends that a claret should be drunk with this dish.

PIGEONS AU BOUZY ROUGE
Pigeons in red wine

PREPARATION TIME: 20 minutes
COOKING TIME: 35 minutes
FOR SIX

6 young pigeons
150 g (5 oz) butter
600 g (1¼ lb) chicken livers
1 tin (400 g, 14 oz size) pâté de
 foie gras or mousse of foie gras
1 small tin of truffles (optional)
20 ml (¾ fl oz) Marc de
 Champagne (or brandy if
 unavailable)
barding fat

1 carrot
1 onion
several parsley stalks
1 bay leaf,
salt, pepper
1 chicken stock cube
1 bottle red wine (preferably
 Bouzy Rouge)
6 slices of white bread
tablespoon of oil

Bouzy Rouge is the still red wine of Champagne. While its use is preferable, it is by no means essential.

Melt a little butter in a pan and cook the chicken livers until grey all over the outside. Mince very finely together the livers, half the foie gras, the truffles; add the Marc. Stuff the cavity of each bird with the mixture, tie barding fat or bacon on to the breasts and truss them. Melt a third of the butter in a large pan, and over a low heat, seal the birds, turning them so they colour all over. Add the carrot cut into round slices, the sliced onion, the chopped parsley stalks and the bay leaf. Season, cover the pan and cook for about 20 minutes.

Remove the birds, take off the barding fat and keep them in a warm place.

While the pigeons are cooking, make a stock with the chicken cube and 250 ml (9 fl oz) of water. Reduce it over a brisk heat to 100 ml (3½ fl oz). Pour the cooking fats from the sauté pan when the pigeons have finished cooking, deglaze the pan with the red wine and the chicken stock stirring vigorously. Reduce by ⅔ over a brisk heat.

Cut the crusts from the bread and fry each slice lightly in the rest of the butter and the oil. Spread the rest of the foie gras on to the croûtons and arrange a pigeon on each slice.

Strain the sauce from the pan through a sieve and serve separately.

CAILLES AU THYM
Quails with thyme

PREPARATION TIME: 15 minutes
COOKING TIME: 20 minutes
FOR SIX

6 quail
salt, pepper
chopped thyme
100 g (3½ oz) butter
6 thin slices of fat smoked bacon

olive oil
12 small chipolata sausages
100 ml (3½ fl oz) dry vermouth
6 slices of white bread

Buy the quail prepared for cooking, but not barded. Work a teaspoon each of salt and freshly-milled pepper, and a tablespoon of chopped thyme into the butter, divide the mixture into 6 knobs and put 1 into the cavity of each bird. Wrap and tie them in the fat bacon and put them in an oven pan with 2 tablespoons of oil. Sprinkle lavishly with chopped thyme, and cook in a hot oven (220°C/425°F/Gas Mark 7) for 20 minutes.

Cook the chipolatas in a pan in olive oil, remembering to prick them all over to prevent them bursting. Remove and keep in a warm place.

When the quail are cooked, remove and pour off the cooking fat from their pan. Scrape the pan with the back of a fork, add the cooking juices from the sausages and deglaze the pan, over a brisk heat, with the vermouth. Check the seasoning, bring the sauce to the boil for 1 minute, skimming off any grease that comes to the surface.

Cut the crusts from the bread and fry them lightly in more butter. Arrange them on a warmed serving dish, place a quail on each and surround with chipolatas. Pour the sauce (reduced to a reasonably thick consistency) over the birds before serving.

NOISETTES DE CHEVREUIL
Venison steaks

PREPARATION TIME: 30 minutes
COOKING TIME (THE SAUCE): 2½ hours
         (THE VENISON): 10–12 minutes

FOR SIX

6 or 8 prepared venison steaks
50 g (scant 2 oz) butter
2 or 3 tablespoons of brandy
60 g (2 oz) dried seedless raisins
2 level tablespoons green
  peppercorns
2 tablespoons pine kernels
butter

For the sauce
500 g (generous 1 lb) venison
  bones and trimmings

1 level tablespoon of lard
4 onions
1 large carrot
bouquet garni
2 tablespoons wine vinegar
1 heaped tablespoon flour
3 medium-sized tomatoes
500 ml (18 fl oz) robust red wine
  (Cahors, for example)
500 ml (18 fl oz) beef stock
salt, pepper

To make the sauce, put the bones and trimmings into the hot melted lard in a saucepan with the sliced onions, the grated carrot and the bouquet garni. When the vegetables are soft, add the vinegar, evaporate it, sprinkle on the flour, stir and cook until browned. Add the skinned and seeded tomatoes, the wine and the beef stock; season and cook for at least 2½ hours over a low heat.

Then strain the contents, return the liquid to the pan and scrape the bottom with the back of a fork. Return to the heat, and reduce the liquid to a syrupy consistency over a brisk heat.

Melt the butter in a pan and cook the venison steaks. Put to one side on a warmed serving dish but make sure the steaks do not continue to cook. Deglaze the pan with the brandy, add the currants (previously swollen by soaking in warm water), the green peppercorns, the pine kernels and the syrupy sauce. Bring to the boil, check the seasoning, remove from the flame and whip in 4 knobs of butter.

Pour the sauce over the venison and serve.

GIGUE DE CHEVREUIL
Haunch of venison with game sauce

PREPARATION TIME: 10 minutes (2 hours in advance)
COOKING TIME: 15–18 minutes per lb
FOR EIGHT TO TEN

a haunch of venison about 2½ kg
  (5½ lb)
1 bay leaf
2 tablespoons olive oil
teaspoon of chopped thyme
salt, pepper, nutmeg

For the game sauce
60 g (2 oz) butter

3 shallots
3 sticks of celery
bouquet garni
200 g (7 oz) venison trimmings
1 bottle of claret
salt, pepper, nutmeg
1 level tablespoon of cornflour
1 liqueur glass of brandy
redcurrant jelly

Crush the bay leaf and mix it into the oil with the thyme, seasoning and grated nutmeg. Coat the haunch of venison with the mixture and leave for 2 hours.

After marinating, put the meat on the grid of a roasting-pan and cook in a hot oven (220°C/425°F/Gas Mark 7). Turn the haunch from time to time, but do not baste it: add 70 ml (2½ fl oz) of water to the pan halfway through the cooking time.

While the haunch is cooking, start to prepare the game sauce. Melt 2 knobs of butter in a saucepan and gently cook the chopped shallots and celery, the bouquet garni and the roughly minced trimmings until the shallots are transparent. Pour in the wine and simmer, with the pan uncovered, until the contents have reduced in volume by half. Squeeze through a fine sieve and put the liquid to one side. Season with salt, pepper and grated nutmeg.

When the haunch has cooked, remove to a serving dish and keep warm. Return the sauce liquid in its pan to the heat and stir in a paste made from the cornflour and a little water. Let the sauce thicken and then add the brandy and 2 level tablespoons of redcurrant jelly. Stir well, remove from the heat and beat in the rest of the butter, knob by knob.

Carve the venison at table and serve with the game sauce and more redcurrant jelly.

SALADE DE POIS CHICHES
Chick-pea salad

PREPARATION TIME: 40 minutes
COOKING TIME: 2–3 hours if using dried chick-peas
FOR SIX TO EIGHT

250 g (about 8 oz) dried
  chick-peas (or large tin
  prepared chick-peas)
onions
head of celery
tablespoons chopped mixed
  herbs (dried herbs will do if
  fresh are not available)
tin of tuna
2 anchovy fillets in oil
clove garlic

1 bunch radishes
150 g (5 oz) black olives
1 small lettuce
4 hard-boiled eggs
4 small tomatoes
Bowl of prepared mayonnaise

For the vinaigrette dressing
5 tablespoons olive oil
1 tablespoon wine vinegar
salt, pepper

If using uncooked chick-peas, soak them overnight in a bowl of water to which a teaspoon of bicarbonate of soda has been added. Drain and put into a saucepan of fresh, unsalted water and cook slowly until they are tender: this will take about 2 or more hours. Rinse in cold water and drain thoroughly. If you are using tinned chick-peas, put them into a sieve and rinse thoroughly under a running cold tap.

Finely chop the onions, the celery and the mixed herbs. Put them all into a dish with the vinaigrette dressing, add the chick-peas, the tuna fish, the anchovy fillets sliced into small pieces, the crushed garlic, the radishes (sliced crossways into rounds) and the black olives. Mix all the ingredients together and leave in the dish for 30 minutes, stirring occasionally.

Take a salad bowl and cover the bottom with the lettuce which has been cut into strips. Add the chick-pea mixture and decorate the salad with the eggs which have been hard-boiled for 10 minutes, and the tomatoes, cut into quarters. Serve with the mayonnaise in a separate bowl. In general, the mayonnaise should not be mixed in with the salad as not everyone will appreciate it. Those who like it can add it to the plate on which their salad is served.

Chick-pea salad will, by itself, make a light and nourishing meal.

COURGETTES EN SALADE
Courgette salad

PREPARATION TIME: 20 minutes
COOKING TIME: 25–30 minutes
FOR SIX

1 kg (2¼ lb) medium-sized
  courgettes
4 tablespoons olive oil
1 teaspoon coriander seeds
1 teaspoon cumin seeds
15 black peppercorns

2 cloves garlic
1 lemon
1 small onion (or shallot)
2 tablespoons chopped mixed
  herbs (fresh, if possible)
salt

Wash the courgettes and peel them lengthways, leaving strips of skin. Cut them into quarters, again lengthways, discarding any loose seeds. Slice into pieces about 3–4 cm (1½ in) long.

Add the oil, coriander, cumin, peppercorns and the whole peeled cloves of garlic to 1 litre (about 36 fl oz) of water and bring to the boil. Add the courgettes, making sure that there is enough boiling water to keep them covered. Cook them just on the boil for 25–30 minutes when the courgettes should still be firm yet give to the point of a knife.

Using a perforated spoon, remove the courgettes and place in the serving-dish. Boiling vigorously, reduce the cooking liquid until about a teacupful remains. Remove from the heat and immediately add the juice of the lemon, the chopped onion and the mixed herbs: salt to taste and pour the mixture over the courgettes. Leave to cool before serving.

[123]

CRUDITÉS EN FONDUE
Raw vegetable dip

PREPARATION TIME: 40 minutes
COOKING TIME: nil
FOR SIX TO EIGHT

1 cauliflower
500 g (generous 1 lb) carrots
1 head of celery
1 bunch of radishes

For the sauce
6 petits-suisses cheeses (if
   unobtainable, use 100 g,
   3½ oz, Philadelphia cheese
   instead)
180 g (scant 6½ oz) Roquefort
   cheese (or any available blue
   cheese)
100 ml (3½ fl oz) crème fraîche
2 tablespoons brandy
tabasco sauce

This dish goes well with aperitifs or it can be served as the first course of a meal.

Break the flower-heads from the cauliflower, wash them well, drain and dry them. Cut the carrots and the celery sticks into thickish strips about 7½ cm (3 in) long. Cut the leaves from the radishes, leaving a short stalk, trim the root end and make an incision in the form of a cross.

Blend together the ingredients for the sauce into a smooth cream dip, using a few drops only of tabasco sauce.

Aïoli also makes a delicious dip for raw vegetables (see page 147). and the dish can be served with either one, or with both of these sauces.

CONCOMBRES À LA MENTHE
Cucumber with mint

PREPARATION TIME: 15 minutes
COOKING TIME: nil
FOR SIX

3 cucumbers
salt
2 tablespoons vinegar
2 cloves garlic

3 small pots of natural yoghurt,
   about 450 g (1 lb)
3 tablespoons olive oil
1 teaspoon fresh chopped fennel
1 teaspoon fresh chopped mint

Peel the cucumbers and split them into four lengthways. Scrape out the seeds and cut the cucumbers into dice. Put them into a colander and sprinkle with 1 teaspoon of salt, leaving them to sweat.

In a bowl, mix the vinegar and the finely chopped garlic and leave for 10 minutes. Take a second bowl and mix together the yoghurt, oil and chopped fennel; then add the vinegar which should be passed through a fine sieve.

Thoroughly wash the cucumber dice, drain and dry them. Put them into the salad bowl in which they will be served and pour the sauce over them. Finally, garnish by sprinkling on the chopped mint.

This dish, which comes from Turkey, should be served chilled and the cucumber and its sauce mixed together just before serving.

SALADE COMPOSÉE
Mixed salad

PREPARATION TIME: 15 minutes
COOKING TIME: nil
FOR SIX

1 endive lettuce
2 crisp eating apples
1 lemon
10 radishes
3 tomatoes
1 head of celery

100 g (3½ oz) shelled walnuts
green peppercorn mustard
salt, pepper
200 ml (7 fl oz) crème fraîche
cider vinegar

Separate the lettuce, wash and dry the leaves thoroughly. Cut into strips using kitchen scissors.

Peel and slice the apples and sprinkle them with lemon juice to prevent discoloration. Top and tail the radishes and slice into discs. Chop the tomatoes into small pieces, and cut the well-washed sticks of celery into dice. Arrange all these ingredients, together with the walnuts, in a salad bowl, finishing with the slices of apple.

Take a bowl and add a dessertspoon of the green peppercorn mustard and salt and pepper. Mix thoroughly together with the cream and 2 tablespoons of cider vinegar.

As with all mixed salads, it is best to serve the dressing separately so the look of the arrangement is not disturbed.

PISSENLITS AU LARD
Dandelion* and bacon salad

PREPARATION TIME: 15 minutes
COOKING TIME: 5–7 minutes
FOR SIX

750 g (generous 1½ lb)
   dandelion leaves
1 teaspoon of mustard
1 tablespoon wine vinegar

salt, pepper
3 tablespoons oil
300 g (10½ oz) of thickly cut
   streaky bacon

* Note If dandelion leaves are unobtainable, the salad is just as delicious when made with curly endive, or with spinach.

Separate the leaves and wash thoroughly in several changes of water. Drain and shake out residual moisture.

Make the dressing in a salad bowl with mustard, vinegar, a little salt, pepper and the oil. Add the salad leaves: do not, at this stage, mix them together with the dressing.

Cut the bacon into strips across the slices, the width being about the same as the thickness of the bacon. Fry them in a thick pan without any added fat. When they are nicely browned, tip them, together with any fat which has come out during the cooking, on to the salad.

Take straight to table, mix bacon, salad and dressing well together and serve immediately.

CHAMPIGNONS EN SALADE
Mushroom salad

PREPARATION TIME: 15 minutes
STEEPING TIME: 10 minutes
FOR SIX

750 g (generous 1½ lb) button mushrooms	olive oil
4 lemons	salt, pepper
	parsley

Choose mushrooms that are quite white and whole and unblemished. Trim the stalks and wash them quickly one by one under running water, drying them on a clean cloth. Drop them whole into a bowl, sprinkling them with the juice of 2 lemons to prevent discoloration. Turn them over so that the lemon juice covers them properly.

Then slice the mushrooms and put them into the serving bowl. Pour over the juice of the remaining 2 lemons, 5 tablespoons of olive oil, season with salt and freshly-ground pepper. Mix all together and sprinkle on a little chopped parsley.

Let the salad steep for ten minutes before serving.

Elle advises that the mushrooms should be sliced with a stainless steel knife as a further precaution against discoloration.

CHAMPIGNONS AU CONCOMBRE
Mushroom and cucumber salad

PREPARATION TIME: 25 minutes
COOKING TIME: nil
FOR SIX

1 cucumber	1 kg (2¼ lb) button mushrooms
500 g (17½ oz) natural yoghurt	mushrooms
1 tablespoon olive oil	salt, pepper
15–20 leaves fresh mint	2 lemons
3 cloves garlic	

Peel the cucumber and cut into large dice. Spread them out on a clean cloth or kitchen paper, sprinkle with table-salt and leave them to sweat for 15 minutes. Dry off on fresh kitchen paper.

Put the yoghurt into a salad bowl and whisk it until frothy. Add the oil, the finely-chopped leaves of mint, the crushed cloves of garlic, and season with salt and pepper. Mix together well.

Trim off the end of the mushroom stalks, wash them and sprinkle with lemon juice to prevent discoloration. According to size, cut each mushroom either in half or in quarters and put them into the salad bowl together with the dried cucumber. Mix all together and serve chilled.

Elle advises not to put too much salt into the dressing as the cucumber will retain some of the salt from its preparation. It may be best to season after the salad has been mixed together.

POMMES DE TERRE EN SALADE
Potato salad

PREPARATION TIME: 30 minutes
COOKING TIME: 25–30 minutes
FOR SIX

1½ kg (3¼ lb) potatoes
300 ml (10½ fl oz) dry white wine
1 teaspoon mustard
2 medium-sized shallots
salt, pepper

1 tablespoon chopped mixed
  herbs (or freshly chopped
  chervil if available)
3 tablespoons wine vinegar
170 ml (6 fl oz) olive oil

Buy potatoes that do not go floury when cooked (Arran Pilot and Desirée are among a number of suitable varieties). Cook them in their skins in plenty of salted water and while still hot, peel and slice into rounds. Put them into a bowl and pour on the white wine, turning them over well so the wine is thoroughly dispersed. Leave them to steep and cool.

Make a vinaigrette dressing with the mustard, finely-chopped shallots, seasoning and the mixed herbs or chervil, the vinegar and the olive oil.

Just before serving the potatoes, add the dressing, taking care when mixing not to break the rounds. This dish is tastiest if still slightly warm.

RHUBARBE EN SALAD
Rhubarb salad

PREPARATION TIME: 20 minutes
COOKING TIME: nil
FOR SIX

500 g (generous 1 lb) rhubarb
1 teaspoon salt
3 small onions
parsley, chervil, chives

1 tablespoon wine vinegar
4 tablespoons salad oil
2 teaspoons sugar

Peel the sticks of rhubarb and cut them into dice. Sprinkle on the salt and mix well; put on one side for 10 minutes.

Make the vinaigrette dressing in a salad bowl with the finely chopped onions, the chopped fresh herbs, the vinegar and the oil. Add the rhubarb to the salad bowl, sprinkle on the sugar and mix everything together. Serve chilled.

Elle advises that this unusual salad requires young and tender rhubarb. It should go without saying that no part of the rhubarb *leaf* should ever be used.

SALADE CARMEN
Chicken and pepper salad

PREPARATION TIME: 20 minutes
COOKING TIME: 40 minutes
FOR SIX

300 g (10½ oz) long-grain rice
2 wings of chicken
2 large red peppers
250 g (about 8 oz) shelled peas
sugar

2 tablespoons chopped fresh
  tarragon
salad oil
wine vinegar
mustard, salt, pepper

Cook the rice in salted boiling water. When cooked, retain the cooking liquid, and rinse the drained rice in running cold water. Drain again and leave to cool. Skin the chicken-wings and cook them in the rice's cooking water. When they are cooked and cool, strip off the flesh and cut into dice.

Halve the red peppers and remove the seeds and inner membranes. Pass them outside-upwards under a grill until the skin can be peeled off and then cut the flesh into strips. Part-cook the peas in boiling salted water to which a lump of sugar has been added. After cooking, the peas should be firm and slightly crunchy.

Make a vinaigrette dressing using three parts of oil to one of wine vinegar, the chopped tarragon, one or two teaspoons of mustard and seasoning.

When all the ingredients for the salad are cold, mix them together in the serving dish with the dressing. Serve chilled.

Elle suggests that hard-boiled eggs and anchovy fillets can also be added to this salad.

SALADE NIÇOISE
Traditional Mediterranean salad

PREPARATION TIME: 45 minutes
COOKING TIME: 20–25 minutes
FOR SIX

250 g (about 8 oz) salted
  anchovies
4 potatoes (Arran Pilot or Desirée
  are best)
250 g (about 8 oz) French beans
1 lettuce
1 head of celery
4 tomatoes

2 green or red peppers (or one of
  each)
100 g (3½ oz) stoned black
  olives
2 hard-boiled eggs
1 tin (200 g, 7 oz) tuna
olive oil, wine vinegar
salt, pepper

Wash the anchovies well in running cold water, at the same time splitting them open and removing their spines. Dry and cover with olive oil. (Note This will be unnecessary if two small tins of anchovy fillets – 50 g, 1¾ oz size – are used instead, but some of the flavour and texture may be lost.)

Cook the potatoes in their skins in boiling salted water, drain, peel and cut into rounds. Leave to cool. Cook the French beans also in boiling salted water for about 20 minutes so that they are still firm and have retained their colour. Drain, cut each one into two or three pieces and leave to cool.

In a large salad bowl, arrange the ingredients in successive layers of potato, beans, lettuce, the celery head cut into thin strips, the tomatoes cut into quarters, the peppers (from which the seeds and inner membranes have been removed) cut into thin rings, the anchovy fillets and some of the olives. The final layer is made up of the hard-boiled eggs cut into quarters, the tuna broken into largish pieces and the remainder of the olives.

Make a vinaigrette dressing in a separate dish, using three parts of oil to one of vinegar; season and pour it over the salad. Mix together just before serving.

SALADE CAMARGUAISE
Salad from the Camargue

PREPARATION TIME: 40–50 minutes
COOKING TIME: 15–18 minutes
FOR SIX TO EIGHT

400 g (14 oz) long-grain rice	125 g (4½ oz) black olives
1 cucumber	1 small tin anchovy fillets
6 firm tomatoes	pepper
1 green pepper	4 tablespoons salad oil
½ tin red peppers	1 tablespoon wine vinegar
2 onions	1 lettuce
1 clove garlic	3 tablespoons mayonnaise
3 tablespoons capers	1 tin (200 g, 7 oz) tuna

Cook the rice in boiling salted water, rinse in running cold water and drain well. The grains should be separate – avoid over-cooking.

Cut 12 thin slices from the cucumber and put on one side for use as decoration. Peel the rest and cut into small dice. Also chop up four of the tomatoes, the flesh of the green pepper (having removed the seeds and inner membranes) and the equivalent of 4 tablespoons of the tinned red peppers. Chop the onions finely and crush the garlic.

Mix all these ingredients together with the capers, half the olives and the chopped anchovy fillets. Add the oil and vinegar, and a twist or two of freshly-ground pepper. Leave for 30 minutes.

Dress a serving-dish with lettuce leaves. Stir the mayonnaise into the salad mixture and make a mound in the middle of the dish. Decorate with the slices of cucumber, the remainder of the olives and some pieces of red pepper. Put chunks of tuna and half-moons of tomato around the edges of the dish.

SALADE DES ROIS
Epiphany salad

PREPARATION TIME: 20 minutes
COOKING TIME: 2 hours
FOR SIX

500 g (generous 1 lb) dried white haricot beans	100 g (3½ oz) lamb's lettuce (if available)
bouquet garni	4 heads of chicory
4 potatoes	salad oil, wine vinegar
4 eating apples	salt, pepper

Put the beans into a large saucepan and amply cover them with cold water. With the lid on the pan, gently bring the beans to the boil, taking at least 45 minutes. As soon as they boil, drain and return to the saucepan together with plenty of boiling salted water. Add the bouquet garni and continue to cook slowly, the pan covered, for a further 1¼–1½ hours. Drain thoroughly and leave to cool.

Choose a variety of potato that is suitable for salads (Arran Pilot and Desirée are good because they do not go floury when cooked). Scrub them and cook in their skins in plenty of cold water. Drain, peel and cut into slices.

Core the apples but do not peel them: cut them into dice. Trim the chicory and peel off a number of outer leaves from each. Put on one side. Slice the remainder into discs.

Make separately a vinaigrette dressing using oil, vinegar and seasoning. In a bowl, mix together beans, potatoes, apples, lamb's lettuce and chicory, with a little of the dressing.

Line a serving-dish with the whole leaves of chicory which were put to one side, and fill the middle with the salad mixture. Garnish with a few leaves of lamb's lettuce and serve the dressing separately. Use watercress as a garnish if lamb's lettuce is unavailable.

Elle advises that it may be simpler to cook the beans and potatoes in advance, or alternatively tinned beans can be used. This salad is traditionally eaten in Belgium on the Feast of the Epiphany.

EPINARDS CRUS EN SALADE
Raw spinach salad

PREPARATION TIME: 15 minutes
COOKING TIME: 10 minutes
FOR SIX

500 g (generous 1 lb) fresh
   spinach
250 g (about 8 oz) button
   mushrooms
2 lemons

300 g (10½ oz) smoked streaky
   bacon
olive oil, wine vinegar
salt, freshly-ground pepper

Separate the spinach leaves from their spines, wash well in several changes of water, drain and thoroughly shake off any surplus moisture.

Trim off the ends of the mushroom stalks and wash them under running water. Dry them and turn them in the juice of the 2 lemons to avoid discoloration.

Put the bacon slices into a pan, cover them with cold water and bring to the boil, keeping on the boil for 3 minutes. Drain, allow to cool and then cut into small dice.

Make a vinaigrette dressing in a salad-bowl and then add the spinach leaves and sliced mushrooms.

Put a teaspoon of oil in a pan and fry the bacon dice until they are golden. Pour bacon and fat on to the salad, mix all together and serve at once.

<u>Elle says</u> that raw spinach makes a delicious salad but it must be young and tender.

TABOULÉ
A Syrian salad

PREPARATION TIME: 30 minutes (2 hours in advance)
COOKING TIME: nil
FOR SIX

200 g (7 oz) packet of couscous
12 small onions
500 g (generous 1 lb) juicy ripe
   tomatoes
2 tablespoons chopped parsley
1 tablespoon chopped fresh mint

2 lemons
6 tablespoons oil, peanut if
   possible
salt, pepper
4 small firm tomatoes

Into a dish put the couscous, eight of the onions chopped finely, 500 g (1 lb) peeled and chopped tomatoes with their juice, the parsley, mint, lemon juice, oil and seasoning. Mix well together and leave in a cool place for 2 hours, stirring from time to time.

Serve chilled in a salad bowl decorated with the firm tomatoes cut into quarters, the remaining onions and a sprig of mint.

The purpose of using the couscous straight from the packet is that it will swell up in the juices of the tomatoes, lemons and in the oil.

<u>Elle says</u> that couscous is a sort of semolina which can be bought at most oriental shops. It also gives its name to Middle-Eastern meat dishes in which it forms a base.

TOPINAMBOURS À L'AÏOLI
Jerusalem artichokes with garlic sauce

PREPARATION TIME: 45 minutes
COOKING TIME: 30 minutes
FOR SIX

1½ kg (3¼ lb) Jerusalem
  artichokes
40 g (scant 1½ oz) butter
100 g (3½ oz) black olives
chopped parsley

For the sauce
3 cloves garlic
250 ml (9 fl oz) olive oil
1 teaspoon wine vinegar
1 egg
salt, pepper

Thoroughly wash all the earth from the artichokes and blanch them in plenty of salted boiling water. They should not be allowed to cook through or they will be impossible to peel. Drain and, when not too hot to handle, peel like boiled potatoes.

Put them in a saucepan with the butter and 4 tablespoons of water, cover the pan and complete the cooking over a very low heat. The artichokes will be done when they can be pierced through with a thin skewer or pointed knife.

Make the aïoli as for mayonnaise, having first put in the bowl the three cloves or garlic crushed to a thin paste. (Note A more complete recipe for aïoli is given on page 147.)

Arrange the artichokes in a serving-dish, if necessary broken into small pieces, garnish with black olives and sprinkle with chopped parsley. The garlic sauce should be served separately.

This dish is at its most delicious when it is served while still warm.

TOPINAMBOURS SAUTÉS
Sautéed Jerusalem artichokes

PREPARATION TIME: 20 minutes
COOKING TIME: 1 hour
FOR SIX

1½ kg (3¼ lb) Jerusalem
  artichokes
70 g (2½ oz) butter (or 2
  tablespoons of goose fat)

salt, pepper
1 tablespoon chopped parsley
garlic

Scrub the artichokes vigorously with a brush in order to remove all traces of earth. Cook them in their skins in plenty of salted water, as for potatoes. Do not cook too far: as soon as a pointed knife will penetrate them, remove, drain and run under cold water. Peel and cut into slices.

Melt three-quarters of the butter in a pan. When it begins to froth, add the artichokes and sauté them gently over a very moderate heat, stirring from time to time to prevent them sticking to the pan. Cooking should be complete in about 20–30 minutes.

Just before serving, season, add the rest of the butter and sprinkle with parsley into which has been mixed a little garlic, chopped fine.

CHOUX DE BRUXELLES AU LARD
Brussels sprouts with bacon

PREPARATION TIME: 45 minutes
COOKING TIME: 25 minutes
FOR SIX

500 g (generous 1 lb) chestnuts	250 g (about 8 oz) streaky bacon
1 litre (1¾ pints) beef stock	lard
750 g (generous 1½ lb) sprouts	salt, pepper

With a pointed knife, make an incision in the rounded side of each chestnut. Plunge them into plenty of boiling water and continue cooking for 1 minute after the water comes back to the boil. Remove the pan from the heat. Peel the chestnuts, taking them from the water one by one.

Heat the stock in a large saucepan and when it begins to simmer add the peeled chestnuts and continue cooking them for a further 15–20 minutes. Cooking should stop if, before then, the chestnuts show signs of breaking up.

Trim and wash the sprouts and cook in salted boiling water, also for about 15–20 minutes. They should retain a certain crispness when cooked.

Cut the bacon into strips across the slice and fry them gently in a tablespoonful of lard until golden. Add first the sprouts then the chestnuts, season and very carefully mix the ingredients together. Warm through in the pan and serve.

Elle suggests that this dish from the Limousin goes particularly well with roast or pan-cooked pork. With a side-salad, it can make a dish of its own.

FÈVES PRINTANIÈRES
Young broad beans with onions

PREPARATION TIME: 30 minutes
COOKING TIME: about 45 minutes
FOR SIX

5 kg (11 lb) young broad beans	1 tablespoon of dried savory (or a
100 g (3½ oz) butter	sprig of fresh)
20 small white onions	sugar
150 g (5 oz) sliced ham	salt, pepper

Shell the beans and put them into 2 litres (3½ pints) of boiling water. Bring back to the boil and immediately remove from the heat. Leave in their cooking water for 5 minutes and then put into a strainer and run them under a cold tap. Skin them by making a slit along the flat edge of the bean (its spine) and squeezing gently so the green inner bean pops out.

Take a thick-bottomed casserole and melt half of the butter. Add the trimmed white onions, the ham sliced into thin strips and the savory. Stirring frequently, cook for 20 minutes. Add the beans, 100 ml (3½ fl oz) of hot water, a teaspoon of sugar and lightly season. Cover the pan and continue cooking over a moderate heat; the beans should not be allowed to break up. Turn them over from time to time.

The exact cooking time will depend very much upon the size and freshness of the beans.

Just before serving, drain any juice from the beans into a small saucepan, and reduce rapidly. Add the rest of the butter and melt it in the juice, then pour the liquid back over the beans.

Elle suggests that this delicious vegetable dish goes particularly well with spring lamb.

CAROTTES EN FRICASSÉE
Fricassée of carrots

PREPARATION TIME: 30 minutes
COOKING TIME: 1 hour
FOR SIX

1½ kg (3¼ lb) carrots	3 tablespoons of lard or goose fat
500 g (generous 1 lb) onions	250 g (about 8 oz) streaky bacon
bouquet garni	salt, pepper, sugar

Peel the carrots and slice them into discs, and skin and trim the onions. Small ones will not break up so easily during cooking.

Heat the lard in a casserole and when it is hot add the vegetables and the bouquet garni. Stirring frequently, heat the ingredients through, then reduce the heat and continue to cook with the pan uncovered for 25–30 minutes until most of the moisture has evaporated.

Cut the bacon into narrow strips and blanch in boiling water for 5 minutes. Drain, dry and add it to the vegetables. Season, add a teaspoon of sugar and cover the pan. Reduce the heat to its absolute minimum and complete the cooking in the closed pan, stirring from time to time.

CÉLÉRI-RAVE EN PURÉE
Purée of celeriac

PREPARATION TIME: 20 minutes
COOKING TIME: 40 minutes
FOR SIX

3 large heads of celeriac	milk
2 lemons	salt, pepper, nutmeg
1 kg (2¼ lb) potatoes	100 g (3½ oz) butter
2 tablespoons of flour	

Trim and peel the celeriac, sprinkling the surfaces with lemon juice as they are peeled to prevent discoloration. Wash them in a solution of water and lemon juice, cut them into slices and weigh them. Allow 250 g (about 8 oz) of peeled potatoes for every 1 kg (2¼ lb) of celeriac.

Bring 3 litres (5¼ pints) of salted water to the boil and stir in the flour-paste and the juice of half a lemon. Add the celeriac and the potatoes, bring back to the boil and cook for 30–40 minutes until the celeriac can be crushed with a fork.

Drain the vegetables and pass them through a Moulinette. Depending on the consistency of the purée required, either moisten it with milk or evaporate any surplus liquid by re-heating the purée. When the right texture is obtained, season, add grated nutmeg, and finally mix the butter well in.

Elle suggests that this delicious purée goes well with any sort of roast, and particularly with roast game.

CÉLERIS EN COCOTTE
Hungarian braised celery

PREPARATION TIME: 15 minutes
COOKING TIME: 30 minutes
FOR SIX

3 good heads of celery
40 g (scant 1½ oz) butter
cube of chicken stock
2 pots of yoghurt, 150 g (5 oz)
  size

salt, black pepper, cayenne
  pepper
1 teaspoon paprika
1 tablespoon wine vinegar
4 hard-boiled eggs
sprig of fresh parsley

Trim the celery top and bottom and take off the outer sticks. Put the hearts to one side and slice the sticks into 1.5 cm (½ in) lengths.

Melt the butter in a casserole, add first the celery pieces and then the celery hearts, cut in half lengthways. Barely cover with cold water and crumble the stock cube over the vegetables. Cook over a low heat for about 30 minutes, remove and allow to cool in the casserole. Drain the remaining liquid from the celery.

Make the sauce while the celery is cooking. Put the yoghurt into a mixing-bowl, season, add a pinch of cayenne pepper, the paprika and the wine vinegar. Whisk together until a really smooth sauce results.

Arrange the celery hearts in a serving dish, pour the sauce over them and decorate with parsley and the yolks of the hard-boiled eggs which have been put through a Moulinette.

Elle advises that the celery can be cooked in advance. The sauce should be chilled before serving.

Cold braised celery is suitable either as a starter or as an accompanying vegetable.

COEURS DE CÉLERI GRATINÉS
Gratin of celery hearts

PREPARATION TIME: 20 minutes
COOKING TIME: 50 minutes
FOR SIX

6 small heads of celery
6 tablespoons clear beef stock
2 tablespoons grated
  Emmenthaler cheese

salt, pepper
100 g (3½ oz) butter

Trim the tops and roots of the celery and remove any damaged or discoloured sticks. Wash thoroughly.

Bring a large pan of salted water to the boil and cook the celery for 20–25 minutes after the water has returned to the boil. Drain, cut each head of celery in half lengthways and arrange them in an oven-proof dish. Moisten them either with stock or with the water in which they were cooked. Season, sprinkle with the grated cheese and dot with butter, using all of it.

Pre-heat the oven for 15 minutes to a temperature of 200°C/400°F/Gas Mark 6. Put the dish of celery in the oven and cook until all the liquid has evaporated. At this point, the butter should be bubbling and the cheese just becoming golden brown. If the cheese looks as though it might brown too quickly, cover the dish with a piece of aluminium foil.

Elle says that as with the previous dish, celery cooked in this way can make either a starter or be an accompanying vegetable.

[134]

COURGETTES AUX LARDONS
Courgettes with bacon

PREPARATION TIME: 5 minutes
COOKING TIME: 25 minutes
FOR SIX

150 g (5 oz) smoked streaky
  bacon
2 onions

1 kg (2¼ lb) courgettes
50 ml (1¾ fl oz) oil
salt, pepper

Cut the bacon into strips across the grain, blanch them for 5 minutes in boiling water, remove and thoroughly drain. Chop the onions, wash and wipe the courgettes, trim them and cut into round slices a little over 1.5 cm (½ in) thick.

Heat the oil in a pan and when it is hot, seal the bacon strips, then add the chopped onions and sliced courgettes. Cook over a moderate heat and turn from time to time so that the mixture does not stick to the pan. Season: because of the bacon, very little salt should be necessary.

The mixture should be cooked when the cut surfaces of the courgettes have a golden-brown appearance. Serve hot.

Elle suggests that courgettes cooked in this way are delicious with any roast or grilled meat.

COURGETTES PERSILLÉES
Courgettes with parsley butter

PREPARATION TIME: 10 minutes
COOKING TIME: 15 minutes
FOR SIX

1½ kg (3¼ lb) courgettes
150 g (5 oz) butter

2 tablespoons fresh chopped
  parsley
salt, pepper

Wash and dry the courgettes and peel them lengthways in alternate strips (see illustration). Cut into round slices just over 1.5 cm (½ in) thick. Bring a large pan of salted water to the boil, put in the courgettes and cook for 3 minutes. Remove and thoroughly drain.

Melt one-third of the butter in a pan, add the courgettes and cook over a low to moderate heat for 10–12 minutes. Work the parsley into the rest of the butter, season; then shape it and put in a cool place.

Serve the courgettes with a slice of parsley butter.

Elle suggests that courgettes cooked in this way go particularly well with any red meat but especially well with lamb.

FENOUILS BRAISÉS
Braised fennel

PREPARATION TIME: 5 minutes
COOKING TIME: 45–50 minutes
FOR SIX

8 small heads of fennel	salt, pepper
2 tablespoons flour-paste	mixed herbs
70 g (2½ oz) butter (or 2 tablespoons goose fat)	

Be sure to buy small fennel as their flavour is more delicate.

Bring 3 litres (5¼ pints) of salted water to the boil, stirring in the flour-paste. Blanch the whole fennel in the boiling water, continuing the cooking until they are soft enough to be pierced through with a fine skewer. Remove the fennel, put them under running cold water, cut them into quarters and dry them on kitchen paper.

Melt the butter (or goose fat) in a pan, add the pieces of fennel and over a very moderate heat complete their cooking, stirring and turning them from time to time. Add a little freshly-ground pepper.

The fennel should not be allowed to brown and for the last part of the cooking the pan should be covered.

They may be served as they are, or sprinkled with chopped mixed herbs.

HARICOTS VERTS
French beans

Two recipes are given for haricots verts which are a very popular vegetable in France.

HARICOTS VERTS FRAIS
Fresh French beans

To each kg (2¼ lb) of beans, allow 5 litres (8 pints) of boiling *unsalted* water, and cook in either an enamel-lined or stainless-steel saucepan. Add the beans in separate handfuls so the water does not fall below boiling point.

Check the progress of cooking frequently since it is very easy to overcook fresh French beans. As soon as the beans no longer break with a snap, they are cooked. Remove from the heat, drain and run the beans under cold water. Return the beans to the pan and warm them through gently, stirring in a good knob of butter. Garnish with either chopped onion or parsley, or crushed garlic.

HARICOTS VERTS À LA PROVENÇALE
French beans provençale

PREPARATION TIME: 15 minutes
COOKING TIME: 40 minutes
FOR SIX

1½ kg (3¼ lb) french beans	50 g (scant 2 oz) butter
4 tomatoes	1 clove garlic
6 small onions	1 bouquet garni
2 tablespoons olive oil	salt, pepper

Trim and string the beans, wash and drain them. Plunge the tomatoes into boiling water for 3–4 minutes, remove and peel them, cut them in half and remove the pips. Peel and halve the onions.

Heat the oil and butter together in a saucepan and, over a gentle heat, glaze the tomatoes and onions. Add the beans, the garlic and the bouquet garni. Season, cover the pan and cook for a further 40 minutes, still over a low heat.

HARICOTS SECS
Haricot beans

PREPARATION TIME: 10 minutes
COOKING TIME: 2–2½ hours
FOR SIX

500 g (generous 1 lb) dried haricot beans	1 onion stuck with a clove
1 bouquet garni	1 clove garlic
1 head of celery	2 small carrots
	salt

The cooking method is exactly the same whether white haricot beans or flageolet beans are used. They should not be soaked: this can lead to partial fermentation of the starch in the beans which is the cause of all complaints made about the taste of dried vegetables.

Cooking takes place in two stages. Wash the beans thoroughly and put them in a large saucepan with plenty of cold water. Cover the pan and very slowly bring the water to the boil, this should take at least three-quarters of an hour. As soon as boiling-point is reached, remove from the heat and allow the beans to cool. By this time, they should have doubled in volume.

Drain the beans and return them to the saucepan. Cover them with plenty of boiling water and add the other vegetables; add salt and then cover the pan. As soon as the water returns to the boil, reduce the heat so that the pan is only just at boiling point, and continue cooking for 1–1¼ hours (depending on the quality of the beans).

By cooking the beans in this way, you will be sure to have them still whole and ready to be prepared for serving in any way that you choose.

FLAGEOLETS EN SALADE
Salad of haricot beans

PREPARATION TIME: 15 minutes
COOKING TIME: 2–2½ hours
FOR SIX

500 g (generous 1 lb) dried haricot beans	2 small carrots
1 head of celery	mustardy vinaigrette
1 onion stuck with a clove	salt, pepper
1 clove of garlic	cervelas sausage (optional)
	chopped fresh mixed herbs

Cook the beans in the same way as in the previous recipe, as far as the end of stage two. Once the beans have cooled, drain them, discard the other vegetables, and dress with a mustardy vinaigrette.

Poach the sausage by putting it into boiling water, removing the pan immediately from the heat and leaving the sausage to swell for 10 minutes. (Frankfurter sausages can be used if cervelas is unobtainable.) Skin the sausage and cut into slices. Use these to decorate the edges of the serving dish after the beans and dressing have been well mixed together. Sprinkle with chopped herbs before serving.

LENTILLES AU LARD
Lentils with bacon

PREPARATION TIME: 20 minutes
COOKING TIME: 50 minutes
FOR SIX

1 onion
150 g (5 oz) green streaky bacon
2 tablespoons lard
1 tablespoon flour
600 g (1¼ lb) brown lentils

1 bouquet garni
2 tomatoes
1 clove garlic
salt, pepper.

Chop the onion and dice the bacon. Blanch the bacon for 5 minutes in boiling water, remove and dry on kitchen paper. Then gently fry in the melted lard until the dice are just golden-brown. Sprinkle and stir in the flour, let it colour for a few moments and then add 1½ litres (2½ pints) of water.

Wash the lentils and sort through to remove any pieces of grit. Then add to the bacon in the saucepan, together with the bouquet garni, the tomatoes (peeled, pipped and chopped), the garlic and seasoning. Bring very slowly to the boil and leave to simmer, the pot covered, for 40 minutes or so.

Add more boiling water during the cooking should it be necessary. Serve with chopped parsley sprinkled on the top.

LAITUES BRAISÉES
Braised lettuce

PREPARATION TIME: 25–30 minutes
COOKING TIME: 30 minutes
FOR SIX

125 g (4½ oz) butter
24 small white onions
sugar, salt

6 cos lettuce (or open, loose
    cabbage lettuce)
pepper
bouquet garni

Take a heavy iron casserole and melt a tablespoon of butter. As soon as it begins to froth, add the onions, a level teaspoon of sugar and a pinch of salt. Glaze the onions over a moderate heat for about 25 minutes until they take on the colour of caramel.

Choose lettuce without firm and tightly-packed hearts. Cut them in half, wash and drain them well. Melt half the remaining butter in a pan and soften the lettuce which should be sprinkled with a little sugar to colour. When soft, take them from the pan, roll each one up on itself and arrange them around the edges of a pan. Season, add the bouquet garni and pile the onions in the centre. Cover the pan and braise the lettuce in the rest of the butter until they are cooked. If, at this time, too much liquid remains in the pan, reduce it by abruptly raising the heat for a minute or so.

Arrange the vegetables in the same way in a serving dish, with the onions in the middle of the lettuce.

Elle suggests that this dish goes well with veal cutlets or pork chops.

POIS MANGETOUT
Mangetout peas

PREPARATION TIME: 30 minutes
COOKING TIME: 45 minutes – 1 hour
FOR SIX

1½ kg (3¼ lb) mangetout peas
1 lettuce heart
12–15 small white onions
slice of ham, about 175 g (about 6 oz)

60 g (2 oz) butter
salt, pepper
sprig of fresh parsley
sprig of thyme

Trim the stalks of the mangetout and, if necessary, string them. Wash and dry them. Cut the lettuce heart into thin strips. Halve the onions and cut the ham into cubes.

Melt the butter in a casserole over a low heat, taking care that it does not brown. Gently cook the pieces of ham and when golden-brown, remove and put on one side. Add all the vegetables to the casserole, season and add the sprigs of herbs. Cover the pan and simmer over a low heat until the mangetout are tender.

Do not overcook. Mangetout peas are like French beans in that their flavour is at its best when they are still firm after being cooked.

Remove the sprigs of herbs, mix in the cooked ham, and serve.

Elle suggests that this vegetable dish is delicious on its own but also goes well with grills or roasts.

OIGNONS MARINÉS
Marinade of onions

PREPARATION TIME: 20 minutes
COOKING TIME: 1¾ hours
FOR SIX

For the tomato purée
500 g (generous 1 lb) tomatoes
2 onions
3 cloves garlic
50 ml (1¾ fl oz) oil
bouquet garni
salt, pepper
sprig of basil (or dried basil)

For the onion dish
1 kg (2¼ lb) small white onions
100 g (3½ oz) seedless raisins
6 tablespoons olive oil
200 ml (7 fl oz) white wine vinegar
80 g (scant 3 oz) caster sugar
bouquet garni
salt, pepper

Begin by preparing the purée of tomatoes. Peel and pip the tomatoes, and put with all the other ingredients into a pan. Simmer together for 30 minutes and then pass everything through a fine sieve. Put to one side.

Trim the onions and put them in a casserole with the tomato purée, 500 ml (18 fl oz) of water, raisins, oil, vinegar, sugar, bouquet garni and the seasoning. Bring all to the boil, reduce the heat and let the ingredients cook slowly uncovered for a good hour. Allow to cool, turn into a serving dish and refrigerate. Serve chilled.

Elle advises that if the onions are on the large side, the cooking time may have to be extended for 15–30 minutes.

PETITS POIS À LA PARISIENNE
French peas

PREPARATION TIME: 25 minutes
COOKING TIME: 20 minutes
FOR SIX

3 kg (6½ lb) young peas
50 g (scant 2 oz) butter
1 tablespoon flour
salt, pepper
4 small onions

sprig of parsley
a few chives
1 cos lettuce
3 egg yolks

Shell the young peas. Make a white sauce in a casserole with the melted butter, flour and 200 ml (7 fl oz) of water, and bring to the boil.

Add the shelled peas, season, then add the onions, parsley, chopped chives and the lettuce (washed, dried and cut into strips). Cover the dish and leave to cook for 20 minutes over a low heat.

Remove from the heat and, one by one, vigorously beat in the egg yolks. Check the seasoning. Serve hot.

Elle advises that if you need to keep this dish warm before serving it, the egg yolks should be beaten in only at the last moment to avoid curdling.

POIVRONS MARINÉS
Marinade of peppers

PREPARATION TIME: 30 minutes
COOKING TIME: 15 minutes
FOR SIX

1 kg (2¼ lb) large red or green
peppers
salt, pepper

clove of garlic
300 ml (10 fl oz) olive oil

Pre-heat the grill for 15 minutes and then put the peppers under the heat, turn them as the skin blackens and bubbles. Remove from the heat, cut in half and, when cool, peel off the outer skins. Remove all the seeds.

Slice the half-peppers into strips, again lengthways, season, sprinkle with crushed garlic and cover them with oil. Leave the strips of pepper to marinate for at least 24 hours.

This dish goes very well with grilled or cold meat; it can also be served as an hors d'oeuvre.

POMMES BOULANGÈRE
Casserole of potatoes

PREPARATION TIME: 25 minutes
COOKING TIME: about 1½ hours
FOR SIX

1½ kg (3¼ lb) potatoes	dried bay leaf
4 tablespoons of lard or goose fat	½ clove of garlic
salt, pepper	tablespoon of chopped parsley
4 sprigs of thyme	

Peel the potatoes and cut them into thin slices. Wash them well in running cold water in order to remove as much starch as possible. Drain well and dry on kitchen paper.

Rub the bottom and sides of a fireproof gratin dish with a good tablespoon of lard or goose fat. Line with one-third of the sliced potatoes, season very lightly, sprinkle with half the herbs mixed together (including the crumbled bay leaf) and a little crushed garlic. Do not increase the quantities of herb specified – they should suggest, rather than impose, their flavours.

Add a second layer of potatoes, sprinkle on the rest of the herbs and put in the final layer of potatoes. Season each layer very lightly. Dot the remaining fat over the surface of the dish and add as much hot water as will just come up to the level of the top layer of potatoes.

Put the dish on a moderate heat and bring to the boil. Reduce the heat and let them simmer until all the water has evaporated and only potato juice remains.

Pre-heat the oven to a temperature of 220°C/425°F/Gas Mark 7. Complete the cooking in the oven; when the surface is lightly golden-brown, reduce the heat to 160°C/325°F/Gas Mark 3, and allow to bubble gently for a further 20 minutes.

Serve with any roast or grilled meat.

POMMES DARPHIN
Potato cake

PREPARATION TIME: 30 minutes
COOKING TIME: 45 minutes
FOR SIX

1½ kg (3¼ lb) potatoes	100 g (3½ oz) lard
salt, pepper	

Peel the potatoes and cut them into thin strips. Press them in a clean cloth or between sheets of kitchen paper, and sprinkle them all over with table salt. Season with a pinch of freshly-ground black pepper.

Heat two-thirds of the lard in a frying pan measuring about 26 cm (10½ in) in diameter, and add the potatoes. Cook over a moderate heat, turning and stirring them to start with and then letting them fry together into a single mass. When a crust has formed on the bottom of the potatoes, turn them out in one piece onto a plate, add the remainder of the lard to the pan and return the potatoes upside-down so a golden-brown crust is formed on both sides.

The dish should be served by cutting the cake into portions at the table.

Elle suggests that this dish goes well with roast or grilled meat or, with a green salad, makes a light meal by itself.

POMMES LYONNAISE
Potatoes with onions

PREPARATION TIME: 25 minutes
COOKING TIME: 30 minutes
PRE-COOKING TIME: 20–25 minutes (2 hours in advance)
FOR SIX

1½ kg (3¼ lb) potatoes
125 g (4½ oz) butter
2 tablespoons cooking oil

500 g (generous 1 lb) onions
salt, pepper
chopped fresh parsley

Cook the potatoes in their skins in the usual way in plenty of salted boiling water. Peel them and allow to cool. Then cut into round slices.

Heat half the butter and one tablespoon of oil together in a frying pan, add the potatoes and warm over a moderate heat.

Chop the onions and, in another pan, cook them slowly in the remaining oil and butter until transparent. (Note There is less risk of burning or overcooking the onions if they are put into the pan with the oil and butter: i.e. do not, in this case, pre-heat the cooking fats.)

While both potatoes and onions are hot, put the ingredients together in one pan and mix well. Season and keep them over a moderate heat for 2 or 3 minutes, stirring occasionally.

Sprinkle with chopped parsley before serving.

POMMES NORMANDE
Stuffed potatoes

PREPARATION TIME: 30 minutes
COOKING TIME: 1½ hours
FOR SIX

5 large potatoes
3 small Neufchâtel cheeses (if
unobtainable, use cream
cheese)

3 egg yolks
2 tablespoons of cream
salt, pepper, nutmeg
1 whole egg

Bake the potatoes in the oven, whole and in their skins. When cooked, cut them in half lengthways and remove all the pulp. While it is still hot mash it well with the cheese, the egg yolks and one tablespoon of cream. Keep working the mixture until it is smooth and creamy; extend with the second tablespoon of cream if necessary.

Because of the saltiness of the cheese, taste the potato mixture before seasoning. Add pepper and nutmeg with a light hand.

Using a forcing-bag fitted with a No. 12 nozzle, or with a serving spoon, fill six of the potato shells with the mixture. Brush the surfaces with egg beaten together with a teaspoon of water.

Pre-heat a very hot oven (240°C/475°F/Gas Mark 9) and put in the stuffed potatoes. When heated through, they will have puffed up and the surfaces will have begun to brown. Serve immediately, before they have collapsed.

Elle advises that this is a filling dish and, with a green salad, makes a meal on its own.

POMMES DE TERRE AU GRATIN
Gratin of potatoes

PREPARATION TIME: 30 minutes
COOKING TIME: 1½–2 hours
FOR SIX

1½ kg (3¼ lb) potatoes
salt, pepper, nutmeg
1 litre (1¾ pints) milk
2 cloves of garlic

100 g (3½ oz) grated Gruyère
  cheese
50 g (scant 2 oz) butter

Peel, wash and wipe the potatoes. Cut them into thin slices; do not wipe or dry them further.

Add salt, pepper and a little nutmeg to the milk and bring to the boil. Put in the potatoes, bring the milk to the boil and then simmer until the potatoes are cooked.

Remove them with a perforated spoon and arrange the slices in two or three layers in a gratin dish which has been rubbed with crushed garlic. Each layer should be sprinkled with grated cheese.

Reduce the milk to the consistency of double cream and pour it over the potatoes. Dot the surface with knobs of butter and put in a hot oven (200°C/400°F/Gas Mark 6) until the surface is golden-brown. If all the milk evaporates in the oven, replace it with 2 tablespoons of double cream.

This dish goes well with either meat or poultry.

POMMES DES VENDANGEURS
Potato and bacon casserole

PREPARATION TIME: 20 minutes
COOKING TIME: 2¼ hours
FOR SIX

1½ kg (3¼ lb) potatoes
500 g (generous 1 lb) smoked
  streaky bacon
500 g (generous 1 lb) green
  streaky bacon

200 g (7 oz) grated Emmenthaler
  cheese
pepper
50 g (scant 2 oz) butter

Peel and wash the potatoes and cut into fairly thick slices. Buy the bacon in thin slices and remove all the rinds.

Take an earthenware casserole and put a layer of slices of smoked bacon on the bottom; add a layer of raw sliced potatoes, a sprinkled layer of grated cheese, and a layer of green bacon. Season with freshly-ground black pepper. Repeat for three more layers, finishing off with a layer of smoked bacon. Dot the surface with knobs of butter.

Pre-heat a very hot oven (230°C/450°F/Gas Mark 8) and put in the casserole. After half an hour, reduce the heat to 200°C/400°F/Gas Mark 6 and continue to cook for a further three-quarters of an hour. Cover the dish with a sheet of aluminium foil and return to the oven for one more hour.

These potatoes go well with roasts of beef, lamb or veal.

The chef of the Paris restaurant 'Le Mazagran' where this Burgundian dish is served, recommends that it be accompanied either by a good Beaujolais such as Juliénas or Chiroubles, or by a Volnay or a Pommard from Burgundy.

TIAN DE POMMES DE TERRE
Gratin of potatoes and tomato

PREPARATION TIME: 25 minutes
COOKING TIME: 40–45 minutes
FOR SIX

1½ kg (3¼ lb) potatoes
300 g (10½ oz) onions
150 g (5 oz) Gruyère cheese
600 g (generous 1¼ lb) tomatoes
sprig of thyme
salt, pepper
150 ml (5¼ fl oz) olive oil

Cook the potatoes in their skins, peel them and cut them into slices. Chop the onions and grate the cheese. Slice the tomatoes.

Take a gratin dish and put in alternate layers of potato, tomato, chopped onion, grated cheese, a few leaves of thyme and seasoning. Finish up with a layer of tomatoes sprinkled with cheese and thyme.

Be sparing with the salt when seasoning because of the saltiness of the cheese. Sprinkle the oil over the dish and put it into a hot oven (220°C/425°F/Gas Mark 7) until the ingredients have melted together and the surface is golden-brown.

Elle suggests that this typically Mediterranean dish goes well with any meat or, with a salad, can make a light meal of its own.

BOHÉMIENNE
Provençale vegetable casserole

PREPARATION TIME: 30 minutes
COOKING TIME: 45 minutes
FOR SIX

1 kg (about 2¼ lb) aubergines
1 kg (about 2¼ lb) tomatoes
300 g (10½ oz) onions
150 ml (5¼ fl oz) olive oil
3 cloves of garlic
8 anchovy fillets in oil
1 tablespoon flour
75 ml (2½ fl oz) milk
chopped parsley
50 g (scant 2 oz) fresh white
   breadcrumbs

Trim the aubergines and cut them into dice. Put them into a sieve, sprinkle them with salt and leave to sweat for 30 minutes. Peel the tomatoes, cut them into quarters and remove the seeds. Chop the onions.

Heat the oil and the onions together and cook gently until the onion is transparent. Wash the diced aubergines and dry on kitchen paper; add them to the onions together with the tomatoes and one whole clove of garlic. Let everything cook slowly together; stir frequently.

In a mixing-bowl, mash the anchovy fillets in their own oil with the flour and milk to make a sort of roux. Add it to the vegetable stew, mixing it well in.

Crush the rest of the garlic and mix it together with the chopped parsley and the breadcrumbs. Cover the surface of the vegetables with this mixture and put into a very hot oven (230°C/450°F/Gas Mark 8) until a crust is formed.

RATATOUILLE VENÇOISE
Ratatouille

PREPARATION TIME: 20 minutes
COOKING TIME: 1–1½ hours
FOR SIX

75 ml (2½ fl oz) olive oil
200 g (7 oz) onions
5 chopped cloves of garlic
4 peeled tomatoes
1 tablespoon tomato purée
½ litre (18 fl oz) dry white wine
sprig of parsley
sprig of thyme
3 large leaves of basil
4 bay leaves
salt, pepper
3 aubergines
2 red or green peppers
5 medium-sized courgettes

In a casserole, heat oil and chopped onions gently together until the onion is transparent. Add the chopped garlic, the tomatoes quartered and seeded, the tomato purée, the wine and all the herbs. Season, stir together and bring to a vigorous boil.

Add all the remaining vegetables: the aubergines cut into dice, the peppers seeded and cut into strips and the courgettes in round slices. Reduce to a moderate heat and cook with the pan uncovered for 40–50 minutes, when the ingredients should be ready.

Elle suggests that this ratatouille is either served hot as an accompanying vegetable to a roast, or on its own as a cold hors d'oeuvre.

SALSIFIS SAUTÉS
Sautéed salsifis

PREPARATION TIME: 35–40 minutes
COOKING TIME: 30–40 minutes
FOR SIX

1½ kg (3¼ lb) white salsifis (or black scorzonera)
juice of 2 lemons
2 tablespoons flour
80 g (scant 3 oz) butter
salt, pepper
chopped parsley
clove of garlic

Peel the salsifis with a vegetable peeler so no more skin is removed than is necessary. Cut into pieces the length of a little finger and put them at once into water mixed with lemon juice so as to prevent discoloration.

Mix the flour into a smooth paste with a little cold water. Heat 2 litres (3½ pints) of water and when it is at the point of boiling stir in the flour-paste and continue stirring until the water boils.

Add the salsifis and reduce to a moderate heat. Continue cooking, but watch carefully and when the salsifis can be pierced through with the point of a knife, remove from the cooking water and run them under a cold tap. Dry on kitchen paper.

Melt the butter in a pan and, when it begins to froth, add the salsifis. Let them simmer, the pan uncovered, for about 20 minutes. Turn them frequently and keep the heat to a level which will ensure they do not go brown.

Season and, a minute or two before serving, sprinkle with chopped parsley mixed with a little chopped garlic.

EPINARDS À LA CRÈME
Creamed spinach

PREPARATION TIME: 1 hour
COOKING TIME: 30 minutes
FOR SIX

3 kgs (about 6½ lb) fresh spinach   salt, pepper
100 g (3½ oz) butter   teaspoon of sugar
250 ml (9 fl oz) single cream   grated nutmeg

Strip the spinach leaves from their stalks and blanch them for a few minutes in plenty of salted boiling water. They should be removed before they are cooked; the leaves should have softened but should not have turned dark green.

Taking the spinach leaves in batches, run each batch under a cold tap and press them together into a ball, extracting as much water in the process as possible. Chop each spinach-ball very finely.

Heat the butter in a deep pan and when it begins to froth, add all the chopped spinach. Stir constantly and cook until all the excess liquid has evaporated, then mix in the cream. Season, add the sugar and grated nutmeg and, over a moderate heat only, complete the cooking with the pan uncovered until the cream has all been thoroughly absorbed (about 10 minutes).

TERRINE DE LEGUMES
Vegetable terrine

PREPARATION TIME: 30 minutes
COOKING TIME: 20–25 minutes
FOR SIX

1 head of celery   1 crisp eating apple
1 head of fennel   salt, pepper
4 aubergines   cumin seed
4 courgettes   fresh mint, fresh chopped
olive oil   parsley
4 tomatoes   several leaves of basil

Trim the heads of the celery and fennel and chop them up. Blanch the pieces in plenty of salted boiling water for 8 minutes, then remove and drain.

Peel the aubergines and the courgettes and cut them lengthways in slices a little less than ½ cm (¼ in) thick. Heat the oil in a pan and fry the slices and, when cooked, dry them on kitchen paper. Slice the tomatoes and the cored and peeled apple.

Take a deep earthenware or Pyrex dish and put in a layer of sliced tomatoes, followed by a layer of apple. Season and add a little cumin seed and a few leaves of mint. Follow this with a layer of courgettes, one of fennel, one of celery and finally a layer of aubergines. Season and add a few more cumin seeds.

Continue to line the pot with layers of vegetables and seasoning in the order described until the top layer is within 1 cm (½ in) of the top. Cover and cook the terrine in a hot oven (220°C/425°F/Gas Mark 7) for 20–25 minutes. Just before serving (the dish can be presented either hot or cold) sprinkle with chopped parsley and basil.

The chef of the Paris restaurant 'd'Olympe' from where this recipe comes, recommends that a red wine from the Loire, served cool, should be drunk with the dish.

AÏOLI & ROUILLE
Two garlic sauces

ANCHOÏADE
Anchovy paste

AÏOLI

PREPARATION TIME: 25 minutes
COOKING TIME: nil
FOR EIGHT

7 cloves of garlic	500 ml (18 fl oz) olive oil
2 egg yolks	½ lemon
salt, pepper	

With a (preferably stone) pestle and mortar, crush the peeled cloves of garlic into a smooth cream. Beat in the egg yolks, season and whip the sauce like a mayonnaise, adding the oil drop by drop. While the sauce is being made add, twice, 2 teaspoons of warm water.

When all the oil has been absorbed, add a few drops of lemon juice to taste.

ROUILLE

PREPARATION TIME: 15 minutes
COOKING TIME: nil
FOR EIGHT

2 cloves of garlic	1 egg yolk
2 small sweet red peppers	150 ml (5 fl oz) olive oil
1 slice of white bread	2 tablespoons of fish stock

Crush the peeled garlic and the flesh of the trimmed and seeded peppers in a pestle and mortar. Trim the crusts from the bread, moisten it with warm water and press it into a ball. Incorporate the damp bread into the garlic and pepper mixture in order to produce a homogeneous paste. Beat in the egg yolk and proceed as for a mayonnaise, adding the oil drop by drop. Lastly, blend in the fish stock.

Rouille has a strong and distinctive flavour and should be eaten sparingly. It is generally used to thicken fish soups and bouillabaisse.

Elle advises that either of these sauces may be made in the blender but the garlic (and peppers) must be crushed first with pestle and mortar.

PREPARATION TIME: 25 minutes (2 hours in advance)
COOKING TIME: nil
FOR SIX

250 g (about 8 oz) salted anchovies or 125 g (4½ oz) tinned anchovy fillets	1 or 2 tablespoons wine vinegar
	250 ml (9 fl oz) olive oil
	freshly-ground black pepper
2 or 3 cloves of garlic	

If using salt-preserved anchovies, open and remove the spines under a cold running tap. Separate the fillets and allow to soak for 2 hours; the water should be changed frequently to take away the salt. If using tinned anchovy fillets, simply drain off the oil and pat with kitchen paper.

Pass the anchovies through the fine grid of a Moulinette (or through a blender). Add the finely crushed garlic, half the vinegar and then the oil which should be poured in very slowly while beating the mixture vigorously with a wooden spoon. Add pepper and the rest of the vinegar to taste.

Anchoïade makes a delicious sauce with grilled, fried or steamed fish. It can also be used as a dip with crudités, or as a spread on toast or bread.

SAUCE À L'AVOCAT
Avocado sauce

PREPARATION TIME: 15 minutes
COOKING TIME: nil
FOR SIX

1 ripe avocado
2 lemons
1 egg yolk
salt, pepper

1 tablespoon Dijon mustard
2 tablespoons olive oil
tabasco sauce

Cut the avocado in half, remove the stone and spoon out all the flesh. Sprinkle thoroughly with the juice of 1 lemon to prevent discoloration.

Cut the flesh into large pieces and put them through a blender. In a mixing bowl, make a sauce with the beaten egg yolk, seasoning, the mustard and the oil whisked in drop by drop. Add the avocado purée, the juice of the second lemon and a few drops of tabasco sauce.

This sauce can be used as an alternative to mayonnaise, or as an excellent dip for crudités.

Elle advises that this sauce should preferably be made immediately before it is to be eaten.

SAUCE BARBECUE
Barbecue sauce

PREPARATION TIME: 10 minutes
COOKING TIME: 25 minutes
TO MAKE 500 ML (18 FL OZ) OF SAUCE

5 tablespoons olive oil
3 onions
200 g (7 oz) tomato purée
4 tablespoons cider vinegar
100 ml (3½ fl oz) white wine
100 ml (3½ fl oz) Worcester
  sauce

3 sprigs thyme
1 bay leaf
2 cloves of garlic
4 tablespoons honey
1 teaspoon Dijon mustard
salt, pepper
tabasco sauce (optional)

In a heavy saucepan, gently heat together the oil and the chopped onions until the onion is transparent. Stir constantly. Extend the tomato purée with the vinegar and add to the onions.

Allow to bubble for 2 minutes and then add the wine, the Worcester sauce, the herbs and crushed garlic, the honey and the mustard. Mix together and adjust the heat so that the sauce simmers. Continue cooking and stirring for 15 minutes until a creamy sauce results.

Season to taste and, if desired, add a few drops of tabasco sauce.

This sauce goes well with roast or grilled fish, poultry or meat, as well as making one of the sauces for a fondu bourguignonne. It keeps well in the refrigerator.

SAUCE CHARCUTIÈRE
A sauce for roast or grilled pork

PREPARATION TIME: 5 minutes
COOKING TIME: 35 minutes
FOR SIX

1 large onion
1 dessertspoon lard
1 heaped tablespoon flour
250 ml (9 fl oz) dry white wine

1 tablespoon capers
3 gherkins
salt pepper

Chop the onion and heat with the lard in a saucepan, cooking gently until the onion becomes transparent. Add the flour at this point and continue the cooking, stirring constantly, until the mixture begins to take a little colour. Add the white wine all at once and bring to the boil while mixing in 75 ml (2½ fl oz) of water.

Continue cooking over a low heat for half an hour, stirring constantly. During this time, the sauce should be reduced in volume by about one-third. Add the capers and the trimmed gherkins cut into round slices; season.

This sauce goes particularly well with roast pork or pan-fried pork chops. The juices in which the meat has been cooked should be deglazed by adding a tablespoon of boiling water, vigorously stirring with the back of a fork, then mixing in with the sauce.

SAUCE AU CONCOMBRE
Cucumber sauce

PREPARATION TIME: 20 minutes (one hour in advance)
COOKING TIME: nil
FOR SIX

Half a good-sized cucumber
200 ml (7 fl oz) crème fraîche
4 sprigs of tarragon

2 tablespoons wine vinegar
salt, pepper

Peel the cucumber and chop it finely by hand. Spread the chopped cucumber on to a dish, sprinkle it lightly with salt and leave to sweat for an hour. At the end of that time, drain it and press it in a clean cloth or between sheets of kitchen paper in order to remove excessive moisture.

Put the cream into a serving bowl and add the cucumber, the chopped tarragon and the vinegar. Season and mix well together.

This sauce should be served, as soon as prepared, with cold poached trout or any other cold fish.

HOLLANDAISE ET BÉARNAISE
Two hot sauces

SAUCE HOLLANDAISE
PREPARATION TIME: 2 minutes
COOKING TIME: 12 minutes
FOR SIX

3 egg yolks	250 g (9 oz) butter
2 tablespoons cider vinegar	1 lemon
salt, pepper	

In the round-bottomed upper vessel of a double-boiler, beat together the egg yolks and the vinegar, seasoned with salt and pepper. Heat the water in the lower vessel until it is hot but *not* boiling. Warm the beaten mixture through and add the butter piece by piece, stirring constantly, until the sauce has the consistency of mayonnaise.

Season and add lemon juice drop by drop, to taste.

SAUCE BÉARNAISE
PREPARATION TIME: 5 minutes
COOKING TIME: 10 minutes
FOR SIX

150 ml (5 fl oz) wine vinegar	salt, pepper
5 chopped shallots	250 g (9 oz) butter
2 tablespoons chopped tarragon	1 tablespoon chopped chervil
3 egg yolks	

Put the chopped shallots, the vinegar and 1 tablespoon of chopped tarragon into the upper vessel of a double-boiler and reduce it over a brisk heat until all the liquid has evaporated. Leave to cool.

Beat in the egg yolks together with 2 tablespoons of water and seasoning. Heat the water in the lower vessel of the double-boiler, then add the butter piece by piece to the shallot mixture in the upper vessel, as with the hollandaise sauce above.

Before serving, mix in the rest of the tarragon, and the chervil.

Elle suggests that as all hot sauces are difficult to make, it may help if the egg yolks are beaten together with a little (half a teaspoon) of flour.

Béarnaise sauce is usually served with grilled meat or fish while hollandaise sauce goes better with vegetables, eggs or fish.

BEURRE AU GENIÈVRE
Juniper butter

PREPARATION TIME: 10 minutes
COOKING TIME: 10 minutes
FOR SIX

6 shallots	salt, freshly-ground pepper
2 cloves of garlic	juice of 2 lemons
16 juniper berries	1 tablespoon chopped parsley
250 (9 oz) butter	1 tablespoon chopped chives

Chop the shallots and crush the garlic. Crush the juniper berries either in a pestle and mortar or with the flat of the blade of a large kitchen knife.

Take a heavy saucepan, break the butter into pieces and melt it very slowly. Add the chopped shallots, crushed garlic and crushed juniper berries, cook together, stirring constantly. The butter must *not* be allowed to darken during the time that the shallots are being cooked.

Remove from the heat, season and stir in the lemon juice, the parsley and the chives.

This sauce goes particularly well with baked or boiled potatoes or with most poached fish.

LES MARINADES AU VIN
Wine marinades

PREPARATION TIME: 5 minutes
COOKING TIME: 25 minutes (for the cooked marinade)
TO MAKE 1 LITRE (36 FL OZ) OF MARINADE

1 onion	6–8 peppercorns
2 carrots	salt
bouquet garni	1 bottle of red wine
2 cloves of garlic	200 ml (7 fl oz) wine vinegar
1 head of celery	100 ml (3½ fl oz) oil
1 clove	

The uncooked marinade
This is used with all cuts of fresh meat and feathered game.

Put the meat into an earthenware dish, cover with chopped onion and chopped carrot, the bouquet garni, the crushed garlic, chopped celery, the clove and seasoning. Mix together with the wine, the vinegar and the oil.

Put in a cool place and turn from time to time.

The cooked marinade
This is used with red meats, for furred game and well-hung game.

Chop the onion, the carrots and the celery together. Cook them very gently in the oil: when they are soft, add the wine, vinegar, the bouquet garni, the garlic and seasoning. Cook together for 25 minutes and then leave to cool. Pour over the meat.

Elle advises that the uncooked marinade will last for 12–24 hours while the prepared marinade is good for 24–48 hours.

PESTO
Garlic and basil sauce

PREPARATION TIME: 15 minutes
COOKING TIME: nil
FOR SIX

1 large sprig of basil	salt, pepper
4 cloves of garlic	250 ml (9 fl oz) olive oil

Mash the basil and the peeled garlic together in a pestle and mortar. Put the mixture into a blender, season and add the oil. Blend briefly until a smooth green paste results.

This marvellous sauce is particularly suited to roast or grilled veal. With grated Parmesan or Emmenthaler cheese, one has a splendid accompaniment to spaghetti or rice dishes.

The sauce will keep for several weeks in a refrigerator.

SAUCE DOROTHÉE
A sauce for potatoes

PREPARATION TIME: 5 minutes
COOKING TIME: 5 minutes
FOR SIX

75 g (generous 2½ oz) butter
75 ml (generous 2½ oz) crème
 fraîche

1 teaspoon wine vinegar
salt, pepper

Melt the butter in a small saucepan. In a mixing bowl, beat together the cream, vinegar and seasoning. Stirring constantly, combine the mixture with the melted butter. Warm the sauce through in a double-boiler. According to some tastes, this sauce is improved by a sprinkling of chopped mixed herbs.

This sauce, always served hot, goes well with mashed or boiled potatoes.

SAUCE GRIBICHE
A sauce for cold fish

PREPARATION TIME: 20 minutes
COOKING TIME: nil
FOR SIX

3 hard-boiled eggs
1 tablespoon Dijon mustard
1 tablespoon wine vinegar
salt, pepper
250 ml (9 fl oz) olive oil
sprig of parsley

3 sprigs of tarragon
6 chives
1 shallot
1 tablespoon capers
1 chilli (optional)

Shell the eggs and separate yolks from whites. Chop up the whites.

Put the yolks into a mixing bowl, mash them and mix in the mustard, the vinegar and seasoning. Add the oil drop by drop and combine it as if making a mayonnaise.

Finely chop the herbs, the shallot and the capers and mix them into the sauce, together with the chopped egg whites.

This sauce goes very well with cold fish.

Elle suggests that to increase the flavour, crush a chilli and mix it in with the sauce.

SAUCE NANTUA
A shellfish sauce

PREPARATION TIME: 1 hour
COOKING TIME: 45 minutes
FOR 500 ML (18 FL OZ) OF SAUCE

For the béchamel
1 onion
1 shallot
30 g (1 oz) butter
35 g (1¼ oz) flour
750 ml (27 fl oz) cold boiled milk
5 sprigs of parsley
1 sprig of thyme
salt, pepper, nutmeg
200 ml (7 fl oz) double cream

For the shellfish butter
125 g (4½ oz) butter
bouquet garni
1 carrot, grated
1 small onion, chopped
1 clove of garlic
salt, pepper
8–10 uncooked Dublin Bay
prawns, or langoustines if
available
vinegar

The béchamel
Chop the onion and the shallot together and cook in melted butter over a low heat until they are transparent. Add the flour and cook for a further 2 minutes, stirring constantly.

Add the milk and bring to the boil while stirring. Then add the parsley, thyme, seasoning and a little grated nutmeg. Simmer over a very low heat; make sure by constant stirring with a wooden spoon that the mixture does not stick to the bottom of the pan. Reduce the volume of the sauce by one-third.

Pass everything through a conical strainer, and then cover with greaseproof paper to prevent a skin forming.

The shellfish butter
Warm 30 g (1 oz) of butter in a pan and cook the herbs, vegetables and garlic together; season them and let them simmer. Thoroughly clean and wipe the prawns. Raise the heat abruptly. Put the prawns in their shells into the pan and add a tablespoon of vinegar: when the prawns have all gone red, reduce the heat, cover the pan and continue cooking for 8–10 minutes. Remove from the heat and allow to cool.

(CONTINUED OPPOSITE)

SAUCE FRAÎCHE
A summer sauce

PREPARATION TIME: 5 minutes (2 hours in advance)
COOKING TIME: nil
FOR SIX

6 individual tubs of natural
yoghurt
3 tablespoons of chopped fresh
mint

1 chopped chilli
pinch of paprika
salt

Put all the ingredients into a blender and mix well together. Transfer the mixture into a bowl and leave in the refrigerator for 2 hours. Just before serving, garnish with a few leaves of fresh mint.

This light sauce goes well with grilled meat or kebabs, especially those made with lamb.

(CONTINUED)

Remove and peel the prawns and put to one side. Crush the complete shells in a grinder, add the rest of the butter, slightly softened, colour (if necessary) with 2 or 3 drops of cochineal and finely sieve the mixture, making sure that all the butter passes through.

Re-warm the béchamel sauce, mix in the cream and cook, stirring constantly until smooth. Put the pan over a saucepan of hot but not boiling water and beat in the shellfish butter knob by knob. Finish by adding the prawns to the sauce.

This is an excellent sauce with all fish.

SAUCE ROBERT
Monday sauce

PREPARATION TIME: 5 minutes
COOKING TIME: 25 minutes
FOR SIX

6 onions
60 g (2 oz) butter
30 g (1 oz) flour
100 ml (3½ fl oz) dry white wine

250 ml (9 fl oz) beef stock
salt, pepper
2 tablespoons Dijon mustard

Chop the onions and cook until transparent in the melted butter, stirring all the time. Sprinkle in the flour and, continuing to stir, cook for a few moments longer.

Add the white wine and the beef stock, and season. Remove from the heat, mix the mustard in well and serve at once.

This sauce goes very well with left-over or re-cooked meat.

SAUCE VERTE
Green sauce

PREPARATION TIME: 15 minutes
COOKING TIME: 5 minutes
FOR SIX

1 sprig of chervil
1 sprig of parsley
1 sprig of tarragon
50 g (scant 2 oz) watercress

50 g (scant 2 oz) spinach
250 ml (9 fl oz) prepared)
   mayonnaise

Weigh the chervil, the parsley and the tarragon so as to have 50 g (about 2 oz) in total. Blanch the herbs for 5 minutes, together with the watercress and the spinach, in salted boiling water. Remove from the heat and drain, then pass under cold running water and drain once more. Squeeze everything through a cloth in order to extract as much moisture as possible. Put through a fine sieve (or a blender) and then thoroughly mix the purée with the mayonnaise.

This sauce is excellent with fish, shellfish or hard-boiled eggs.

SAUCE PALOISE
A sauce for lamb

PREPARATION TIME: 10 minutes
COOKING TIME: 15 minutes
FOR SIX

tablespoons of fresh chopped mint	3 egg yolks
chopped shallots	salt, pepper
00 ml (3½ fl oz) wine vinegar	250 g (9 oz) butter

Put the chopped mint, chopped shallots and the vinegar together into a saucepan. Reduce over a brisk heat until all the liquid has evaporated.

Remove from the heat and whisk in the egg yolks, followed by 2 tablespoons of water; season. Put the mixture into a double-boiler and mix in the butter piece by piece, whisking all the time.

The chef of the 'L'Archestrate' restaurant in Paris from where this recipe comes, recommends that this sauce, intended to be served with lamb, be accompanied by a youngish claret.

SAUCE SOUBISE
Onion sauce

PREPARATION TIME: 20 minutes
COOKING TIME: 35 minutes
FOR SIX

2 kgs (4½ lb) onions	500 ml (18 fl oz) thick béchamel sauce
500 ml (18 fl oz) beef stock (or the same quantity of milk)	salt, pepper, nutmeg

This sauce is, in effect, a second vegetable to accompany meat dishes. With the traditional dish of a leg of lamb and haricot beans, it is particularly appreciated.

The flavour of the sauce will depend upon whether the onions are cooked in stock or in milk.

Chop the onions. Put them into boiling water and leave to blanch for 2 minutes after boiling point has been regained. Turn out into a strainer and run under cold water. Drain well.

Put the onions into a pan and just cover with either stock or milk. Cook slowly. When the onion has been reduced to a purée, evaporate any remaining liquid over a vigorous heat, stirring constantly.

Pass the onion purée through a fine sieve and mix it in with the béchamel sauce. Return to the heat and mix it together well without it coming to the boil. Season with salt, pepper and grated nutmeg.

Keep the sauce warm, dotting it from time to time with knobs of butter in order to avoid a skin forming. Stir well before serving.

SAUCE TOMATE
Tomato sauce

PREPARATION TIME: 10 minutes
COOKING TIME: 45 minutes
FOR SIX

1½ kgs (3¼ lb) tomatoes
2 cloves of garlic
2 small onions
150 ml (5 fl oz) olive oil
1 bay leaf

1 sprig of parsley
5 leaves of basil (or a sprig of
tarragon)
sugar
salt, pepper

Peel and halve the tomatoes and remove the seeds. Put them into a casserole together with the crushed garlic, the chopped onion, the oil and all the herbs. Cook the mixture over a vigorous heat until the tomato liquid has evaporated.

Taste the sauce and if it seems to be somewhat acid, add a little sugar. Pass through a sieve, and season.

The quality of the tomatoes used will determine the consistency of the sauce. If it seems to be too thin, reduce it quickly over a vigorous heat until the desired consistency is obtained.

Elle advises that this sauce will keep for a week in a refrigerator.

SAUCE THYM & SAUCE MOUTARDE
Thyme and mustard sauces

THYME SAUCE
PREPARATION TIME: 10 minutes
COOKING TIME: 10 minutes
FOR SIX

1 liqueur glass of white wine
1 teaspoon dried thyme
1 lemon
5 egg yolks

salt, pepper
300 g (10½ oz) butter
a little flour

Warm the white wine and soak the dried thyme in it for 20 minutes. In the upper vessel of a double-boiler, put the juice of half a lemon, the egg yolks, seasoning, the wine and thyme mixture, 100 g (3½ oz) butter cut into knobs and a pinch of flour. Whisk well together.

As soon as the mixture has taken, add 100 g (3½ oz) of the butter and when that has been amalgamated, the remainder of the butter. Allow to thicken in the double-boiler until the sauce attains the consistency of a good mayonnaise. If the sauce shows any tendency to separate, remove from the heat, add a tablespoon of iced water and whisk vigorously until the proper consistency is regained.

This sauce goes well with poultry.

MUSTARD SAUCE
Make the sauce in the same way as for the sauce above, but omit the chopped thyme, do not warm the white wine and extend it with 2 tablespoons of Dijon mustard.

This sauce goes well with grilled fish.

GÂTEAU DE THOISSEY
Orange chocolate cake

PREPARATION TIME: 40 minutes
COOKING TIME: 45 minutes
FOR SIX TO EIGHT

The filling	The cake mix
100 g (3½ oz) candied orange peel	4 eggs
80 ml (2¾ fl oz) orange liqueur	125 g (4½ oz) caster sugar
150 g (5 oz) plain cooking chocolate	125 g (4½ oz) flour
100 g (3½ oz) butter	75 g (good 2½ oz) softened butter
250 ml (9 fl oz) whipped cream	50 g (scant 2 oz) cocoa
	100 ml (3½ fl oz) orange liqueur

Prepare the filling first: finely chop the candied peel, cover with the orange liqueur and leave overnight.

Melt the chocolate over a low heat, and beat in the butter, the whipped cream, the chopped peel and liqueur. Mix well and leave to one side.

For the cake mix, break the eggs into a large saucepan and add the sugar. With a wooden spoon, gently work them together over an extremely low heat. When the ingredients are thoroughly mixed together, remove from the heat and continue to beat until the mixture has completely cooled. Shake the flour into the pan through a sieve and mix it without actually beating it in. Add the softened butter and cocoa powder, mix in these ingredients and put the mixture into a greased and floured cake tin.

Put the tin into a slow oven (140°C/275°F/Gas Mark 1) for 25 minutes. Then turn the cake out on to a wire cake rack and leave to cool. Cut the cake into 3 horizontal slices, soak each one with orange liqueur, coat them with filling and put them back together. Keep a little cream for spreading on the top and sides, cover the whole cake with chocolate (vermicelli) and serve very cool.

The chef of 'Le Chapon Fin' at Thoissey recommends a dry champagne to be drunk with this cake.

SUCCÈS
Layered meringue cake

PREPARATION TIME: 1 hour
COOKING TIME: 45 minutes
FOR A 25 cm (10-in) CAKE

The meringue slices	The filling
5 whites of egg	400 g (14 oz) sugar
1 teaspoon of flour	5 egg yolks
125 g (4½ oz) ground almonds	500 g (17½ oz) unsalted butter
125 g (4½ oz) caster sugar	200 g (7 oz) praline

In a bowl, whip the egg whites until they are quite stiff. While still whipping, incorporate the flour, the ground almonds and the sugar. Put the mixture into an icing bag with a large nozzle and make three 25 cm (10-in) spiral discs on a large greased baking sheet. Put these into a moderate oven (160°C/310°F/Gas Mark 2–3) for 45 minutes until they are crisp and a light golden colour. Remove them from the baking sheet and trim off any irregularities: keep these trimmings.

To make the filling, gently melt the sugar in a saucepan to the point where a drop falling from a fork forms a soft ball. Beat the egg yolks while adding the boiling syrup in the thinnest of streams, until the egg yolks whiten and can be lifted with a fork without breaking. Whip the butter into a cream, mix in praline made in the usual way and, whipping continuously, add this mixture to the eggs and sugar.

Put this mixture into an icing bag with a fluted nozzle. Take 1 of the meringue slices and cover with filling, working inwards from the outside edge. Leave a space in the middle which should be filled with the meringue trimmings.

Put the second slice on top and proceed to cover it with filling and meringue trimmings, as for the first slice. Spread the underside of the third slice thinly with the rest of the filling and cap the cake.

Refrigerate for at least 2 hours and sprinkle with icing sugar just before serving.

REINE DE SABA
Chocolate and hazelnut cake

PREPARATION TIME: 30 minutes
COOKING TIME: 1 hour
FOR A ROUND CAKE TIN OF 23 cm (9 in) IN DIAMETER AND 5 cm (2 in) HIGH

250 g (9 oz) plain cooking
   chocolate
250 ml (9 fl oz) clear honey
250 g (9 oz) butter
6 eggs

100 g (3½ oz) flour
2 teaspoons baking powder
125 g (4½ oz) chopped roasted
   hazelnuts

Put the pieces of chocolate on to aluminium foil in an open hot oven. Warm the honey so that it is quite liquified and very runny. When the chocolate is soft enough to be able to stick a finger into it, mix it into the honey. Add the butter (soft, but not melted) and the egg yolks. When the mixture is smooth, sieve the flour and baking powder into it and add the finely-chopped nuts. Beat the egg whites until stiff and then gently fold into the mixture. Pour the mixture into the cake tin, previously buttered and dusted with flour.

Put the cake into a fairly hot oven (200°C/400°F/Gas Mark 6) for an hour. Check the progress of cooking by inserting the blade of a knife which will come out clean when the cake is done.

Turn the cake out on to a wire cake rack to cool.

Elle advises that this cake will keep well for up to a week in a cool place. Thick honey can also be used quite satisfactorily.

CHARLOTTE AUX NOIX
Walnut charlotte

PREPARATION TIME: 45 minutes (the day before)
COOKING TIME: 5 minutes
FOR SIX

170 g (6 oz) butter
170 g (6 oz) caster sugar
100 g (3½ oz) crushed walnuts
200 g (7 oz) sponge fingers

The filling
2 egg yolks

25 g (scant 1 oz) caster sugar
200 ml (7 fl oz) milk

The sauce
100 g (3½ oz) plain cooking
   chocolate
40 g (1½ oz) butter

Cream the butter in a bowl and add the sugar little by little until a smooth mixture results. Add the finely-chopped nuts and mix well.

In another bowl, beat the egg yolks and the sugar together, then whisk in the milk. Pour into a heavy-bottomed saucepan and stir over a medium heat until it becomes a creamy custard; do not let it boil.

Remove from the heat and allow to cool. Then pour it over the butter mixture: stir them well together and put the filling on one side.

Line the bottom and sides of a charlotte mould with sponge fingers, flat sides inwards. Pour in half the filling, add a layer of fingers, then the rest of the filling, and finally another layer of fingers, this time flat-side outwards. Keep in the refrigerator overnight.

Just before serving, make the sauce by melting the chocolate and butter together with 2 tablespoons of water. Whip into a smooth consistency. Turn the charlotte out on to its serving dish and pour the chocolate sauce over it.

Elle advises that this dish from the Perigord is equally good when made with other types of biscuit.

BISCUIT À LA FRAMBOISINE
Raspberry jelly charlotte

PREPARATION TIME: 10 minutes
COOKING TIME: nil
FOR SIX TO EIGHT

5 tablespoons of Kirsch
300 g (10½ oz) sponge fingers
2 packets raspberry jelly, 142 g
 (5 oz) size
20 g (scant ¾ oz) flaked almonds

The Chantilly cream
250 ml (9 fl oz) double cream
vanilla essence

Melt the packets of raspberry jelly in 300 ml (10½ fl oz) boiling water, then add cold water to make up to a total volume of 1.15 litres (2 pints). Flavour it with 2 tablespoons of Kirsch, and leave to cool.

Dilute 3 tablespoons of Kirsch with about the same amount of water and very lightly sprinkle over the sponge fingers so that they are flavoured, but they must not become soft. Line the bottom and sides of a glass serving bowl with the fingers. Pour half the melted jelly into the serving dish, add a layer of sponge fingers, then the rest of the jelly. Sprinkle the surface with flaked almonds and leave to cool for at least 2 hours.

While the pudding is cooling, make the Chantilly cream by whipping a few drops of vanilla essence to taste into the double cream. Put into a cool place.

Serve the pudding directly from the dish, with the whipped cream separately.

Elle advises that this dish can easily be made the day before.

MOUSSE DU CHAT
Chocolate mousse

PREPARATION TIME: 15 minutes (the day before)
COOKING TIME: 5 minutes
FOR SIX

400 g (14 oz) caster sugar
500 g (17½ oz) plain cooking
 chocolate
8 eggs

400 g (14 oz) butter
packet of langues de chat
 biscuits

Put the sugar into a saucepan, just cover it with water and melt over a moderate heat, bringing the syrup to the boil.

Remove from the heat and stir in the chocolate, broken into lumps, until it is thoroughly melted and smooth. Then add the beaten egg yolks, and the butter added knob by knob, and continue to stir.

Whip the egg whites into stiff peaks and gently fold them into the chocolate mixture. Grease a 22 cm (8½ in) cake tin with butter and pour in the chocolate mixture; leave overnight in a refrigerator.

Just before serving, turn out on to a serving dish and decorate with langues de chat biscuits.

The chef, Madame Point, of the famous restaurant 'Pyramide' at Vienne, from where this recipe comes, says that a glass of cold water should be the only accompaniment to this dish.

PARFAIT AUX MARRONS
Chestnut parfait

PREPARATION TIME: 30 minutes (8–12 hours in advance)
COOKING TIME: nil
FOR SIX TO EIGHT

1 large tin of chestnut purée,
439 g (15½ oz) size
125 g (4½ oz) butter
150 g (5 oz) chopped marrons
glacés

100 ml (3½ fl oz) maraschino or
rum
375 ml (13 fl oz) double cream
50 g (1¾ oz) caster sugar
level teaspoon vanilla sugar
marrons glacés for decoration

Work the chestnut purée and the softened butter together into a smooth cream. Soak the chopped marrons glacés in the maraschino or rum. Whip ¾ of the cream and 30 g (1 oz) of sugar together, and fold into the chestnut cream, adding at the same time the chopped marrons glacés and the liquid they were soaked in.

Lightly grease a deep cake tin and pour in the chestnut mixture. Cover, and refrigerate overnight – but not in the freezer compartment.

Just before serving, put the mould briefly into warm water to release the parfait and turn out on to a serving dish. Whip the remaining cream, fold in the rest of the caster sugar and the vanilla sugar. Decorate the parfait with whipped cream and several whole marrons glacés.

CRÈME MOUSSEUSE AU CARAMEL
Caramel cream

PREPARATION TIME: 20 minutes
COOKING TIME: 15 minutes
FOR SIX TO EIGHT

200 g (7 oz) caster sugar
80 g (scant 3 oz) flour
3 large (or 4 smaller) eggs

1 litre (1¾ pints) milk
3 tablespoons caster sugar for
the caramel

Sieve sugar and flour together into a mixing bowl, make a well and put in the egg yolks. Mix well together, adding little by little enough cold milk to make a smooth cream. If necessary, beat to remove any lumps.

Boil the remaining milk and pour it, still boiling, into the cream, stirring vigorously. Put the mixture into a saucepan and bring to the boil, stirring all the time. Remove from the heat when the first large bubble appears. Allow to cool, stirring occasionally to prevent a skin forming.

Make a caramel with the 3 tablespoons of sugar and a little water. Have 100 ml (3½ fl oz) of hot water ready and pour it into the caramel as soon as it begins to colour; mix to dissolve it into the water. Pour the caramel into the cream mixture, again mixing well. Allow to cool thoroughly.

Whip the whites into stiff peaks and gently fold into the caramel cream. Serve really cold, accompanied by sweet biscuits.

ARDÉCHOIS
Chocolate chestnut pudding

PREPARATION TIME: 30 minutes – mostly in advance
COOKING TIME: 20 minutes – in advance
FOR A 1½ LITRE (2¾ PINT) CHARLOTTE MOULD

2 kg (4¼ lb) chestnuts
200 g (7 oz) caster sugar
150 g (5 oz) plain cooking
   chocolate

22½ g (scant ¾ oz) vanilla sugar
300 ml (10½ oz) single cream

A simple way to peel chestnuts is to cut a slit on their rounded sides and drop them into hot oil. They will open and shed their skins easily.

Put the peeled chestnuts into a pan of salted boiling water until they are cooked. Do not boil so vigorously that the chestnuts break into pieces. Drain and make a purée, either by using a vegetable mill followed by a fine metal sieve, or in a chopper attachment. The smoother the chestnut purée, the more delicious the dish will be.

Make a caramel with 125 g (4½ oz) of sugar, moistened with water and when it is boiling, remove from the heat, add the softened choco late, half the cream and two-thirds of the vanilla sugar. Stir together, and then mix it all into the chestnut purée.

Grease the mould and sprinkle it lightly with caster sugar, pour in the chestnut mixture and leave in a cool place for at least 4 hours and up to 12 hours if possible.

Whip the remainder of the cream, fold in the rest of the vanilla sugar and 75 g (2½ oz) caster sugar. Turn out the chestnut pudding on to a serving dsh and decorate it with the whipped cream, using a piping bag with a fluted nozzle.

RÉDUIT DE MONT-DE-MARSAN
Outlandish pudding

PREPARATION TIME: 15 minutes
COOKING TIME: 1 hour
FOR SIX

1 litre (1¾ pints) milk
250 g (9 oz) sugar
7½ g (¼ oz) vanilla sugar

6 eggs
15 g (½ oz) butter

Boil the milk in a large saucepan. Remove from the heat and stir in the sugars until dissolved.

Break the eggs into a bowl and beat them as if for an omelette. Continue beating and slowly add the hot milk, thoroughly mixing together.

Take ¾ of this mixture and put it into a greased round cake tin. Cook in a moderate oven (180°C/350°F/Gas Mark 4) for about 50 minutes. Allow to cool and turn out on to a serving dish.

Put the rest of the mixture into a saucepan and thicken it over a low heat, stirring frequently with a wooden spoon. It must not be allowed to boil, and will be ready when it coats the back of a spoon. Allow the cream to cool and then pour over the pudding.

Elle says that this is a light dish from the Landes and will be welcome at the end of a heavy meal.

FROMAGE BLANC AUX AMANDES
Almond cheese

PREPARATION TIME: 10 minutes, plus 15 minutes for the cream
COOKING TIME: 5 minutes
FOR SIX

500 g (17½ oz) fromage blanc, or cottage cheese	The cream
	2 eggs
125 g (4½ oz) ground almonds	40 g (scant 1½ oz) caster sugar
125 g (4½ oz) caster sugar	20 g (¾ oz) flour
150 g (5 oz) seedless raisins	250 ml (9 fl oz) milk
1 lemon	pinch of vanilla sugar

Put the fromage blanc or cottage cheese into a sieve and let it drain.

Prepare the cream. Beat the eggs and sugar together in a pan, then add the flour, continuing to beat until completely smooth. Boil the milk together with the vanilla sugar and add it slowly to the cream, stirring continually with a wooden spoon. Put the pan on the heat and, still stirring, bring to the boil; after 1 or 2 big bubbles have appeared, remove from the heat and allow to cool.

Mix the ground almonds and sugar together. Put the cheese into a bowl and mix in the almond-sugar mixture, the prepared cream, the raisins and a little grated lemon peel. Turn into a serving dish, decorate with twists of lemon peel and a few raisins and chill before serving.

Elle advises that the amount of grated lemon peel used should be carefully judged. Its flavour should be evident without dominating either that of the cheese or the almonds. The dish can be made in advance.

SURPRISE À L'ORANGE
Orange surprise

PREPARATION TIME: 30 minutes
COOKING TIME: 20–25 minutes
FOR SIX

The Genoese cake	175 g (6 oz) caster sugar
2 eggs	5 egg yolks
75 g (2½ oz) caster sugar	12 g (scant ½ oz) powdered
pinch of salt	gelatine
75 g (2½ oz) flour	2 oranges
20 g (¾ oz) butter	250 ml (9 fl oz) double cream
	cochineal
The cream	10 sponge fingers
500 ml (17½ fl oz) milk	2 tablespoons of rum

Make a Genoese cake in a tin 3 cm (1 in) deep and 22 cm (8½ in) in diameter. Begin by beating the eggs, sugar and salt together in a saucepan: warm the mixture through until it is too hot for the touch beating all the time. Remove from the heat and continue beating until the mixture has doubled its original volume, and a ribbon falls when an immersed wooden spoon is lifted clear of the surface. Mix in the flour and then the melted butter and put the mixture into the cake tin lined with greaseproof paper. Cook in a moderate oven (170°C 320°F/Gas Mark 3) for 20–25 minutes.

Next make the cream. Boil the milk with ½ the sugar. Beat the rest of the sugar and the egg yolks together in a saucepan and, over a gentle heat, pour on the milk slowly until the cream coats the back of a wooden spoon. Remove from the heat and stir in the gelatine which should have been dissolved in a little of the juice from 1 of the oranges. Stir until the gelatine has thoroughly dissolved, and add the chopped peel of the 2 oranges. Let the mixture cool, beating from time to time.

Whip the cream, colour it with a few drops of cochineal and fold it into the cream mixture. Put the Genoese cake on to its serving plate and surround it with halved sponge fingers. Sprinkle the cake with a mixture of rum and the remaining orange juice, putting any surplus into the cream. Pour the cream over the cake and refrigerate until just before serving.

PARFAIT GLACÉ AUX FRAMBOISES
Iced raspberry parfait

PREPARATION TIME: 1 hour
FREEZING TIME: 6 hours (or overnight)
FOR AN OBLONG CAKE TIN 24 cm (9 in) LONG

350 g (¾ lb) caster sugar
8 egg yolks
200 g (7 oz) raspberries
400 ml (14 fl oz) double cream

raspberry essence
cochineal
250 g (9 oz) sponge fingers
2 liqueur glasses of Kirsch

Using 250 g (9 oz) of the sugar and 250 ml (9 fl oz) of water, bring to a gentle boil to make a syrup, and continue boiling until it reaches the soft-ball stage (115°C/238°F on a sugar thermometer).

Take a thick-bottomed saucepan and beat the egg yolks; adding the syrup bit by bit. Put the pan over a low heat and continue beating until the mixture forms a ribbon when the whisk is lifted above the surface. Do not let it boil. Remove from the heat and continue beating until the mixture has thoroughly cooled.

Mash ¾ of the raspberries into a purée, and whip the same amount of the cream. Mix together in a bowl the egg and syrup mixture, the purée of raspberries, and the whipped cream. Flavour with a few drops of raspberry essence and colour with a little cochineal.

Make a thin syrup with the rest of the sugar, 200 ml (7 fl oz) of water and flavour it with the Kirsch. Quickly soak the sponge fingers in this syrup.

Line the cake tin with greaseproof paper and put a layer of mixture in the bottom. Cover with a layer of sponge fingers, and continue with successive layers of mixture and sponge fingers, ending with a layer of mixture. Put into the freezer for at least 6 hours.

Turn out the parfait on to a rectangular serving dish. Whip the rest of the cream and use this and the remaining raspberries to decorate the dish.

TARTE NORVÉGIENNE
Norwegian meringue

PREPARATION TIME: 30 minutes
COOKING TIME (PASTRY): about 25 minutes
(FINAL): 15 minutes
FOR SIX

1 packet of frozen puff pastry,
370 g (13 oz) size
400 g (14 oz) raspberries
125 g (4½ oz) caster sugar

1 litre block (35 fl oz) vanilla ice
cream
3 egg whites
icing sugar

Roll out the pastry to a thickness of 4 mm (⅙ in) and line a greased round cake tin of about 24 cm (9 in) in diameter. Leave to rest in a cool place for at least 30 minutes.

The pastry case should be blind-baked. Cut a circular piece of greaseproof paper big enough to give a border of at least 4 cm (1½ in) all round the edge of the cake tin, and put it over the pastry, pressing it lightly down into shape. Cover the bottom of the cake tin with dried beans, putting in enough to be able to pile them up around the sides. Heat an oven to 220°C/425°F/Gas Mark 7 and put in the pastry: when the edges are firm, discard the dried beans and greaseproof paper and continue in the oven until the base of the pastry case is quite cooked. Remove the case from its tin and leave to cool.

During this time, sprinkle sugar over the raspberries, mixing gently so none of the fruit is bruised. About 20 minutes before the dish is to be served, drain the raspberries and arrange them in the pastry case. Then add the vanilla ice cream, cut into slices, and place in layers over the fruit. Beat the egg whites very stiffly, sieving in about 100 g (3½ oz) caster sugar, and spread thickly over the ice cream.

Decorate the surface with a fork, dust with sieved icing sugar, and put the dish for 15 minutes in an oven, pre-heated to its maximum until the meringue surface is crisp and the peaks golden-brown. Serve at once

SORBET AUX PÊCHES
Peach sorbet

PREPARATION TIME: 1 hour (the day before)
COOKING TIME (PEACHES): 20 minutes
FOR SIX TO EIGHT

The Sorbet
500 g (good lb) peaches
2 ripe apricots
300 g (10½ oz) caster sugar
2 tablespoons lemon juice

Peach mixture
4 peaches
150 g (5 oz) caster sugar
maraschino (optional)

Peel and stone 500 g (1 lb) of peaches and the apricots and put them in a blender. Make a purée, and add sufficient water to make 1 litre (1¾ pints) of liquid. Add the 300 g (10½ oz) of sugar and blend until the sugar is absorbed. Strain through a fine sieve and stir in the lemon juice.

Put the liquid into an electrical ice-cream machine and make a sorbet in the freezer. When the machine has completed its cycle, stir the sorbet, cover and leave in the freezer for at least 6 hours more. If an ice-cream machine is not available, make the sorbet in the traditional way.

Plunge the 4 peaches briefly into boiling water and peel them. Cut each peach into 6 segments. Take a wide-bottomed saucepan and with the 150 g (5 oz) of sugar and 6 tablespoons of water, make a light syrup. Put the peach segments into the syrup, return to the boil and then immediately remove the pan from the heat. Allow to cool.

Divide the peaches among the required number of sundae glasses, and just cover the fruit with syrup, if necessary reducing the syrup over a brisk heat. Put in a cool place.

Just before serving, add a teaspoon of maraschino to each glass and top the fruit with a ball of sorbet formed with an ice-cream scoop or rounded spoon.

COUPES GLACÉES AUX PRUNEAUX
Iced prune whip

PREPARATION TIME: 15 minutes (the day before)
COOKING TIME: 20 minutes
FOR SIX

250 g (9 oz) dried prunes
100 g (3½ oz) caster sugar
250 g (9 oz) fromage blanc or cottage cheese

15 g (½ oz) vanilla sugar
150 ml (5 fl oz) double cream
6 prunes preserved in Armagnac

Soak the prunes in water for 12 hours and then cook them in the same water for 15–20 minutes over a low heat. Drain and stone them and put them through a blender.

Vigorously beat together the prune purée, the caster sugar and the drained fromage blanc or cottage cheese. Add the vanilla sugar to the double cream and whisk to the point where the cream just begins to stiffen and then incorporate it into the prune mixture. Using an icing bag, fill individual sundae glasses with the prune whip and put into the freezer. The glasses should be transferred into a refrigerator for an hour before serving.

As a final touch, top each glass with a preserved prune.

Elle advises that this dish can be kept for some days in the freezer.

CAFÉ ET CHOCOLAT LIÉGOIS
Coffee and chocolate whip

PREPARATION TIME: 10 minutes
COOKING TIME: 15 minutes
FREEZING TIME: 6 hours
FOR FIVE OR SIX

The ice cream	instant coffee
1 litre (1¾ pints) milk	50 g (scant 2 oz) coffee beans
8 egg yolks	50 g (scant 2 oz) cocoa powder
100 g (3½ oz) sugar	50 g (scant 2 oz) caster sugar
15 g (½ oz) vanilla sugar	500 ml (17½ fl oz) double cream

Begin with the ice cream. Make a crème anglaise (custard) with the ingredients given. If a coffee flavour is required, stir black coffee to taste into the custard while it is still warm, remembering that the subsequent freezing will reduce the depth of flavour. For a chocolate flavour, mix the cocoa powder into the milk before boiling it, and increase the quantity of sugar by half.

Freeze the ice cream either in a machine or by the traditional method. After the ice cream is made, keep it in the freezer for at least 6 hours before proceeding to the next phase.

Just before serving, whip the cream to double its volume, stopping just before it begins to stiffen. Put in the refrigerator. Then continue with one of the following methods:

Coffee Whip: Make 250 ml (9 fl oz) of black coffee to your own taste. Sugar sparingly. Chill it in the refrigerator, together with the required number of sundae glasses. Put 2 tablespoons of coffee in the bottom of each glass and fill it with coffee ice cream: do not press the ice cream down so that the glasses are completely filled. Top each one with chilled whipped cream and decorate with a few coffee beans.
Chocolate Whip: Fill the chilled glasses with chocolate ice cream, top with chilled whipped cream and dust with cocoa powder or chocolate vermicelli.

MOUSSE AUX MARRONS
Chestnut mousse

PREPARATION TIME: 20 minutes
COOKING TIME: nil
FOR SIX

250 g (9 oz) icing sugar	300 ml (10½ fl oz) double cream
200 g (7 oz) butter	200 g (7 oz) chopped marrons
2 liqueur glasses of rum	glacés
1 kg (2¼ lb) vanilla-flavoured	6 whole marrons glacés
chestnut purée	

Work the sugar, the softened butter and the rum together in a bowl. Add the chestnut purée and mix everything well together.

Whip the cream to double its volume and fold it gently into the chestnut mixture with a spatula, trying to maintain the lightness of the whipped cream. Add the chopped chestnuts at the same time.

Using an icing-bag with a fluted nozzle, divide the mousse among individual serving glasses. Decorate each one with a whole marron glacé and serve chilled.

SALADE D'ORANGES
Orange salad

PREPARATION TIME: 20 minutes (4 hours in advance)
COOKING TIME (SYRUP): about 5 minutes
FOR SIX TO EIGHT

8 oranges
200 g (7 oz) black grapes
250 g (9 oz) caster sugar

Thoroughly wash the skins of the oranges. Slice 2 of them into rings, collecting any juices escaping.

Peel the remaining oranges, divide them into segments and peel each of these. Again, collect any resulting juice.

Line the inside of a glass fruit bowl with orange rings and pile the centre with orange segments and black grapes. If preferred, remove the pips from the grapes. Cover with any remaining orange slices and pour in the juice collected during peeling and slicing.

Add a glass (7 fl oz) of water to the sugar and boil to a syrup. Pour this over the oranges, decorate with a few more black grapes and serve chilled.

Elle suggests that a fruit-based liqueur may be poured on to this dish as it is served. A red Côtes de Fronsac is the recommended wine to drink with this dish.

POMMES AUX AMANDES
Apples with almonds

PREPARATION TIME: 10 minutes
COOKING TIME: 25 minutes
FOR SIX

6 eating apples
1 lemon
6 slices of bread
40 g (1½ oz) butter
75 g (good 2½ oz) ground
  almonds
100 g (3½ oz) brown sugar
100 ml (3½ fl oz) double cream
1 tablespoon of rum or Kirsch,
  etc.

Peel the apples and core them without hollowing them all the way through. Sprinkle with lemon juice to prevent discoloration.

Cut the crusts from the slices of bread and butter them thickly on one side. Arrange them side by side, butter side downwards, in an oven-proof dish and put an apple on to each slice.

Mix the ground almonds, the brown sugar and the cream together into a paste and flavour it with the tablespoon of liqueur. Fill the centres of the apples with the mixture and put the dish into a fairly hot oven (200°C/400°F/Gas Mark 6) until cooked.

Serve warm with cream, and with caster sugar sprinkled over them.

Elle advises that apples which keep their shape during cooking should be used: Cox's Orange Pippins are ideal.

[166]

FIGUES À LA CRÈME
Figs in cream

PREPARATION TIME: 10 minutes
COOKING TIME: nil
FOR SIX

18 fresh figs
250 ml (9 fl oz) double cream
2 tablespoons of brandy
2 tablespoons of crème de cacao (liqueur)

Mix the cream with the brandy and liqueur and keep in a cool place.

Trim, wash and dry the figs and cut them in quarters. Arrange the pieces in individual serving bowls, cover them with cream and serve chilled.

Elle advises that it is better to make this dessert 2 hours in advance of serving so that the fruit can soak up some of the flavour of the liqueurs.

COURONNE DE FRUITS EN GELÉE
Fruit and jelly ring

PREPARATION TIME: 45 minutes
COOKING TIME (JELLY): 5 minutes
SETTING TIME: 4–5 hours
FOR A 24 cm (9 in) DIAMETER RING MOULD

1 packet of orange jelly, 142 g (5 oz) size
1 tin of sliced peaches, 411 g (14½ oz) size
1 tin of mixed fruits, 822 g (1 lb 13 oz) size
250 g (9 oz) fresh strawberries

Melt the orange jelly according to the instructions. Drain the syrup from the peaches and mixed fruit and add to the melted jelly. Pour just under 1 cm (½ in) of jelly into the bottom of the ring mould and put in the refrigerator until it has just set.

Arrange all the fruits in a varied pattern around the inside of the ring mould, taking care not to press them too close together. Fill the ring mould with more jelly, seeing that it penetrates into all the spaces between the fruit. Pour the rest of the jelly into a flat dish and put both ring mould and dish into a refrigerator for at least 4 hours, when they should both have set quite firmly.

Put the mould in warm water briefly until the fruit and jelly ring turns out easily on to its serving dish. Chop up the sheet of jelly from the dish and use it to decorate the interior and surrounds of the jelly ring. Serve with double cream.

SOUPE AUX QUATRE FRUITS
Four-fruit salad

PREPARATION TIME: 20 minutes
COOKING TIME: 5 minutes
FOR SIX

300 g (10½ oz) strawberries
250 g (9 oz) raspberries
250 g (9 oz) cherries
250 g (9 oz) redcurrants
300 g (10½ oz) caster sugar
2 tablespoons of Kirsch

Rinse and dry the strawberries and remove their stalks. Make a purée of them in a blender, remove to a pan, add the sugar and put over a low heat until the sugar has completely dissolved. Allow to cool, then add the Kirsch.

Rinse and drain the other fruit, remove their stalks and stone the cherries. Mix them all together in the serving bowl, pour on the strawberry purée and put in a refrigerator for 2 hours. Serve with whipped cream.

Elle advises that this delicious dessert can be prepared the day before.

FRAISES AU VIN
Strawberries in wine

PREPARATION TIME: 10 minutes
COOKING TIME: 5 minutes
FOR SIX

1 kg (2¼ lb) strawberries
1 litre (1¾ pints) good red wine
1 stick of cinnamon
1 vanilla pod
3 cloves
150 g (5 oz) caster sugar

Put the wine into a saucepan with the cinnamon, vanilla pod, the cloves and sugar. Bring it to the boil, remove from the heat and let it cool.

Wash the strawberries, removing their stalks and dry them on kitchen paper. Arrange them in a glass serving bowl and pour the wine over them through a strainer. Cool in the refrigerator before serving.

Elle advises that the wine should not be added to the strawberries more than an hour before serving, or the fruit will lose its firmness.

CHAUD-FROID DE FRUITS ROUGES
Hot and cold fruit pudding

PREPARATION TIME: 10 minutes (1 hour in advance)
COOKING TIME: negligible
FOR SIX

200 g (7 oz) wild strawberries
200 g (7 oz) raspberries
1 lemon
100 g (3½ oz) caster sugar

750 ml (26 fl oz) vanilla ice
cream
50 ml (about 3 tablespoons)
fruit-based liqueur or
eau-de-vie

Hull the strawberries and put them with the raspberries into a dish, sprinkle them with the juice of the lemon and the sugar. Leave to one side for about an hour.

Chill the serving bowl in the refrigerator. Just before serving, put 6 large scoops of ice cream into the bowl and return it to the refrigerator.

Pour the fruit, their juices and the sugar into a small saucepan and quickly bring to the boil. As soon as the liquid bubbles, remove from the heat and pour in the liqueur. Flame it and pour the contents of the pan into the serving bowl at once.

Elle advises that the serving bowl must be able to withstand the rapid changes in temperature during the preparation of this dish.

RØDGRØD DE FRUITS ROUGE
Compote of red berries

PREPARATION TIME: 5 minutes
COOKING TIME: 30 minutes in advance
FOR SIX

3 packets of frozen unsweetened
strawberries, 225 g (8 oz) size
3 packets of frozen unsweetened
raspberries, 225 g (8 oz) size

semolina
caster sugar
2 lemons
500 ml (17½ fl oz) double cream

Remove the strawberries and raspberries from their packets and put them in blocks into a saucepan and defrost them over a low heat. Pass the contents through a fine sieve and measure the volume of fruit purée obtained. Put it back into the pan and bring to the boil.

To each litre (1¾ pints) of purée, add 60 g (2 oz) semolina, 80 g (scant 3 oz) of sugar and the juice of 2 lemons. Cook together for 15 minutes, stirring frequently. Pour into a serving bowl, allow to cool and refrigerate for at least 2 hours.

Just before serving, whip the cream with 50 ml (scant 2 fl oz) of very cold water. The aim is to chill the cream and not to make a chantilly. Each person should serve himself separately with compote and chilled cream.

Elle says that fresh fruit can, of course, be used when in season. This Danish compote is very good made only with either strawberries or raspberries.

MOUSSE À L'ORANGE
Orange mousse

PREPARATION TIME: 10 minutes
COOKING TIME: 10 minutes
FOR SIX

25 g (scant 1 oz) flour
3 eggs
100 g (3½ oz) caster sugar

grated peel of 1 orange
3–4 oranges to produce 250 ml
(9 fl oz) juice

In a saucepan, mix together the flour, egg yolks, ¾ of the sugar and the grated orange peel. Stir in the orange juice.

Bring the contents of the pan slowly to the boil, stirring constantly with a wooden spoon. The cream will thicken and will be ready when it coats the back of the spoon. Allow to cool, stirring occasionally to prevent a skin forming.

Beat the egg whites stiffly until peaks can be formed, mixing in the rest of the sugar at the same time. Using a spatula, fold the egg whites carefully into the cream, lifting and incorporating gently.

Put the mousse into its serving bowl and chill before serving.

Elle says that this mousse makes a good dessert at the end of a heavy meal. Serve with plain sweet biscuits.

SOUFFLÉ SALZBOURGEOIS
Salzburg soufflé

PREPARATION TIME: 10 minutes
COOKING TIME: 15–18 minutes
FOR SIX

4 egg yolks
1 lemon
8 egg whites
pinch of salt

75 g (generous 2½ oz) caster
sugar
7½ g (¼ oz) vanilla sugar
50 g (1¾ oz) flour

Pre-heat a very hot oven (230°C/450°F/Gas Mark 8).

Beat the egg yolks and mix in the grated rind of the lemon. Beat the egg whites and, when they have begun to stiffen, sieve in the caster and vanilla sugars. Continue beating the whites until they are very stiff.

Using a spatula, fold 1 spoonful of beaten whites into the beaten yolks. Then, in reverse, put the yolk mixture into the whites, quickly shake on the flour through a sieve and carefully fold the mixture together, lifting it up with the spatula.

Generously butter an oval dish. Turn the mixture into the dish, making 3 separate mounds (which will run together). Put the dish on to the lowest shelf of the oven. Cook for 15–18 minutes; when ready, the soufflé will be golden-brown on the surface and will still be soft inside.

Sprinkle with icing sugar and serve immediately.

Elle advises that it is easier to cook this soufflé properly if a metal dish (either copper or stainless steel) is used.

SOUFFLÉ GLACÉ
Iced soufflés

PREPARATION TIME: 1 hour
FREEZING TIME: 6 hours
FOR 12 SMALL RAMEKINS OR A SINGLE DISH 18 cm (7 in) IN DIAMETER

400 g (14 oz) caster sugar *70 ml (2½ fl oz) white rum*
10 egg yolks *3 tablespoons cocoa powder*
1 litre (35 fl oz) double cream *oil*
2 tablespoons of raspberry syrup

With a pastry brush, lightly paint the insides of the ramekins with oil
and sprinkle them with a little sugar. Put a band of greaseproof paper
or foil 8 cm (3 in) wide around each dish so that the top stands 4 cm (a
good 1½ in) above the edge.

Put the sugar into a saucepan, moisten it, and boil it to the soft-ball
stage (115°C/238°F on a sugar thermometer). Beat the egg yolks
together in a bowl, then, continuing to beat, add the boiling syrup in a
thin stream, as one would do with oil when making mayonnaise. Put
the pan over a low heat and go on beating until the mixture, when lifted
up with the wooden spoon, forms a ribbon. (If wished, this stage can
be done the day before: in this case, the egg-syrup should be kept in
an airtight jar.) Allow to cool thoroughly.

Lightly beat the cream to a chantilly and fold the egg-syrup into it.
Divide into 3 parts and mix in to each one of the chosen flavours.

Fill each ramekin up to the level of the top of the paper collar and
freeze for 6 hours before serving. These soufflés will keep frozen for
more than a week, but put them in the refrigerator for an hour before
serving.

Elle says that a lighter soufflé can be made by using egg whites
instead of the yolks.

SOUFFLÉ AU GRAND MARNIER
Grand marnier soufflé

PREPARATION TIME: 15 minutes
COOKING TIME: 30–35 minutes
FOR SIX: A SOUFFLE DISH 18 cm (ABOUT 7 in) IN DIAMETER

50 g (scant 2 oz) butter *40 g (scant 1½ oz) caster sugar*
50 g (scant 2 oz) flour *3 eggs*
15 g (½ oz) cornflour *liqueur glass of Grand Marnier*
7½ g (¼ oz) vanilla sugar *1 sponge finger*
250 ml (9 fl oz) milk

Heat the butter in a large saucepan until it foams. Put the flour and
cornflour in all at once and remove the pan from the heat; mix the flour
and butter together. Add the vanilla sugar.

Bring the milk to the boil, stir in the sugar and pour into the large
saucepan. Stir well and bring the mixture to the boil, allow it to thicken
slightly, then add the egg yolks one by one, beating each one in
thoroughly.

Soak the sponge finger in Grand Marnier and add the rest of the
liqueur to the mixture in the saucepan.

Beat the egg whites stiffly and carefully fold them into the mixture,
using a spatula. Generously butter the inside of the soufflé dish and
dust the whole of the greased surface with caster sugar. Half-fill the
dish with soufflé mixture, sprinkle the surface with broken pieces of
the soaked sponge finger, then fill the dish to the top with the rest of the
mixture.

Pre-heat a fairly hot oven for 20 minutes (200°C/400°F/Gas Mark 6)
and cook for about 25 minutes. The top should be brown and a thin
skewer plunged into the centre should come out clean.

OMELETTE SOUFFLÉ
Fluffy omelette

PREPARATION TIME: 20 minutes
COOKING TIME: 12–15 minutes
FOR SIX

6 eggs
150 g (5 oz) caster sugar
pinch of salt
rum or any preferred liqueur

30 g (1 oz) cornflour
12 sponge fingers
icing sugar

Separate whites and yolks, and lightly beat the yolks, with a tablespoon of sugar, a pinch of salt and 2 tablespoons of the chosen liqueur.

Beat the whites until stiff and add the rest of the sugar bit by bit, continuing to beat until the whites are very stiff and shiny.

Sieve the cornflour into the egg yolk mixture, and then immediately fold this mixture into the beaten whites, lifting carefully with a spatula.

Take an oval ovenproof dish and place 4 sponge fingers, soaked in liqueur, in the bottom. Cover them with a layer of soufflé mixture, then 4 more sponge fingers and more mixture until biscuits and mixture are used up. Shape the edges of the mixture with a spatula, clean off the edges of the dish and generously sprinkle the soufflé with icing sugar.

Cook in an oven, pre-heated to its maximum, for 12–15 minutes. As soon as the surface of the soufflé becomes golden-brown, cover with a piece of kitchen paper, pre-cut to shape, while it finishes cooking.

OMELETTE AU RHUM
Rum omelette

PREPARATION TIME: 5 minutes
COOKING TIME: 10 minutes
FOR SIX

8 eggs
pinch of salt
caster sugar

60 g (2 oz) butter
100 ml (3½ fl oz) rum

When ready to make the dish, beat the eggs together well, add a pinch of salt and a level dessertspoon of sugar (too much sugar will over-brown the omelette during cooking).

Put the butter into the omelette pan and heat to the point where it is about to darken. Pour in the beaten eggs all together and shake the pan during cooking so that the omelette cooks without forming a thick skin. If necessary, stir the mixture with the back of a fork. While the surface of the omelette is still runny, fold it in half and allow the joined edges to finish cooking. Turn the omelette out into a warmed serving dish and generously sprinkle with sugar.

Warm the rum in a small saucepan, pour it over the omelette, light it and carry the dish to the table at once. This quickly and easily improvised dish will give great pleasure.

CRÊPES AUX BANANES
Banana pancakes

PREPARATION TIME: 30 minutes (part 1 hour in advance)
COOKING TIME (BANANAS): 25 minutes
(IN OVEN): 10–12 minutes

FOR SIX

6 bananas
200 g (7 oz) butter
6 pancakes
caster sugar
rum

The pancake batter (sufficient for
10–12 pancakes)
100 g (3½ oz) flour
1 egg
1 egg yolk
2 tablespoons melted butter
1 teaspoon sugar
4 tablespoons milk
4 tablespoons water
pinch of salt

Make the pancake batter and leave it to stand for 1 hour. It should be thin enough to cover the bottom of the pan, or griddle, quickly. The pancakes can be made the day before and kept in a cool place, covered with a damp cloth. They should be thin ones.

Melt the butter over a very low flame and cook the peeled bananas until they take on a golden colour and are beginning to soften. Generously sprinkle them with sugar, and pour in 3 tablespoons of rum. Put the pan into a warm oven, basting occasionally, until the bananas are caramelised. (The success of the dish depends upon the skill with which this is done.)

Roll each banana in a pancake and arrange them in a flat ovenproof gratin dish. Dot with butter, sprinkle with sugar and with rum; heat through in a fairly hot oven (200°C/400°F/Gas Mark 6).

If desired, the pancakes can be served flambéed with rum.

Elle suggests that any pancakes made and left over may be frozen and used later.

CRÊPIAU AUX POMMES
Apple pancake

PREPARATION TIME: 15 minutes
COOKING TIME: 8–12 minutes
FOR SIX, USING A PAN 28 cm (11 in) IN DIAMETER

3 eating apples
icing sugar
200 g (7 oz) flour
pinch of salt

4 small eggs
250 ml (9 fl oz) milk
125 g (4½ oz) butter

Peel and core the apples and cut them into thin slices and sprinkle them with a good tablespoon of icing sugar. Turn them so that they are covered in sugar on both sides, and then leave to stand while the pancake mix is prepared.

Put the flour, salt and the eggs into a bowl and mix them thoroughly together before adding the cold milk. The result should be a thick pancake batter; it may be necessary to thin it with a little water.

Melt a good half of the butter in the pan and when hot, pour in half of the batter. Cook until the bottom has taken and then arrange the sliced apples on top. Pour on the rest of the batter and continue cooking over a low heat until the bottom is golden-brown. Shake the pan frequently so that the bottom does not stick.

Turn the pancake and slowly cook the second side similarly so that the inside is thoroughly cooked through.

Serve either dotted with butter and sprinkled with sugar, or with honey poured over it.

Elle says that this is a simple but delicious last-minute pudding.

[173]

CRÊPES DE LA ROCHELLE
La Rochelle pancakes

PREPARATION TIME: 15 minutes
COOKING TIME: 3 minutes per pancake
FOR SIX

2 oranges	500 ml (17½ fl oz) milk
200 g (10½ oz) flour	250 ml (9 fl oz) water
3 eggs	50 g (scant 2 oz) melted butter
50 g (scant 2 oz) caster sugar	100 ml (3½ fl oz) brandy
pinch of salt	

Scrub the oranges, grate the rind of one of them and squeeze the juice of both. Put the flour into a large bowl and make a well in the centre. Put in the whole eggs, sugar and salt, and start to mix with a whisk. Incorporate first the milk and then the water, so a smooth light batter results. Finally, mix in the melted butter, the orange juice and the grated rind.

Make pancakes in the usual way, keeping them warm on a dish in the oven with its door ajar. When about to serve, fold each pancake into quarters, arrange them on a metal serving dish, pour on the brandy and serve flambé.

Elle advises that time will be saved if 2 or 3 pans can be used at the same time to make the pancakes.

PÂTE À CRÊPES & PÂTE À BEIGNETS
Pancake and fritter batters

PANCAKE BATTER
PREPARATION TIME: 10 minutes (2 hours in advance)
COOKING TIME: 3 minutes per pancake
FOR ABOUT 15 PANCAKES

250 g (9 oz) flour	500 ml (17½ fl oz) milk
4 eggs	tablespoon of oil
pinch of salt	

Put the flour into a bowl, make a well and put in the eggs and salt. Mix together with a wire whisk, adding bit by bit first the milk and then the oil. Leave to rest for at least 2 hours.

When about to make the pancakes, extend the mixture with warm water until it is thin enough to spread easily across the bottom of the pan.

Really thin pancakes should never be tossed, but turned with a spatula.

FRITTER BATTER
PREPARATION TIME: 10 minutes (1 hour in advance)
COOKING TIME: 5 minutes for each round
FOR 20 FRITTERS

250 g (9 oz) butter	500 ml (17½ fl oz) milk
3 whole eggs	tablespoon of sugar
2 egg whites	rum or Grand Marnier
teaspoon of salt	

Make the batter as above but using 3 egg yolks and 1 egg white only. Leave to rest for an hour.

When ready to cook the fritters, mix in 3 tablespoons of the chosen liqueur. Beat the remaining 4 egg whites stiffly and fold into the mixture, using a spatula, until the whites are completely incorporated.

PÂTE À FONCER
Flan pastry

PREPARATION TIME: 20 minutes (30 minutes in advance)
COOKING TIME: 40 minutes–1 hour (according to filling)
FOR A 26 cm (10 in) DIAMETER PASTRY TIN

250 g (9 oz) flour
1 teaspoon of salt
50 g (scant 2 oz) granulated
   sugar
2 eggs
100 g (3½ oz) butter

Put the flour into a mixing bowl and make a well, into which put salt, sugar, eggs and the softened butter. Work all together with the finger-tips, from time to time moistening the pastry with a very little cold water. The aim is to have a soft and flexible pastry. If possible, leave to rest for 30 minutes although you can go on to the next stage without delay.

Grease the inside of the tin with butter and dust it with flour. Roll out the pastry and line the tin so that pastry overlaps the edges: pass the rolling pin over the tin in order to trim off the surplus which may, if wished, be used for decoration.

Leave for 30 minutes in a cool place to ensure that the pastry shell will not shrink during cooking. Prick the base of the tin with a fork and then fill with fruit or whatever other mixture is to be cooked.

Elle says that this pastry is particularly suitable for tarts of such fruits as plums, apricots or cherries. Made without sugar, it is excellent for pâtés en croûte and savoury flans.

PÂTE À BRIOCHE
Brioche dough

PREPARATION TIME: 30 minutes (4–6 hours in advance)
FOR 500 g (17½ oz) OF DOUGH

300 g (10½ oz) flour
10 g (⅓ oz) fresh yeast
70 ml (2½ fl oz) warm milk
½ teaspoon salt
1 tablespoon sugar
4 eggs
150 g (5 oz) butter

The leaven: make a ball of dough with a ¼ of the flour, the yeast and some of the warm milk. Drop it into the bowl of warm water where it will double in volume in 15–20 minutes.

The dough: Put the rest of the flour into a mixing bowl. Add the salt and sugar and moisten the flour with the rest of the warm milk. Break in 3 of the eggs and, when everything is thoroughly mixed together, add and combine the leaven.

Knead the dough, lifting it and beating it on the pastry board. Fold the dough over on itself, spread it out again so that it absorbs air, and keep kneading it until it comes away cleanly from both fingers and pastry board.

Beat and roll out the butter until it has the same consistency as the dough and then, using a third of the butter at a time, work it well into the dough. When all the butter is thoroughly incorporated, put the dough into a bowl, cover it with a cloth and leave it in a warm place for 4–6 hours.

When the dough has doubled in volume, put it back on to the pastry board and flatten it to expel its air. It is now ready for use. Brush with beaten egg just before putting the brioches into the oven.

Elle advises that the dough will keep for 3–4 days if formed into a ball, covered with aluminium foil and refrigerated.

CLAFOUTIS
Traditional cherry pudding

PREPARATION TIME: 20 minutes (2 hours in advance)
COOKING TIME: 45 minutes
FOR SIX, USING A 22 cm (8½ in) FLAN DISH

750 g (1½ lb) black cherries	pinch of salt
150 g (5 oz) flour	2 tablespoons sugar
3 eggs	200 ml (7 fl oz) milk

The cherries should not have the stones removed as they add an element to the flavour of the dish. Wash and drain the cherries and remove their stalks. Arrange them in the buttered flan dish.

Make a batter as if for pancakes. Sieve the flour into a bowl, add the whole eggs, salt and sugar. Whisk it together, moistening with milk added bit by bit. Stop adding milk as soon as the batter is creamy and free from lumps. Leave to rest for 2 hours.

Pre-heat a fairly hot oven (200°C/400°F/Gas Mark 6). Mix any remaining milk into the batter and pour the mixture over the cherries. Sprinkle with sugar and cook for 40–45 minutes.

The dish will rise during cooking and fall again when taken out of the oven. Serve warm.

PAPIN
Boulonnais flan

PREPARATION TIME: 30 minutes (partly 2 hours in advance)
COOKING TIME: 1½ hours
FOR SIX TO EIGHT

The pastry	The filling
500 g (17½ oz) flour	1 litre (35 fl oz) milk
20 g (¾ oz) fresh yeast	1 good sprig of thyme
2 eggs	3 egg yolks
100 g (3½ oz) butter	175 g (6 oz) caster sugar
	125 g (4½ oz) flour

Put the flour on to a pastry board and rub the yeast well in. Make a mound with a well in the middle and break in the eggs, one by one. Add the softened butter and work everything together into a smooth dough. Leave to rest in a warm place for at least 2 hours.

In the meantime, prepare the filling. Bring the milk to the boil, remove from the heat and put in the thyme to infuse for about 10 minutes.

Mix the egg yolks and sugar together in a bowl, sieve in the flour and mix well, and then very slowly pour in the milk, beating all the time so a smooth, creamy consistency results. Transfer to a saucepan and bring the mixture to the boil: let it bubble twice, remove from the heat and take out the thyme.

Roll out the pastry dough to a thickness of 5 mm (just under ¼ in) and line a buttered flan dish with it. Pour in the filling. Cook the flan for 1½ hours in a fairly hot oven (200°C/400°F/Gas Mark 6).

Elle advises that dried thyme can be used but it should be wrapped in a piece of muslin first.

FLAN AUX PRUNEAUX
Prune flan

PREPARATION TIME: 30 minutes (partly 4 hours in advance)
COOKING TIME: 35 minutes
FOR A 26 cm (10 in) FLAN DISH

The pastry	The filling
200 g (7 oz) flour	400 g (14 oz) dried prunes
100 g (3½ oz) butter	1 tea bag
1 egg	1 egg
pinch of salt	1 teaspoon of cornflour
1 tablespoon of granulated sugar	60 g (2 oz) caster sugar
1 glass (5 fl oz) water	2 tablespoons of orange liqueur
	150 ml (5 fl oz) single cream
	30 g (1 oz) butter

Make enough weak tea to cover the prunes and leave them to soak for 4 hours. Drain and stone them.

Make a pastry with the ingredients given and line the flan dish. Add the prunes. Put into a fairly hot pre-heated oven (200°C/400°F/Gas Mark 6).

Beat the egg, the cornflour, the sugar and the liqueur into the cream and, as soon as this is done, pour it over the prunes. Dot with a few knobs of butter and return the flan to the oven. Check the progress of cooking by the colour of the pastry: when cooked, turn out the flan on to a wire rack.

Serve either hot or cold.

FLAN AU CITRON
Lemon flan

PREPARATION TIME: 10 minutes
COOKING TIME: 40–50 minutes
FOR SIX

A flan case made with Pâte à foncer, see p. 175	4 egg yolks
1 lemon	2 egg whites
500 ml (17½ fl oz) milk	20 g (¾ oz) butter
40 g (scant 1½ oz) flour	75 g (good 2½ oz) caster sugar
75 g (good 2½ oz) sugar	icing sugar

Grate the rind of the lemon, avoiding the white as much as possible. Add it to the milk and bring to the boil. Remove from the heat and allow to cool.

Mix flour and sugar together, then beat in the egg yolks. Strain the milk to remove the lemon rind and add it to the mixture together with the juice of half the lemon. Brush the inside of the flan case with melted butter, sprinkle it with sugar and pour in the mixture.

Pre-heat a fairly hot oven (190°C/375°F/Gas Mark 5) and cook the flan on an upper shelf for 20–25 minutes.

Beat the egg whites stiffly and add the caster sugar, continuing to beat until the meringue mixture makes stiff peaks. Spread the meringue over the surface of the flan and put into a slow oven and continue cooking for a further 20–25 minutes, until the meringue is lightly browned.

TOURTE AUX AMANDES
Almond tart

PREPARATION TIME: 15 minutes
COOKING TIME: 35 minutes
FOR SIX, USING A 22 cm (8½ in) DIAMETER FLAN DISH

100 g (3½ oz) blanched almonds	*2 egg yolks*
150 g (5 oz) caster sugar	*grated rind of 1 lemon*
375 g (13 oz) flour	*vanilla essence*
135 g (4¾ oz) butter	*pinch of salt*

Coarsely chop the almonds and spread them on to a baking sheet. Sprinkle them with a little sugar and put them under the grill until they are lightly browned.

Put 100 g (3½ oz) sugar into a bowl with the sieved flour, butter cut into knobs, the egg yolks, the grated lemon rind, a few drops of vanilla essence and a pinch of salt. Add the warmed almonds and work the ingredients together, using the fingertips, for about 2 minutes. Put a quarter of this mixture to one side.

Butter the flan tin and put the larger part of the mixture in the centre. Using the palm of the hand, spread the mixture over the whole of the bottom of the flan tin.

Take the last quarter of the mixture kept to one side and add to it 3 tablespoons of water. Mix well together and pour into the flan tin. Sprinkle the rest of the sugar over the tart and cook in a moderate oven (180°C/350°F/Gas Mark 4) for about 35 minutes.

Elle says that this Italian dish is best cooked in a tin with a removable base, to make it easier to turn out.

TARTE RUSTIQUE AUX ABRICOTS
Country tart with apricots

PREPARATION TIME: 15 minutes (partly 1 hour in advance)
COOKING TIME: 45–50 minutes
FOR A FLAN TIN OF 26 cm (10 in) IN DIAMETER

1 kg (2¼ lb) apricots	*1 teaspoon salt*
250 g (9 oz) flour	*50 g (scant 2 oz) sugar*
125 g (4½ oz) butter	*70 ml (2½ fl oz) water*

Choose small, ripe apricots for this dish.

On a pastry board, make a well in the flour. Add the softened butter, salt and a tablespoon of sugar. Work all the ingredients together with the fingertips, quickly working them into a firm and supple dough. Leave to rest for an hour.

Roll out the pastry to a thickness of 4 mm (about ⅙ in) thick, butter the flan tin, dust with flour and line it with the pastry. Prick the base all over with a fork and sprinkle with a good tablespoon of sugar.

Cut the apricots in half and remove their stones. Arrange them cut-side upwards and slightly overlapping, within the flan case. Put into a hot oven (220°C/425°F/Gas Mark 7) for 20 minutes; then reduce the heat to 180°C/350°F/Gas Mark 4 and sprinkle the fruit with another tablespoon of sugar. Cook for a further 20–25 minutes. The bottom of the tart should be quite firm and stiff when it is properly cooked.

Serve hot, or cold dusted with icing sugar.

TARTE GROSEILLES MERINGUÉE
Redcurrant meringue tart

PREPARATION TIME: 30 minutes
COOKING (PASTRY): 20–25 minutes
(MERINGUE): 1 hour
FOR A FLAN TIN OF 24 cm (9½ in) DIAMETER

The pastry	The filling
250 g (9 oz) flour	6 egg whites
120 g (good 4½ oz) butter	250 g (9 oz) caster sugar
pinch of salt	300 g (10½ oz) redcurrants
1 egg yolk	100 g (3½ oz) chopped grilled
1 level tablespoon granulated	hazelnuts
sugar	icing sugar

Make a pastry with the ingredients shown and line the flan tin. Leave it to rest in a cool place for 30 minutes, in order to prevent it shrinking during cooking. Bake blind, as instructed on p. 26.

In the meantime, beat the egg whites. When they are stiff, add the sugar, spoonful by spoonful, continuing to beat until the whites become very stiff. Put aside 4 or 5 large spoonfuls of beaten egg white and mix the redcurrants, with their stalks removed, into the remainder. Spread the chopped hazelnuts on the bottom of the flan case and then cover them with the redcurrant meringue. Put the rest of the beaten whites over the top, spreading it evenly with the blade of a spatula.

Sprinkle icing sugar generously over the surface and put the dish into a very cool oven (110°C/225°F/Gas Mark ¼) for an hour to cook without browning.

This splendid tart may be served either hot or cold.

TARTE-GALETTE
Apple tart

PREPARATION TIME: 30 minutes
COOKING TIME: 20–25 minutes
FOR SIX

400 g (14 oz) frozen puff pastry   caster sugar
4 good ripe eating apples

Normally, frozen puff pastry is in 4 layers. Roll it out on a floured pastry board and, returning it to its original size and shape, fold it twice more. Now roll out the pastry to a thickness of 4 mm (about ⅙ in) and lay it on to a baking sheet which has been wiped with a damp cloth. Using an inverted plate, cut the largest possible disc from the pastry.

Peel and core the apples and cut them into very thin slices. Arrange them on the pastry in overlapping rings or spirals beginning 1 cm (⅖ in) in from the edge.

Put into a hot oven (220°C/425°F/Gas Mark 7) and cook until the dish takes on a light and pleasing colour. Serve sprinkled with sugar.

Elle says that cooking the tart on a dampened baking sheet will prevent it losing its shape during cooking.

TARTE AU FROMAGE BLANC
White cheese tart

PREPARATION TIME: 30 minutes (partly 1 hour in advance)
COOKING TIME: 45–50 minutes
FOR A FLAN TIN OF 26 cm (10 in) IN DIAMETER

The pastry
250 g (9 oz) flour
125 g (4½ oz) butter
70 ml (2½ fl oz) water
1 teaspoon salt

The filling
600 g (21 oz) drained fromage
  blanc or cottage cheese
125 ml (4½ fl oz) double cream
2 eggs
2 egg yolks
175 g (6 oz) caster sugar
1 tablespoon of flour
pinch of salt
7½ g (¼ oz) vanilla sugar
grated rind of 1 lemon

Make a pastry with the ingredients given, form it into a ball and let it rest for an hour in a cool place.

Put the cheese through a sieve and then whip it into the cream. When the mixture is thoroughly smooth, mix in first the whole eggs, one by one, then the extra egg yolks, the sugar and flour mixed together, the salt and either vanilla or lemon flavouring.

Butter the flan dish and dust it with flour. Line it with the pastry rolled out to a thickness of 4 mm (about ⅙ in). Prick the base all over with a fork and then pour in the cheese mixture. Put into a hot oven (220°C/425°F/Gas Mark 7) for 20 minutes then lower the temperature to 180°C/350°F/Gas Mark 4 and cook for 25 more minutes. If the dish should rise too much, prick it with a fork to deflate it.

The dish can be served either hot, or cold and sprinkled with icing sugar.

TARTE AUX MENDIANTS
Oasis pudding

PREPARATION TIME: 25 minutes
COOKING TIME: 40 minutes
FOR SIX

The pastry
1 egg
60 g (2 oz) sugar
pinch of salt
250 g (9 oz) flour
125 g (4½ oz) softened butter

The filling
200 g (7 oz) dates
200 g (7 oz) dried figs
100 g (3½ oz) raisins
50 g (scant 2 oz) shredded
  almonds
3 eggs
150 ml (5 fl oz) crème fraîche
50 g (scant 2 oz) caster sugar
pinch of salt

Beat 1 egg in a bowl together with the sugar and salt. Sieve the flour and add it all at once to the beaten egg. Work all these ingredients into a lumpy mixture and then, knob by knob, incorporate the butter so a smooth and supple pastry dough results. Roll out.

Butter a flan dish with a removable base and line it with pastry. Line the case with stoned dates, chopped figs, raisins and shredded almonds.

Beat together the 3 remaining eggs, the crème fraîche, sugar and salt. Pour the mixture over the dried fruit and put the dish into a fairly hot oven (200°C/400°F/Gas Mark 6) for 40 minutes. Turn out the dish and serve either warm or cold.

POIRAT DU BERRY
Pear pie

PREPARATION TIME: 40 minutes
COOKING TIME: 1 hour 10 minutes–1 hour 20 minutes
FOR A TIN ABOUT 20–22 cm (8–8½ in) SQUARE

1½ kg (3¼ lb) pears
6 tablespoons of Calvados or brandy
200 g (10½ oz) granulated sugar
pinch of ground white pepper
400 g (14 oz) frozen puff pastry
1 egg
100 ml (3½ fl oz) double cream

Peel and core the pears and divide each one into eight. Put them in a dish with the Calvados or brandy, the sugar and the pepper. Turn and stir and leave to soak for at least 30 minutes.

Roll out the pastry to a thickness of 4 mm (about ⅙ in) and, having buttered the tin and dusted it with flour, line it with pastry. Trim off the surplus from the edges. Drain the pears, putting the juices to one side, and arrange the slices in the pastry case.

Roll out the pastry left over. Brush the edges of the pastry case with beaten egg and cover the dish with the rolled out pastry having first put a pie funnel in the centre. Leave a fairly large hole in the pastry to allow steam to escape during cooking. Mould any trimmings into decorations and stick them down with the beaten egg. Finally, brush the pie all over with the rest of the egg.

Pre-heat a fairly hot oven (200°C/400°F/Gas Mark 6) and cook the pie for 15 minutes. Then lower to a moderate heat (180°C/350°F/Gas Mark 4) and complete the cooking, judging it by the colour and consistency of the pastry case.

Finally, stir together the cream and the pear juices which were put to one side and pour them in through the hole in the pastry lid. Serve hot.

TARTE AUX PÊCHES AU FROMAGE
Peach pie

PREPARATION TIME: 30 minutes (2 hours in advance)
COOKING TIME: 50 minutes
FOR A ROUND FLAN DISH 24 cm (9½ in) IN DIAMETER

The almond pastry
125 g (4½ oz) butter
125 g (4½ oz) granulated sugar
7½ g (¼ oz) vanilla sugar
125 g (4½ oz) powdered almonds
pinch of salt
250 g (9 oz) flour
1 egg

The filling
3 sponge fingers
4 ripe peaches
250 g (9 oz) fromage blanc or cottage cheese
25 g (scant 1 oz) flour
75 g (good 2½ oz) caster sugar
75 g (good 2½ oz) softened butter
pinch of salt
grated rind of half a lemon
milk

To make the pastry, work the butter, sugar, vanilla sugar, powdered almonds and the pinch of salt thoroughly together with the palms of the hands. Then mix in the flour and the egg, working until a supple pastry results. Form it into a ball and put it in a cool place for 2 hours.

Roll out the pastry to a thickness of 5 mm (⅕ in) and line the dish. Trim off the surplus pastry around the edges and prick the bottom with a fork. Crumble the sponge fingers and peel, stone and chop the peaches (well-drained tinned peaches can be used). Put in first a layer of sponge finger crumbs and cover it with the chopped peaches.

Beat the drained cheese together with the flour, sugar, softened butter, salt and grated lemon rind. If too thick a mixture, dilute with milk. Spread this cheese mixture over the peaches and cover the whole pie with a lattice work of pastry strips.

Put into a hot oven (210°C/410°F/Gas Mark 6–7) until the pastry is browned to taste. Serve cold.

BRIOCHE AUX CERISES
Brioche of cherries

PREPARATION TIME: 45 minutes (partly 2–3 hours in advance)
COOKING TIME: 35 minutes
FOR SIX, USING A 25 cm (10 in) IN DIAMETER FLUTED FLAN DISH

The pastry
250 g (9 oz) flour
30 g (⁷⁄₁₀ oz) fresh yeast
6 tablespoons milk
1 egg
100 g (3½ oz) butter
½ teaspoon of salt
1 tablespoon granulated sugar

The filling
750 g (good 1½ lb) cherries
125 g (4½ oz) caster sugar
1 tablespoon powdered
    semolina
1 egg yolk

Begin by preparing the leaven. Form the flour into a hollow pyramid on a pastry board and put in the yeast which should have been dissolved in 3 tablespoons of warm milk. Work the yeast and about a third of the flour together and form a ball; cover this with the remaining flour and leave it to rise.

When the surface of the flour begins to crack, work it all in to the leaven together with the whole egg, the softened butter, the salt, the sugar and 2 or 3 tablespoons of milk. When a smooth and supple pastry results, form it into a ball, cover it with a cloth and put it aside until it has doubled in volume.

Stone the cherries, put them into a bowl with the sugar and the semolina and mix them all together.

Roll out ⅔ of the pastry to a size that will line the flan dish and leave an overlap all round. Put the cherry filling into the pastry case and cover with the remainder of the pastry, pressing the edges all round with the fingers to seal top and bottom together. Decorate the top with any pastry trimming left over and brush the whole surface with beaten egg. Cook in a fairly hot oven (200°C/400°F/Gas Mark 6).

Elle says that this Limousin pie may be either served direct from its dish or turned out on to a serving plate.

POGNE DE ROMANS
A Dauphiné cake

PREPARATION TIME: 45 minutes (10 hours in advance)
COOKING TIME: 40 minutes
FOR SIX TO EIGHT

15 g (½ oz) fresh yeast
70 ml (2½ fl oz) milk
350 g (12 oz) flour
3 eggs
1 teaspoon of salt

125 g (4½ oz) softened butter
75 g (2½ oz) granulated sugar
1 tablespoon orange essence
1 egg yolk

Begin with the leaven. Dissolve the yeast in warm milk. Put 2 tablespoons of flour into a mixing bowl, stir it together with the milk and yeast and put the bowl into a saucepan of warm water (it should come up almost to the lip of the bowl). Cover with a cloth and leave for 20 minutes when the leaven should have doubled in volume.

In the meantime, proceed to make the dough. Put the rest of the flour into a bowl, break in an egg, add the salt and work everything together with the fingertips. Continue with the second and third eggs and, after the third, knead the dough with the palm of the hand to lighten it. Work in the softened butter, the sugar and the orange essence and, when a smooth dough results, incorporate the leaven. Continue to knead the dough which should have the consistency of bread dough and come away in one lump from the mixing bowl. If necessary, dust with flour occasionally during kneading.

Sprinkle the lump of dough with flour, cover with a cloth and leave it to rest in the kitchen for 10 hours.

Put the dough on to a floured pastry board and press it with the hands into a flat round shape. Form a central hole with the fingers so a thick ring of dough results. Cut little slashes all around the top surface and brush with beaten egg yolk. Cook in a hot oven (210°C/410°F/Gas Mark 6–7) for 40 minutes.

This light cake is delicious for a special continental breakfast.

Elle advises that if the dough is made well in advance, knead it again just before forming the ring in order to remove any air.

GÂTEAU AU VIN BLANC
White wine cake

PREPARATION TIME: 10 minutes
COOKING TIME: 30 minutes
FOR SIX TO EIGHT

2 eggs
pinch of salt
200 g (7 oz) caster sugar
80 ml (3 fl oz) peanut oil

100 ml (3½ fl oz) dry white wine
200 g (7 oz) flour
teaspoon of baking powder

Break the eggs into a bowl and add the salt, the sugar, the oil and the white wine. Beat them all together with a wooden spoon, then add bit by bit the flour (which should have been mixed with the baking powder). Work everything together into a thin, smooth mixture.

Pour the mixture into a buttered cake tin 22 cm (8½ in) in diameter. Cook in a fairly hot oven (200°C/400°F/Gas Mark 6) for 30 minutes.

The cake will rise and become very light. Serve either with ice cream or crème anglaise.

The chef of the Paris restaurant 'La Coquille' from where this recipe comes, recommends a sweet champagne to be drunk with this cake.

GALETTE BRETONNE
Twelfth-Night cake

PREPARATION TIME: 30 minutes (2 or 3 days in advance)
COOKING TIME: 40–45 minutes
FOR A 26 cm (10 in) CAKE

100 g (3½ oz) hazelnuts
250 g (9 oz) granulated sugar
7½ g (¼ oz) vanilla sugar
125 g (4½ oz) salted butter
3 eggs

500 g (17½ oz) flour
100 g (3½ oz) crystallised fruits
1 teaspoon baking powder
1 egg yolk

Put the shelled hazelnuts into a moderate oven (180°C/350°F/Gas Mark 4) just long enough for their skins to go crisp which will make them easier to remove. Chop the nuts finely in a moulinette or grinder.

Put the ground-up nuts, sugars and butter on to a pastry board and work them all together with the fingertips, adding the eggs one by one. Put in the sieved flour and baking powder all at once and work this in, working from the outside towards the centre. Chop and add the crystallised fruits and continue kneading until a smooth dough results. Form it into a ball and leave it covered in a cool place for 2 or 3 days.

Butter a baking sheet, dust it with flour. Roll out the dough to a thickness of 15 mm (a good ½ in) and place it on to a baking sheet. Use an inverted plate to cut a round disc of dough. Brush it with the egg yolk, beaten twice with a few minutes' interval between. Score the dough with a fork in a diamond pattern, and bake in a hot oven (200°C/400°F/Gas Mark 6) for 40–45 minutes. Check the progress of cooking by watching the colour of the cake.

The trimmings can be used to make small galettes which can be baked at the same time, but only for 15–20 minutes.

MACARONS
Macaroons

PREPARATION TIME: 30 minutes
COOKING TIME: 25 minutes
FOR 36 SINGLE OR 18 DOUBLE MACAROONS

1 kg (2¼ lb) marzipan
6 egg whites
350 g (12 oz) icing sugar
7½ g (¼ oz) vanilla sugar
apricot preserve (optional)

Put the marzipan into a bowl and work in 1 egg white until it is thoroughly absorbed. Repeat with a second egg white; the mixture should now be smooth and workable. Add the icing sugar and vanilla sugar all at once and the rest of the egg whites and mix until a smooth paste results. A tablespoon of strained apricot preserve added at this point will give a softer macaroon, but whether or not it is used, the paste must be smooth, without lumps and stiff enough to hold its shape without running.

Cut a piece of rice-paper to the size of the baking sheet being used and, with a piping bag, form round macaroons on it. They should be 4 cm (a good 1½ in) across and with space between them. Put a large pastry brush into cold water, shake it out and use it to flatten and form each macaroon.

Bake in a fairly hot oven (190°C/375°F/Gas Mark 5) on a shelf about one-third up from the bottom, for 20–25 minutes, keeping a watch on the colour.

Remove from the oven and run half a glass of cold water between the rice-paper and the baking sheet. Leave to cool and then remove from the sheet: if double macaroons are required, they should be stuck back-to-back at this point.

After 24 hours, the macaroons should be put into an airtight container, where they will keep for several weeks.

CROQUETS AUX AMANDES
Almond cake

PREPARATION TIME: 10 minutes
COOKING TIME: 30–35 minutes
TO MAKE 2 CAKES

500 g (17½ oz) flour
1 teaspoon baking powder
120 g (scant 4½ oz) ground almonds
500 g (17½ oz) granulated sugar
5 egg whites
250 g (9 oz) blanched almonds
3 tablespoons orange essence
1 egg yolk

Sieve the flour and baking powder together and mix in the ground almonds and the sugar. Make a hollow pyramid and fold in the egg whites one by one, the blanched almonds and the orange essence. Mix until a smooth dough results.

Divide the dough in half and roll each one into a sausage shape 5 cm (2 in) thick, put them on to a buttered baking sheet and flatten them with the heel of the hand. Brush with beaten egg and score a diamond pattern on them with a fork.

Pre-heat a hot oven (220°C/425°F/Gas Mark 7) for 15 minutes and bake the cakes for 30–35 minutes. Remove from the oven and, while still warm, cut them into slices.

Elle says that although the recipe suggests baking the cakes in loaf form, they could equally well be made in more amusing shapes by, for example, using gingerbread cutters or pastry moulds.

PAIN D'ÉPICE
Spice loaf

PREPARATION TIME: 30 minutes (8 hours in advance)
COOKING TIME: 2½ hours
FOR A CAKE TIN 23 × 11 × 6.5 cm (9 × 4½ × 2½ in)

500 g (17½ oz) honey
500 g (17½ oz) granulated sugar
1 kg (2¼ lb) flour
30 g (1 oz) baking powder
pinch of salt
½ teaspoon of cinnamon

½ teaspoon of quatre-épices (see p. 29)
5 egg yolks
100 g (3½ oz) sugar (for the caramel)

Do not use an over-refined thin honey. Put the honey into a saucepan over a very low heat until it has just melted and then add the sugar, mixing it with the honey still over a very low heat. Pour the syrup into a bowl and when it has cooled a little, add the flour (sieved together with the baking powder), salt and spices. Mix together, beating in the egg yolks at the same time.

Moisten the caramel sugar and melt it gently. Bring it to the boil and when it reaches a rich red-brown colour, remove from the heat and pour in a tablespoon of cold water. Add this caramel, spoonful by spoonful, to the dough until it reaches the desired colour. Turn out the dough on to a floured pastry board and knead it until the dough is smooth and supple. Form it into a ball and leave in a cool place for at least 8 hours.

Butter the cake tin and line it with greaseproof paper. Fill it ¾ full with dough and bake in a cool oven (120°C/250°F/Gas Mark ½) for 2 hours, being sure not to open the oven door during the first 25 minutes. The spice loaf will be ready when an inserted skewer can be withdrawn cleanly. Turn the loaf out on to a wire rack and leave for several hours before serving.

Elle says that made in this way, the spice loaf is not sticky. It will be easy to cut into slices and will keep for at least a week.

BROYE DU POITOU
Poitou cake

PREPARATION TIME: 30 minutes
COOKING TIME: 12–15 minutes
FOR SIX TO EIGHT

250 g (9 oz) butter
250 g (9 oz) caster sugar
pinch of salt

2 tablespoons of rum
500 g (17½ oz) flour
1 egg yolk

Work the butter, sugar and salt together in a bowl, mix in the rum and then add the flour all at once. Continue to work all together into a smooth dough, roll it into a ball and put it on to a buttered baking sheet. Roll out the dough to a thickness of 1 cm (⅖ in) in as round a shape as possible. Use an inverted plate to trim the dough into a neat disc.

Shape the edges of the disc with a pointed knife and brush all over with beaten egg. Decorate in a diamond pattern by scoring the surface with a fork.

Bake in a fairly hot oven (200°C/400°F/Gas Mark 6) for 12–14 minutes.

CONFITURE DES QUATRE FRUITS
Summer fruit preserve

PREPARATION TIME: 45 minutes
COOKING TIME: 50 minutes

For 1 kg (2¼ lb) stoned cherries   *1 kg (2¼ lb) strawberries*
   use: *1 kg (2¼ lb) raspberries*
1 kg (2¼ lb) redcurrants   *4 kg (9 lb) sugar*

Use English cherries if possible. Remove the stalks from the redcurrants and soften them by boiling in 2 or 3 tablespoons of water. Pass them through a fine sieve.

If possible, use a jam kettle made of copper. Put in the redcurrant juice, the sugar and a glass of water. Bring to the boil and, stirring constantly, boil for 10 minutes. Then add the stoned cherries, bring back to the boil for 10 minutes, and then add the strawberries. Finally, after 10 more minutes, add the raspberries and, still stirring, boil for 10 minutes more. Skim the surface from time to time.

Leave to cool a little before turning out into sterilised jars.

CONFITURE DE MARRONS
Chestnut preserve

PREPARATION TIME: 40 minutes
COOKING TIME: 1 hour

For 3 kg (6¾ lb) whole   *pinch of salt*
   chestnuts: *2½ kg (5½ lb) granulated sugar*
cooking oil   *2 vanilla pods*

Make a slit crossways through the skin of the rounded part of each chestnut. Heat some oil in a deep pan and when it is simmering plunge in the chestnuts for a few minutes, until the slit has opened. Drain the chestnuts, and it will then be easy to remove both skins.

Put the peeled chestnuts into a saucepan with a pinch of salt and just cover them with cold water. Keep at a slow boil for 30 minutes; the chestnuts should crush easily between finger and thumb.

In the meantime, put the sugar into a jam kettle with the vanilla pods slit in half. Moisten with a little water and melt the sugar to a syrup. Bring to boiling point and continue to the regular large bubble stage.

Pass the chestnuts through a fine sieve; the smoother and finer the purée obtained, the better the preserve will be. Time this stage to be completed when the syrup is boiling in large bubbles so that the chestnut purée does not cool down before being added to the syrup.

Stirring constantly, continue boiling for 30–35 minutes. Remove the vanilla pods and turn the preserve out at once into jars and do not cover them until the following day. Keep the preserve in a cool place.

<u>Elle advises</u> that this preserve tends to ferment rather easily. If you want to keep it for any length of time, turn it out into sterilised jars as soon as the syrup returns to the boil after adding the chestnut purée and go on boiling the jars in water for a further 30 minutes.

CONFITURE DE TOMATES
Tomato preserve

PREPARATION TIME: 30 minutes
COOKING TIME: 1 hour

4 kg (9 lb) tomatoes
4 kg (9 lb) granulated sugar

2 lemons
1 kg (2¼ lb) apples

Use late-season tomatoes that are barely ripe. Wash and dry them and cut them into quarters. Put them into a jam kettle with their same weight of sugar and the juice and grated rind of both lemons.

Bring to the boil, stirring constantly, and keep at a slow boil until the mixture begins to thicken. Peel and core the apples and cut them into thin slices; add them to the mixture and, still stirring, simmer for 30 minutes more.

Turn out into sterilised jars and cover this delicious preserve.

MARMELADE DE RHUBARBE
Rhubarb marmalade

PREPARATION TIME: 50 minutes
COOKING TIME: 55 minutes
TO MAKE 6 kg (13½ lb) OF MARMALADE

3 kg (6¾ lb) rhubarb
3 kg (6¾ lb) granulated sugar
8 oranges

6 lemons
250 g (9 oz) walnut kernels

Trim the rhubarb and remove any stringy parts. Cut into lengths of 3–4 cm (1¼–1½ in) and put them into a copper jam kettle (a large stainless steel pan may be substituted). Add the juice of 2 oranges and of 3 lemons, bring to the boil, cover and simmer gently for 15 minutes when the rhubarb will be soft.

Add the sugar and, stirring constantly, keep at a slow boil for 20 minutes. Grate the rind of 3 oranges and of 3 lemons and put to one side. Peel the remaining fruit (6 oranges and 3 lemons) and then divide into segments; peel each segment, retaining only the pulp. Put fruit pulp and grated rind into the marmalade and continue cooking for 30 minutes more.

Add the walnut kernels and take the jam kettle from the heat. Leave to cool, stirring from time to time. When quite cold, pour into sterilised jars.

CERISES À L'EAU-DE-VIE
Cherries in brandy

PREPARATION TIME: 30 minutes
COOKING TIME: nil
FOR A 2 LITRE (3½ PINT) JAR

1 litre (35 fl oz) eau-de-vie de cuisine (or cheap brandy may be used instead)　*2½ kg (5½ lb) cherries*
200 g (7 oz) caster sugar

Choose only cherries that are without blemish and not too ripe. Trim the stalks to within 2 cm (⁴/₅ in) of the fruit, wash and dry the cherries and fill the jar. Pour in the spirit up to the brim and put an airtight seal on to the jar.

After 3 weeks or a month, add the sugar and re-seal. Three days later, shake the jar, still sealed, so the sugar is dispersed. Repeat 2 or 3 times more, at the same interval.

Keep the preserved cherries in a dark place. They will be ready for eating after about 2 months.

ABRICOTS AU SIROP
Preserved apricots

PREPARATION TIME: 45 minutes
COOKING TIME: nil
STERILISING TIME: 10 minutes

For 3 kg (6¾ lb) apricots　*1 vanilla pod*
500 g (17½ oz) granulated sugar

Choose unblemished fruit that is just ripe. Wash the apricots and cut them carefully in half with a stainless steel knife. Remove and crack the stones, and pick out the best kernels. Blanch the kernels in boiling water and peel them.

Take preserving jars which have been sterilised and well dried, and fill them with apricot halves. Do not press them down into the jar but fill each jar right to the top, then put in peeled apricot kernels, about 12 to each 1 litre (35 fl oz) jar.

Mix the sugar with 1 litre (35 fl oz) water and, with the vanilla, boil for 5 minutes. Remove the syrup from the heat and allow to cool for 5 minutes, then pour it into each jar up to the level of the neck. Seal with airtight lids and sterilise the jars in boiling water for 10 minutes. Allow the jars to cool down in the sterilising water and then store in a cool, dark place.

Elle says that apricots preserved in this way can be used for tarts and puddings, for making ice cream or for fruit drinks.

PRUNEAUX AU VIN
Prunes in wine

PREPARATION TIME: 10 minutes
COOKING TIME: 5 minutes

For 600 g (generous 1¼ lb)
  prunes
1¼ litres (44 fl oz) strong red
  wine

80 sugar lumps (40 French-size
  lumps)
2 vanilla pods
200 ml (7 fl oz) rum

Put the wine, sugar and the vanilla pods, split in half, into a saucepan and heat the contents until a white foam covers the surface of the liquid. Remove from the heat and pour in the rum. Take out the vanilla pods.

Push a skewer or larding needle through each prune from end to end. Fill a jar with prunes and pour in warm wine until they are covered. Seal with airtight lids and leave the prunes to soak for 3 to 4 weeks before using them.

Elle advises that these preserved prunes are so quickly prepared that several jars could be made at the same time. They make very acceptable Christmas presents.

CHAMPAGNE CUP
To Elle and Us

PREPARATION TIME: 10 minutes (1 hour in advance)
FOR EIGHT TO TEN

3 bottles of brut champagne
3 tablespoons of brandy
3 tablespoons of orange liqueur

2 oranges
125 g (4½ oz) black grapes
125 g (4½ oz) white grapes

Put the champagne to cool in the refrigerator. Cut the unpeeled oranges into thin slices, trim the stalks from the washed grapes and put all the fruit into a glass punch-bowl. Pour in the brandy and the orange liqueur, cover the bowl with a piece of aluminium foil and refrigerate for an hour.

When ready to serve, bring out the chilled bowl and pour in the contents of the bottle of champagne. Stir gently and serve at once.

Elle advises that this drink is at its best when quite chilled. It may therefore be best to make it in a number of bowls, bringing each one out as required.

Index